RETHINKING EARLY LITERACIES

Rethinking Early Literacies honors the identities of young children as they read, write, speak, and play across various spaces, in and out of (pre)school. Despite narrow curricular mandates and policies, the book highlights the language resources and tools that children cultivate with families, communities, and peers. The chapters feature children's linguistic flexibility with multiple languages, creative appropriation of popular culture, participation in community literacy practices, and social negotiation in the context of play. Throughout the book, the authors critically reframe what it means to be literate in contemporary society, specifically discussing the role of educators in theorizing and rethinking language ideologies for practice. Issues influencing early childhood education in trans/national contexts are forefronted (e.g., racism, immigration rights, readiness) throughout the book, with a call to support and sustain communities of color.

Mariana Souto-Manning is Associate Professor and Director of the Early Childhood Education and Early Childhood Special Education Programs at Teachers College, Columbia University, USA.

Haeny S. Yoon is Assistant Professor in the Early Childhood Program at Teachers College, Columbia University, USA.

Changing Images of Early Childhood
Series Editor: Nicola Yelland

Books in this forward-thinking series challenge existing practices in early childhood education and reflect the changing images of the field. The series enables readers to engage with contemporary ideas and practices of alternative perspectives which deviate from those theories traditionally associated with the education of young children and their families. Not only do these books make complex theory accessible, they provide early childhood educators with the tools to ensure their practices are backed by appropriate theoretical frameworks and strong empirical evidence.

Titles in the *Changing Images of Early Childhood* series include:

Early Childhood Qualitative Research
edited by J. Amos Hatch

Shift to the Future: Rethinking Learning with New Technologies in Education
by Nicola Yelland

Playing it Straight: Uncovering Gender Discourse in the Early Childhood Classroom
by Mindy Blaise

Childhood and Postcolonization: Power, Education, and Contemporary Practice
by Gaile S. Cannella and Radhika Viruru

Rethinking Parent and Child Conflict
by Susan Grieshaber

Rethinking Early Literacies: Reading and Rewriting Worlds
by Mariana Souto-Manning and Haeny S. Yoon

RETHINKING EARLY LITERACIES
Reading and Rewriting Worlds

Mariana Souto-Manning
and Haeny S. Yoon

Routledge
Taylor & Francis Group

NEW YORK AND LONDON

First published 2018
by Routledge
711 Third Avenue, New York, NY 10017

and by Routledge
2 Park Square, Milton Park, Abingdon, Oxon, OX14 4RN

Routledge is an imprint of the Taylor & Francis Group, an informa business

Library of Congress Cataloging-in-Publication Data
Names: Souto-Manning, Mariana, author. | Yoon, Haeny S., author.
Title: Rethinking early literacies : reading and rewriting worlds / Mariana Souto-Manning and Haeny S. Yoon.
Description: New York, NY : Routledge, 2018. | Series: Changing images of early childhood | Includes bibliographical references.
Identifiers: LCCN 2017024844 (print) | LCCN 2017050932 (ebook) | ISBN 9781315650975 (e-book) | ISBN 9781138121393 (hbk) | ISBN 9781138121416 (pbk) | ISBN 9781315650975 (ebk)
Subjects: LCSH: Reading (Early childhood). | Language arts (Early childhood)—Computer-assisted instruction. | Literacy—Social aspects.
Classification: LCC LB1139.5.R43 (ebook) | LCC LB1139.5.R43 S65 2018 (print) | DDC 372.4—dc23
LC record available at https://lccn.loc.gov/2017024844

ISBN: 978-1-138-12139-3 (hbk)
ISBN: 978-1-138-12141-6 (pbk)
ISBN: 978-1-315-65097-5 (ebk)

Typeset in Bembo
by diacriTech, Chennai

We dedicate this book to:
Phillip Baumgarner,
Alison Lanza,
Carmen Lugo Llerena,
Jessica Martell,
Maria Helena Mendonça Buril,
Abigail Salas Maguire,
Debbie White,
and all of the teachers whose teaching and learning are portrayed in this book. May they continue shedding light onto what is possible when we critically rethink early literacies.

CONTENTS

CHANGING IMAGES OF EARLY CHILDHOOD

Series Editor: Professor Nicola Yelland, Victoria University, Melbourne, Australia

The books in the *Changing Images of Early Childhood* series consider contemporary and alternative theoretical perspectives in the domain of early childhood education. The aim of the series is to introduce the reader to new theoretical perspectives and to make them accessible so that their relevance to everyday practices is highlighted. The topics span classroom, family, and community settings, and provide readers with *rich* descriptions of everyday lives in global contexts. The books in the series enable us to engage in meaningful conversations around the personal and complex sets of interactions that we experience in the early childhood years. Our focus centers on their relevance to the lived experiences and the everyday practices of adults who interact with young children in a myriad of environs, thus enabling educators to create learning environments which are underpinned by a respect for all participants, equity, and social justice.

The *Changing Images of Early Childhood* books challenge and confront educators with a wide range of topics. They reflect the complex nature of our lives in a postmodern world where issues around globalism, capitalism, democracy, and the multifaceted nature of our contemporary experiences are not easily resolved, but need to be confronted. They have been created to bring to the forefront the issues faced by marginalized groups so that they might be interrogated with respect and from perspectives that are relevant to the nature and culture of those groups and individuals. Additionally, we want to share the innovative practices of educators who are at the forefront of thinking dynamically about the challenges inherent to living in the twenty-first century.

In this volume, we are provided the opportunity to interrogate and discuss our framing of literacy in contemporary times. As the authors indicate, this is particularly relevant in times when policymakers and others, who are deemed to be responsible for the provision of schooling, seem to be focused on a definition of literacy that is grounded in "print literacy." The same people also seem to be fundamentally concerned about the acquisition of skills for decoding that are reminiscent of strategies from previous eras. This book opens up the debate as to how becoming literate is a basic prerequisite for living in the twenty-first century and illustrates the diverse and practical ways in which new definitions of literacy that give agency to young learners can be enacted in everyday learning experiences. The authors theorize about literacy for young children by challenging us to consider what it means to be literate today as well as to incorporate the diverse manifestations of multiple literacies across a broad range of experiences.

The book has three parts, beginning with a view of young children as competent and autonomous learners. The discussion then moves to the present, looking at ways in which relational literacy is relevant today using empirical examples from diverse classroom contexts with children in the age range of birth to eight years of age. In the final part, the authors present the argument for rethinking early literacy, with a consideration of children's literate identities at the forefront. They discuss opportunities to communicate and make meaning in new and dynamic ways because of adopting this reconceptualist stance. The authors create new spaces to "orchestrate complex literacies, making visible the ways in which children negotiate multiple spaces and construct multiple sets of participatory rules" (p.xvii). They achieve this by exploring the potential of curriculum to provide exciting contexts for learning, describing classroom interactions that promote communication and the sharing of ideas, as well as linking theory and classroom contexts in order to shape productive spaces for children to participate, practice, and negotiate opportunities to engage in multiliteracies. These are powerful ideas that in turn help us to understand the profound impact of being literate in the twenty-first century and provide a stark contrast to the reductionist approach taken by those who view literacy as a narrowly defined set of skills that can be tested. Young children can explore and become multiliterate in a variety of planned and spontaneous settings that require us, as educators, to rethink literacies with a more critical approach to texts and communication in relation to aspects of power, autonomy, and identity. This rethinking of literacy as a range of cultural practices that are related to social and cultural practices, affiliations, beliefs, and values enable us to uncover and learn from the diverse sets of practices that can contribute to a more socially just world.

ACKNOWLEDGMENTS

As we read and rewrote early literacies in the process of coauthoring this book, we learned from and with incredible young children and adults—within and across schools and communities. We had the privilege of being both teachers and learners in diverse learning communities in Arizona, Georgia, Illinois, and New York; in the U.S. and in Brazil. As you turn the pages and start reading this book, we hope that our words capture the richness and depth of the learning experiences we witnessed.

Throughout the years, we have been honored and humbled to be entrusted with such powerful learning journeys and rich family funds of knowledge. Thus, here, we affectionately acknowledge the children, their teachers, and families, whose stories and questions we share in this book. Our stories are their stories.

The children whose stories and pictures we portray in this book invited us to expand the concept of literacies. It was because of them that we came to see literacies as relational. Although we cannot use their real names, here we thank each one of them sincerely. We learned much from their unique stories and rich journeys; from the ways in which they learned how to make meaning within and across time and space. Whether infants or second graders, through words, gestures, and actions, they invited us to witness their writing and rewriting of the world—in hopeful and powerful ways. We are grateful that their families allowed us to bear witness to their learning and to capture counterstories of promise.

In addition to the children and their families, we offer our deepest gratitude to the teachers who welcomed us into their classrooms and (pre)schools over the course of our careers as educators, allowing us to grow in unforeseeable ways—regardless of whether we share their stories here. But because so many of the stories shared here come from settings where we spent years, we offer our greatest thanks—and dedicate this book—to several teachers whose stories are portrayed in this book. They are Phillip Baumgarner, Alison Lanza, Carmen Lugo Llerena, Jessica Martell, Maria Helena Mendonça Buril, Abigail Salas Maguire, and Debbie White.

Phillip Baumgarner is a Head Start teacher in Georgia, in whose classroom and (pre)school Mariana had the pleasure of spending two years. Baumgarner was always enthusiastic about the power of children's communicative practices and the richness of their family and community literacies—even when they were absent from the Creative Curriculum, adopted by his (pre)school. He inspired coauthor Mariana Souto-Manning to think of theater and performance as powerful avenues for teaching and learning, and he was always excited to learn from Souto-Manning's observations of his class. We acknowledge Baumgarner's stance as a learner of children's multiple ways with words.

Alison Lanza, a teacher in New York City's Central Park East II, a progressive public school in East Harlem, invited Souto-Manning to consider intersectionalities within the context of early childhood education. Always seeing young children as capable, full participants of a society needing transformation, she engaged her students in learning from Walter Dean Myers and Christopher Myers. She repositioned practices typically found outside of the early childhood classroom and (pre)school walls within the context of her classroom and school community, including graffiti and hip-hop. Souto-Manning started learning with Lanza in 2015.

Carmen Lugo Llerena, a teacher in an inclusive primary grade in New York City, teaches children with and without disabilities (her class is made up of children with autism spectrum disorders and children with/without individualized education programs [IEPs]). Both Mariana Souto-Manning and Haeny S. Yoon had the pleasure to learn with Llerena over the past four years, having spent much time in her classroom. With Llerena, we learned to make space for superhero play, *Star Wars*, and childhood cultures. In her class, she consistently cultivated peer literacies. Over the past two years, Yoon and Llerena worked together to create curriculum with children and create spaces for play and meaningful learning. Llerena listens to children with careful attention, honors the diversities that children embody, and is always asking thought-provoking questions to children and adults alike. Yoon is grateful to the National Council of Teachers of English (NCTE) Professional Dyads and Culturally Relevant Teaching (PDCRT) for bringing Llerena into her life as a curricular partner. Being in Llerena's classroom continues to make our work better. This classroom work led to wider networks of thought partners who also challenged our ideas.

Tran Templeton, an extraordinary doctoral candidate and multitalented scholar at Teachers College, Columbia University in New York, offered her time, energy, and valuable insights to expand curricular opportunities in Llerena's classroom. Her scholarship and research expertise reinvigorated the classroom project, but also served to expand our perspectives on teaching young children with a social justice stance. Included in this group is Nick Martin, Llerena's coteacher, whose good humor and artistic gifts brought energy and possibilities to the curriculum. They are more than colleagues; they are treasured friends.

Jessica Martell, a New York City public school teacher, welcomed Souto-Manning weekly into her classroom for years. Souto-Manning and Martell cotaught, cothought, and cowrote their relationship as well as the classroom's curriculum and teaching. They learned from the young children who made up Martell's classroom community—from their histories and through their families and neighbors—as they sought to delve into culturally relevant early literacy teaching. This long-term multiyear learning journey was initially supported by the NCTE PDCRT and resulted in a coauthored book, *Reading, Writing, and Talk: Inclusive Teaching Strategies for Diverse Learners, K–2*. Whether in person or electronically, since 2013 they have been in touch almost daily. They continue to learn from and with each other. They have other projects in the works.

Maria Helena Mendonça Buril, an Early Head Start teacher in Georgia, looked closely and listened carefully to the young children with whom she taught and learned. When Souto-Manning first met Mendonça Buril, she immediately noticed how her passion for and knowledge of education were contagious. In her classroom, Mendonça Buril positioned very young children as agents, who could shape the learning that went on in her classroom—by resignifying objects, redesigning mealtime to honor their families' and communities' ways of sharing meals, and blurring time and space boundaries. While in Georgia, Souto-Manning had the privilege of learning from and with Mendonça Buril and the children she taught. Mendonça Buril and Souto-Manning went to the same school in Brazil, Instituto Capibaribe, a Freirean nonprofit community school in the city of Recife.

Abigail Salas Maguire, a dual language (Spanish/English) teacher in a New York City public school, invited Souto-Manning to think of the power of cross-grade collaborative learning experiences. From 2011, Salas Maguire has shown Souto-Manning transformative and innovative ways of engaging families, honoring their lives. She meets families in city parks and libraries, instead of expecting them to enter the school building during more traditional hours. She positions families as partners, acknowledging and valuing their knowledge and abilities.

Debbie White, who is now a retired kindergarten teacher from Illinois, graciously opened up her classroom for Yoon's dissertation research. In coauthoring this book, Yoon is reminded of White's wisdom and love for children. White opened up every school year with *Mrs. Spitzer's Garden*, a book that acknowledges the importance of cultivating with great care the things (or, in this case, the people) you love. It was evident that White believed in the potential of all young children, especially advocating for children who needed someone in their corner. Her classroom was a place of joy and laughter. It was a privilege for Yoon to be a part of this space filled with the sounds of young children at play and work (mostly both at the same time). The space she gave children to grow allowed them to build relationships, explore ideas, ask meaningful questions, and cultivate their unique identities. The conversations documented in this book are a testament to White's brilliance as an early childhood educator. Although she is now raising her grandchildren full-time, we hope these descriptions of her classroom serve as examples of what is possible when young children are entrusted with curriculum.

In addition to the early childhood and elementary teachers we named earlier, we also thank the teachers whose pseudonyms are Ms. Bailey, Ms. Mary Martin, Mary Hill, Jessica Garcia, Ms. Silva, and Ms. Hernandez. Ms. Silva, Jessica Garcia, and Mary Hill showed us some of the obstacles early childhood education teachers are navigating in the name of a standardized notion of quality. Ms. Bailey, Ms. Mary Martin, and Ms. Hernandez invited us to consider the power and possibility of repositioning family funds of knowledge and community literacies centrally in early childhood classrooms. We hope you enjoy learning from their practices as much as we did. We are indebted to them.

In addition to acknowledging those portrayed in the lines and figures of this book, we acknowledge those who are present in between the lines (or parentheses) and behind the curtains. That is, we acknowledge our many teachers over the years across time and space. In particular, we acknowledge our professors and colleagues Anne Haas Dyson, Celia Genishi, Luis Moll, and Betsy Rymes. Their work and words have helped us rethink who we are and the work we do. These scholars taught us to rewrite our world by modeling generosity, kindness, and commitment to children and their communities. There are other friends and colleagues in academia too numerous to name. We honor the work that many friends are doing to bring critical conversation around equity and social justice for young people, especially in these trying political times. We also thank Professors Barbara Comber (University of South Australia) and Jackie Marsh (University of Sheffield, UK) for their generous endorsements of our book. And a special thank you to Nicola Yelland for such a lovely foreword and to Luis Moll for an inspiring afterword. Each of these luminaries in the field has inspired our scholarship in wonderful ways. Their words humble us.

We acknowledge our roots and thank our parents and siblings. If we see young children as being at promise, it is because as children of color we were seen as at promise by our families, being loved, nurtured, and encouraged. We sincerely thank our partners, Dwight and Neal, who have unfalteringly believed in us and in the work we do. Their nurturing has been essential to this collaboration. Souto-Manning thanks her children, Lucas and Thomas, for their support of and enthusiasm for her professional life and work.

We owe much gratitude to Nicola Yelland, series editor, for encouraging us to develop the proposal for this book. We are indebted to her for her kindness, patience, and enthusiasm. We thank Alex Masulis, from Routledge, and Christina Nyren, from Taylor & Francis, for their support in bringing this project across the finish line.

Finally, we would be remiss if we did not acknowledge each other. This is our first project together and certainly not our last. We feel fortunate to have the opportunity to work and learn and grow together. We hope you have as much fun reading this book as we had writing it. May it account for the expansiveness and inclusiveness of the literacies children from minoritized backgrounds embody each day.

INTRODUCTION

Our overall goal with this book is to theorize the literacy of young children in a way that invites early childhood educators and researchers to rethink theoretical constructs framing understandings of literacy in contemporary society. This is especially important within the current landscape of early education; where (pre)school is positioned as an investment and traditional literacy notions dictate what counts as reading and writing. Working to reclaim early literacy in ways that honor young children's brilliance (Hilliard 2009) and timelines (Genishi and Dyson 2009), we see the need for challenging the early learning "goal of standardization and for shifting the spotlight from teachers straining to be accountable to the group we are to educate, children in early childhood settings. Indeed, we urge a change in the cast on the classroom stage, along with a change in scripts" (Genishi and Dyson 2012, 18).

As we rethink early literacies, we consider reconceptualizations of children's literate identities, challenging how we define diverse language learners (e.g., English learners as multilingual learners) within a context in which "difference and diversity are the new normal" (Genishi and Dyson 2009, 10). We reconsider and expand the notion of texts to multimodal creations as well as the inclusion of creative texts that popular culture has inspired—graffiti, movies, toys, and other cultural artifacts related to childhood(s). Throughout, we consider issues influencing early childhood and how young children are positioned given transnational social and political issues while acknowledging that too often the field views "the languages, literacies, and cultural ways of being of many students and communities of color as deficiencies to be overcome in learning the . . . dominant language, literacy, and cultural ways of schooling" (Paris 2012, 93).

This book has three parts:

- Part I considers young children as competent literate beings.
- Part II defines the concept of relational literacy from feminist and Afrocentric standpoints (Irvine 1991; Licona and Chávez 2015).
- Part III rethinks early literacies, considering children's literate identities in contemporary times, specifically in institutional spaces such as (pre)school.

Laying the foundation of the book (Part I: Young Children as Literate Beings), we regard young children as capable literate beings. We offer an overview of historical, social, and cultural theories that have defined and redefined literacy in the twenty-first century. In doing so, we explore issues of identity, culture, and agency as foundational to early literacy. We challenge prevalent conceptions of young children as incapable and young children from minoritized backgrounds as deficient, propagated by the current educational discourse related to the closing of achievement and opportunity gaps.

From this new understanding of early literacy, in Part II: Spaces of Belonging: Relational Literacies, we invite the field to consider literacies across relational contexts—the spaces where children belong. Informed by rhetoric and composition studies, we draw on relational literacies from the standpoint of "women-of-color feminisms and literacy studies" (Licona and Chávez 2015, 96). Jacqueline Jordan Irvine's call (1991) for Afrocentric teaching and learning provides an ontological perspective that emphasizes collective responsibility and shared commitment within African American communities. Undergirding Afrocentric teaching is the inherent value of "communal well-being" (King and Swartz 2014, 3) and the preservation of cultural and historical legacies as integral to communities across the African diaspora. Therefore, knowledge of and participation in literacies is born of interconnected networks, relationships between elders and youth, familial connections that move fluidly between families, and shared practices collectively explored through interactions. These relational literacies move beyond everyday practices, but embody literacies as interdependent and interconnected across time and space (Irvine 1991; King and Swartz 2014). Through a variety of examples, we contemplate languages and literacies in families and homes, considering concepts such as home literacies (Gregory, Long, and Volk 2004a), family funds of knowledge (Moll, Amanti, Neff, and González 1992), assets inventories (García and García 2012), and family cultural practices (Valdés 1996). "Understood as practices, relational literacies imply the labor of making meaning, of shared knowledges, or of producing and developing new knowledges together" and imply "the desire and possibility for shared action" (Licona and Chávez 2015, 96). Thus, we position families and homes within the context of neighborhoods and communities and reaffirm children as active members of multiple communities (Boutte and Johnson 2014; Haight and Carter-Black 2004; Ladson-Billings 1995; Long, Volk, Baines, and Tisdale 2003; Souto-Manning 2013b). Finally, we consider the languages and literacies of peer culture within the context of play, popular culture, and the digital landscape.

After understanding theories shaping early literacy and children's identities and considering relational literacies across time and space (inspired by Anzaldúa 1987; Licona and Chávez 2015; Martin 2013), we invite you to rethink early literacy, expanding what counts as literacy and moving toward multiple early literacies. In Part III: Rethinking Early Literacies: Children's Literate Identities in Contemporary Times, we engage in rethinking (pre)school literacies and challenge reductionist practices shaping children's identities. We consider the complexity of children's literate identities and challenge socially constructed literacies related to gender identity, race, socioeconomic status, and linguistic repertoires.

Throughout the book, drawing on examples from young children from birth to eight years of age, we seek to orchestrate complex literacies, making visible the ways in which children critically negotiate multiple spaces and construct multiple sets of participatory rules (Bhabha 1994; Gutiérrez 2008; Gutiérrez, Morales, and Martínez 2009), even within current social and political discourses and policies that seek to standardize and constrain possibilities. In doing so, we examine the potential of curriculum, classroom interactions, and research in bringing theories and practices together in ways that create productive and authentic spaces for children to practice "multiple" literacies.

PART I

Young Children as Literate Beings

Young children are literate beings. This is the assumption that undergirds this book. They read words and worlds. They are capable. They don't enter schools without literacy or without language. They are sophisticated symbol readers and symbol weavers (Dyson 1990). Although the specific literacy practices in which they engage may not be immediately visible (or valued) by adults, young children are purposeful communicators who negotiate literacies in deliberate ways—through actions and interactions. To explain what we mean by the statement that young children are literate beings, in this book, we explore theoretical constructs through examples from a variety of sites involving diverse children from birth to eight years of age (the early childhood years).

In Chapter 1, we delve into issues of identity, culture, and agency. Chapter 1 portrays young children as communicatively and culturally competent long before they enter classroom spaces. In it, we explore the multiple contexts of children's language development in their sociocultural worlds, emphasizing the rich resources and communicative repertoires that all children uniquely possess. We give an overview of theories that address identities as lived, produced, and conceptualized through activities in social contexts, through practice. These activities are inevitably situated in how children are positioned in their own communities, within social institutions (e.g., schools, churches), and within the larger society (Archer 2000, 2003; Carter and Goodwin 1994; Corsaro 2011; Dyson 1993; Freire 1970; Holland, Lachicotte, Skinner, and Cain 2001; James 2011; Tatum 1992). Drawing on the work of Hilliard (2009), we explore children's literate identities, making visible how all children are gifted. We challenge the idea of the achievement gap, elucidating how there is no achievement gap at birth (Delpit 2012) and move to deconstruct the idea that children need to race to catch up (Genishi and Dyson 2012) or to master the so-called basics (Dyson 2013).

Chapter 2, Reading and Rewriting Worlds and Words, takes a sociopolitical approach toward definitions of literacy, arguing for broadened and expansive understandings of reading, writing, and speaking. Through examples from multiple settings, we advocate for the rethinking of literacies by repositioning texts, power, and identity centrally (Bauman and Briggs 2003; Collins and Blot 2003; Dyson 1990; Genishi and Dyson 2009; Gutiérrez, Martínez, and Morales 2009; Lewis, Enciso, and Moje 2007). At the same time, we deconstruct the idea of "readiness" (Graue 1992), reenvisioning it as a concept used to marginalize children whose language practices are misaligned with linguistic norms (Souto-Manning 2013a). Instead, we move away from traditional definitions of reading and writing by exploring the sophisticated communicative repertoires that children embody (Alim 2005; Dyson and Smitherman 2009; Heath 1983; Paris 2009; Razfar 2005).

Chapter 3 explores young children's multiple social communicative contexts, recognizing that they are exposed to and develop language before entering school—in homes and communities, with peers, and across environments. Their language usage is a tool to engage with others in their immediate contexts—to interact with adults, to connect with other children, and to take part in sociocultural activities. That is, children develop identities through active participation in their social and cultural communities using language as a mediating tool. Thus, in Chapter 3, we explore the social, cultural, and political contexts that influence children's language interactions, and move toward critically redefining what it means to be literate. Through examples from a variety of settings, we explain how being literate in one social context, especially in the digital, contemporary age, does not always translate into being literate in another context (Marsh 2005a)— and how meaning making is context-dependent. Young children often navigate within and across multiple social worlds (Gutiérrez 2008) that are organized by their own sets of rules, interactions, and social practices, and instead of complying they can engage in challenging and changing them (Vasquez 2014).

Starting with these three chapters, which make up Part I, we invite you to rethink children's positionings in literacy—from consumers to producers; from passive recipients of knowledge to change agents. Through examples from a variety of early educational and community settings, we rethink literacies in expansive and inclusive ways, centrally accounting for issues of power and identity (Bauman and Briggs 2003; Collins and Blot 2003; Dyson 2013; Genishi 1992; Gutiérrez 2008; Martínez 2010; Orellana 2009). In doing so, we move away from traditional definitions of reading and writing as fully comprising literacy, using cultural historical activity theoretical tools to re-mediate literacy (Cole and Griffin 1983; Gutiérrez, Morales, and Martínez 2009). Throughout Part I, we trouble prevalent discourses in early literacy—such as readiness and basics (Dyson 2013; Graue 1992)—and invite readers to see children's varied and sophisticated communicative repertoires.

1

IDENTITY, CULTURE, AND AGENCY

Lou: Look, I made a heart. [Lou turned his paper over and drew a box on the back of page 2. He made a shape that looked like a sideways heart.]

Jaquan: That's no heart.

Lou [to Haeny]: Ain't this a heart? Ain't this a heart?

Tonea: No, no, no, no, no, no, no. A heart is like this. [She tries to draw one on Lou's paper. He quickly snatches it out of her reach.]

Jaquan: A heart is like this. [He starts drawing a heart on his own paper.]

Tonea: I love my mommy.

Lou: You don't love your mommy, and I *know* your mommy.

Tonea: Who is my mommy?

Lou: Your mom. . . . Your mom, she works . . . she works at a nursing home. Don't your momma work at a nursing home? [Tonea does not respond.]

Jolene: Tonea is the best girl at this table.

Lou, Jaquan, Jolene, Tonea (and Jon, introduced later) were all kindergartners who occupied the same table at a school in the midwestern U.S. Lou, Tonea, and Jaquan were African American children who lived in the same neighborhood within a small urban community, making it likely that they knew each other outside of school. All three children received free or reduced-price lunch (a U.S. marker of low-/no-income). Although it was unclear whether or not Tonea's mother worked at the nursing home, the conversations followed trajectories like the one above where one of the children tried to bring up people who others might know (e.g., an older sibling, an auntie, or a parent).

They attempted to connect with each other using language varieties (e.g., "Ain't this a heart?"), popular cultural artifacts, references to people and places within the neighborhood, and lessons on literacy. They taught each other how to write words and draw shapes, they incorporated different phrases that became group norms, they praised one another excessively, and they judged one another's work harshly. Most importantly, they became a distinct social group that did not just exist in a physical space, they were "mobilized or otherwise 'called into being' . . . on the basis of shared representation and undertakings" (Collins and Blot 2003, 105). This particular group of storytellers held diverse ideas made visible in the company of one another; they expanded these ideas in conversation with each other, but at other times, they defended ideas in genuine conflict. In the background were texts featuring children's literacy attempts (e.g., letters, shapes, drawings, and markings), constructed through the interplay of text and talk (Collins and Blot 2003).

Throughout the school year, the children were building a literacy repertoire through interactions like the one above, appropriating tools provided by the teacher and suggested by the curriculum as well as tools distinctive of the individual children in the group. The children in this classroom sat at rectangular tables assigned by Debbie White, their teacher. In the official classroom space, this grouping was arbitrarily named Table 1, because the table was physically arranged closest to the door. Over time, table numbers became "mini-communities," a term insightfully coined by Debbie White as she joyfully watched ensuing social scenarios as well as the formation of unpredictable bonds. Children often referred to themselves by table numbers in order to make distinctions among themselves. For instance, the children described above would say from time to time, "This is Table 1," or "Table 1 is the best table," explaining their small group in relation to other tables. In a sense, table numbers became an emic term that children adopted to signify their group identity within the larger classroom context. Debbie carefully chose the configurations of these tables saying that she tried to mix up the table groups by abilities, interests, and relational connections. She looked beyond academic qualifiers, highlighting children who were attuned to helping, who thrived on verbal acuity, who were excessive rule followers, who were creatively subversive, and who typified a good role model.

Being a teacher for more than twenty years, Debbie White was amused by children's divergent thinking and by how they created spaces for conversation and talk, even in regulated curricular boundaries where silence and independence were valued. In the first month of school, children were moved to different tables for various reasons (e.g., fighting, off-task behavior, reconfiguring of group dynamics), but by October many of the groups remained consistent for the year—a purposeful decision by Debbie to create smaller communities within the larger classroom community. She reminds us of the important role of teachers in facilitating the growth of social relationships by orchestrating the physical, intellectual, and contextual spaces for interactions to flourish. In other words, seemingly ordinary tasks like arranging seats, scheduling literacy events, choosing books, providing materials, and asking questions are much deeper ideological decisions. These decisions either open up children's identities or force them to go undercover. In sharing the stories at Table 1, we seek to reveal the rich, literate practices children undertake when given the curricular flexibility to play out their identities in the company of their peers.

Tonea: Identities in Motion

For Tonea (an African American girl who was labeled below average in reading), moving to Table 1 at the end of September revealed a different side of her identity which had remained hidden prior to that time. At the beginning of the school year, Tonea seemed disengaged and disinterested in literate activities—it took her a while to complete activities, she often stared off into the distance seemingly lost in her own thoughts, and she relied on her tablemates to help her since all of them quickly "came to her rescue" even when she did not ask.

When she attempted writing, the boy sitting next to her teased her and discredited her authorial attempts:

> Jeff: You know what you're doing? You know what you're doing? You're writing scribble scrabble.
> Tonea: Okay, don't look at it. [She covers her whole paper with her arms and her head.]
> Jeff: [giggles and tries to look at it] Writing scribble scrabble. Writing scribble scrab.

Debbie also noticed that Tonea was getting a lot of assistance from another girl at the table, who was trying to be helpful. Instead of allowing Tonea to be an equitable participant in the group, this positioned her (by no fault of the others) at the periphery of participation, as someone who needed help and was deemed incompetent (as Jeff's comment alluded to). In a child's world, "scribble scrabble" is viewed as an insult directed at those who cannot write.

For example, in the children's book *Scribble* (Freedman 2007), the older sister criticizes the younger child's "scribble kitty," proclaiming that her illegible markings looked merely "like a scribble." Early on, children begin to understand the types of communication deemed valuable and appropriate for the mainstream world: neatly formed drawings and letters. While Emma (the author of the scribble kitty) crafted a coherent storyline replete with active characters, her sister dismissed her efforts as messy. Therefore, both adults and other children impose and silence the written approximations of young children via curriculum, standards, benchmarks, and language ideologies. Missing from imposed benchmarks is the purpose of writing, to make connections with others, self, and the world. Consequently, Tonea struggled and became disconnected in the social groupings of this table, choosing not to connect with her peers. Like Emma in *Scribbles*, she pulled away from those who did not validate her communicative attempts. Unlike Emma, who reacted with anger, hurling insults at her sister (i.e., "You don't know *anything!*"), Tonea withdrew, grew silent, and remained seemingly reclusive. She also was seen as struggling in school assessments, classroom performance measures, and Debbie's initial observations. She was positioned—at her table, in her classroom, and by the school—as someone who needed help, from a deficit perspective.

Moving Tonea to Table 1 was an intentional, ethical choice made by Debbie White that moved beyond pedagogy, teaching, and curriculum. Tonea's lack of participation was not lost on Debbie's watchful and concerned gaze. As Holland and colleagues (2003) remind us, identities are shifting and fluid via interactions between social actors, the rules negotiated between members of a group, the practices that are taken up, and the ideas that are valued. Children appropriate these varying roles as they decide which practices are sustained, discarded, and transformed in collective participation (Holland et al. 2003; Wenger 1998). Therefore, Tonea's move meant that Debbie believed that the contexts in which we sit (physically and metaphorically) potentially changes the way we see ourselves and position others. Tonea found her voice within this group dynamic, in the presence of a new group of children (not better or worse than her previous group), where everything "magically clicked," as Debbie would say.

Figured Worlds: Building Practices in Figured Worlds

Beginning with the practice of the community at one table, we illustrate how identities are socially organized and "figured" (Holland et al. 2003) by the individuals who participate in that world. Within this social world, individuals are cast and recast in different positions. Simultaneously, they learn to build a set of shared practices and ways of responding that characterize that world. The conversation that opens up this chapter began with attempting to draw a heart to place on their texts. Jaquan and Tonea wanted to share with Lou how to draw a heart, making textual footprints on their own paper. However, these markings were the beginning of a larger story when they discussed love, mothers, and admiration. Hearts were the beginning of multiple ideas: Tonea's love for her mom, Jolene's declaration of Tonea as the "best girl," criticism of drawing attempts, self-declarations of competence, and allusions of connections outside of school. The texts were peripheral to the ongoing social dramas that unfolded within the table group. In this case, texts refer to the construction of written artifacts, "situated by time and place, multimodal in scope, guided and facilitated by the available resources in the sociocultural world" (Yoon 2016, 3). Therefore, children's stories or texts are not just words and drawings on paper, but indicators of the intentions and motivations surrounding their production. In fact, throughout this chapter, the texts are records or artifacts of the children's personal relationships, but do not "do justice to the symbolics of monumental display" (Collins and Blot 2003, 21). In other words, children's texts are representations of power and identity, stored on paper as remnants of their personal histories.

Therefore, identities are narrative constructions that are in process more than fixed or stable. The practices and behavior of children are outward manifestations of sociocultural tools (modes of communication, the symbolic tools, the available resources, and the practices used to mediate experience—reading, writing, talking, etc.) that children decide to take up (Marsh 2005b). However, we cannot deny that children, within varying degrees, are limited in their agency by the structures and boundaries set up by societies. Across the globe, images of childhood portray children in different ways ranging from adults-in-the-making to helpless victims. These portrayals influence public policies and organize institutional norms that privilege certain kinds of childhood(s) while marginalizing others. The children described earlier were writing their identities within their larger cultural world, and were given labels and institutional categories for simplifying who they were. Within these layered contexts, educators afford children varying amounts of flexibility based on views of childhood enacted within their situated contexts. Thus, identities are always in motion as individuals get positioned and repositioned within classroom contexts (as seen with Tonea) but also within the world of (pre) school assessments, as well as in the cultural landscape including but not limited to raced, classed, and gendered identities.

While identities are always in motion, they are also socially, culturally, and historically located and valuated; that is, they have been historically instituted. Identities, which have been historically disprivileged and minoritized (McCarty 2002), such as being a person of color and employing nondominant language practices (Paris 2009), as Tonea does, influence the ways in which one's situated identities are constructed. Thus, Tonea's identity of being below grade level in reading intersects with her racial and linguistic identities and how these are positioned within the context of her table and classroom, and in the society in which she lives. Tonea's language identity also reflects her misalignment with the language of power in schooling and what is deemed appropriate, both of which are culturally located concepts (Delpit 1988, 2012). The historical discursive construction of languages other than dominant American English as "lesser than" reflects the unequal power attributed to specific languages, thus further contributing to children who engage in nondominant language practices (albeit sophisticated and rich linguistically) being seen as unready, lesser than, and below average. At the macro level, the discursive construction of Tonea's identity intersects with inferiority and cultural-deficit paradigms (Goodwin, Cheruvu, and Genishi 2008), positioning and constructing the identities of children of color, their families, and communities. Here we note that such identities, and the powerful discourses that have historically demeaned them, influence the making and remaking of one's identity as a student, as a friend, and as a member of communities and affinity groups (Souto-Manning 2013a).

Identity in the Making: The Social Organization of Being in the World

Our identities are "subject to positioning by whatever powerful discourses they happen to encounter—changing state policies that dictate new ways of categorizing people in the census, educational diagnostics that label some children 'at risk'" (Holland et al. 2003, 27), and other institutional categories that set norms and standards. For young children, discourses on childhood and social activities related to participating in social worlds act as mediating devices that organize experiences and meaning making (Bakhtin 1981; Holland et al. 2003; Vygotsky 1978). Figured worlds, according to Holland and colleagues, are configured and situated within activities that are socially constructed and reproduced within historically instituted encounters. However, the ways that individuals participate in figured worlds are hardly static, and cultural appropriations are marked by individual interpretation and actions. Bakhtin (1981) calls these unique appropriations "speech genres," connoting social forms of language where individuals take up multiple voices. This allows individuals to orchestrate their unique enactment, authoring self in a world fraught with differential power and privilege. Thus, whether children are reproducing social norms, resisting societal constructions, or transforming culture, they are exerting agency with their ability to contribute to social life creatively and actively (Corsaro 2011; James 2011).

Looking back to the story in the book *Scribble*, Emma was enraged at her sister's dismissal of her drawing. For Emma, her text was personal, closely tied with her own perception of a drawer and writer of stories. Her kitty represented relational conflict between two sisters, the disheartenment of critique, and the difficulties of standing up for one's work. The intentions behind the words we choose, the decisions we make on how we arrange language forms, and the kinds of literacies that we privilege are accumulated cultural experiences and preferences. We take up language in order to participate in communities and respond to others in relationships. Dyson's body of work (1993, 2003a, and 2013) undergirds this idea that social relations root identities as children solidify friendships through birthday party invites, cultivate local childhood cultures through shared interests and pop culture knowledge, and navigate conflict and discord through counternarratives. These literate acts are situated in "their ventures into writing in the relational ethics of childhood cultures, where children sometimes wanted to be named, to get their turn, and to be included in the fun" (Dyson 2013, 173). Children's identities in process work with, against, and through relationships, what Bomer and Laman (2004) refer to as "discursive identities," taken up in social negotiation with each other. As a result, writing is a performance between child writers who are navigating conflict, jockeying for position, and establishing friendships.

Children also take up literate identities as ascribed or embodied by the macrodiscourses in the larger society. Historically, standardized tests and other arbitrary measures consistently marginalize children of color in low-income neighborhoods, as well as children from linguistically diverse families. When educators label children as reading failures in school, they scrutinize and devalue their identities (Combs and Nicholas 2012). Consequently, teachers give these discursive identities to children and adolescents as static or fixed, further alienating those who speak language varieties and dialects that are nonstandard (Dyson and Smitherman 2009; Kirkland 2009; Paris 2009).

> When looking for bad writing or failure, teachers don't just find it because tests construct it or perhaps overconstruct it. They find it in particular places, students, and kinds of writing because those places, people, and texts are already reified as failure. (Inoue 2014, 335)

Failure, as many scholars have articulated, is disproportionately represented in nondominant communities (see Dutro 2010; Genishi and Dyson 2009; Souto-Manning and Martell 2016; Yoon 2015). We discuss this further in the following section because these issues of language failure are too serious to ignore. Children continue to find themselves struggling because of mismatched ideologies between their home culture with that of school. In a sense, they are forced to choose between the multiple worlds in which they participate. Inability to assimilate into the dominant culture continue to marginalize certain groups of people. As hooks (1994, 179) articulates, "Students who enter the academy unwilling to accept without question the assumptions and values held by privileged classes tend to be silenced, deemed troublemakers."

The Social Constructions of Identity and Difference

Just as much as identity is about belonging, it can also be a way to disenfranchise children whose identities exist outside of the dominant culture. In Debbie White's classroom (as is true in many U.S. schools), education mandates, policies, and assessments served to label and categorize kindergartners by discrete skills related to phonemic awareness and letter recognition. Of the twenty-five children in the classroom, eight were identified as below average. More troubling was that seven of those eight children were African American and identified as coming from low-income families (including Tonea, Lou, and Jaquan). Within this classroom, all seven of the African American children found themselves on the warning list (below or well below average), which simultaneously intersected with income status (see Yoon 2015). These assessments denoted prescribed categories that obviously marginalized the children of color who strayed from the predetermined basics—letter identification, letter formation, and letter-sound correspondence. However, a closer look at children's literacy practices consistently revealed abilities and resources that were immeasurable by current assessment metrics. Nevertheless, a student's "identity-in-person" was constructed by perceived literacy abilities with intersecting deficit discourses, reifying a master narrative about Black and Brown children;

this narrative reinforced the "physical, intellectual, and cultural superiority of Whites, which are undeniably part of the history of race relations in the United States" (Shapiro 2014, 399).

Socioeconomic background frames children's experiences similarly. For example, Anyon's (1981) work on curricular resources in schools within low-income areas revealed astonishing gaps in variety, substance, depth, and inquiry when compared to their affluent counterparts within the same geographical location. Since the 1980s, when the study took place, little has changed in terms of closing the opportunity gap, while conversations about the achievement gap have intensified (Delpit 2012; Genishi and Dyson 2012; Ladson-Billings 2006). Race and class have been associated with and reified as failure in the lives of diverse minoritized families within the current discourse. The term "achievement gap" places the fault on the individual child and on his/her family (we further explore this in Chapter 2), and ignores a history of colonialism and domination, which has historically and contemporarily positioned children of color as inherently inferior or as full of deficits (resulting from factors such as supposedly inadequate upbringing). Therefore, discussions around the failure of children of color in the U.S. (and throughout the world) need to be coupled with honest and critical conversations about race beyond shallow markers and unspoken inequities (Pollock 2008).

Carter and Goodwin (1994) discussed racially biased events over the previous decade, which exacerbated presumptions of inferiority, cultural deprivation, and difference as deficit. Unsurprisingly, these same issues and images persist (in popular culture, in media, and in schools). While cultural pluralism is a politically correct notion, the failure for truly critical multicultural ideas aiming to foster justice and equity to integrate into school curriculum continues to position children of color marginally (Carter and Goodwin 1994; Souto-Manning 2013b). Multicultural social justice education deals "with oppression and social structural inequality based on race, social class, gender and dis/ability. Its purpose is to prepare future citizens to take action to make society better serve the interests of all groups of people, especially those who are of color, poor, female, or have disabilities" (Banks and Banks 2009, 67). This approach requires that democracy be practiced in (pre)schools, agentively repositioning students, and that students learn how to read and problematize inequities, developing critical consciousness. Yet, this is rarely the case, as illustrated by how recently a school in New York City was threatened and criticized for a student-produced mural entitled, "We Pledge Allegiance to An International Flag" (McKay 2016), honoring the countries where students and their families came from by overlaying those countries' flags onto the U.S. flag. Conservative news outlets were quick to accuse the school of left-wing propaganda, indoctrinating young children to lose focus on preserving their national identity in exchange for a global one. The hateful rhetoric targeted at projects like the international mural typify the struggles with diversifying curriculum and engaging in multicultural social justice education. Further, such rhetoric continues to inequitably regard Eurocentric curricula and teaching as acultural, simply defining it as "normal" (Goodwin, Cheruvu, and

Genishi 2008), thus imposing Eurocentric beliefs, practices, and values onto children, families, and communities of color.

Inequities are an inherent part of institutions and contexts within and beyond schooling. In fact, Ladson-Billings and Tate (1995, 48) posited, "Race continues to be a significant factor in determining inequity in the United States." "Race runs in the background" (Hilliard 2009, 24) and is an ever-constant identifier across the globe and within educational institutions, yet "discussions of race and racism continue to be muted and marginalized" (Ladson-Billings and Tate 1995, 47). When there isn't silence around issues of race, there are often single stories (Adichie 2009), which foster and reinforce stereotypes through singular (simplistic and incomplete) images of people of color and/or those living "in poverty." These continue to marginalize certain groups (such as African Americans and immigrant families). Prejudice and racism are motivated by racialized stereotypical assumptions made about groups, hegemonic structures that maintain dominance, and unexamined fear of the "other." Rather than cultivating diverse identities alongside access to knowledge of power, children of color are often assimilated into the dominant culture (e.g., in the U.S. this is White and Eurocentric), foregoing their cultural identities, as illustrated by these two short vignettes (Souto-Manning 2013b, 1):

> Three-year-old Antonia went to a toy store with her preschool class to buy a doll. Even though her own skin is brown and her hair is black, she spearheaded the argument for buying a White doll with blond hair because "she is prettier."

> Two four-year-old children—Felicia and Tom—engaged in pretend play in their preschool classroom. They found two stuffed bunnies—one pink and one blue—and designated the pink one to be a girl and the blue one to be a boy. Then, when they needed a villain, Tom ran across the classroom and found a Black doll to play the "monster."

The images offered by the larger culture shape the dominant narrative of racial groups, but they also play a hand in how individual perceptions form. As seen in the examples above, children begin to adopt notions of who is better, who is physically appealing, who is scary, and what is deemed appropriate for whom early on.

Identifying Oneself vs. Being Identified: Living Out Identities in Contexts

Identities are lived out in contexts. These contexts can support a child's practices or move them to the periphery. Language is a social practice that is tied to identity, similar to the categories of race and class described above. Heath's (1983) classic work *Ways with Words* highlights the language variation of sociocultural groups within a single geographical area in the U.S. Her ethnographic study on distinct linguistic communities points toward the diverse collection of literacy practices and events embodied by different cultural spaces. The larger issue was not that certain cultural communities lacked literacy or were "illiterate;" the problem was that specific communities enacted "ways with words" (Heath 1983) that were misunderstood and misaligned with school and how educators defined school success. The families who were closer to the dominant group's ways of being and communicating were identified as successful, while other groups (mostly racially, linguistically, and/or socioeconomically nondominant) were consistently reified as failures, lacking literacy. She underscored the "inadequacy of unilinear models of child language development" and proposed the need for "a broad framework for sociocultural analysis" of early language and literacy practices for understanding the development of communicative competence (Heath 1982, 49).

Since then, many scholars have argued for multiple literacies that take into consideration the distinct social practices that connote language use (spoken, written, and read) in everyday life (Dyson 1993; Gee 2004; New London Group 1996). Moreover, multiple literacies provide a conceptual framework that is inclusive of a myriad of cultural practices related to reading, writing, speaking, and hearing—in other words, the range of changing literacy practices in historically situated times (Collins and Blot 2003). Long, Volk, Baines, and Tisdale (2013, 422) offer "critical syncretism" as the process of creating transformative literacy practices, invented by children and teachers who bring "multiple bodies of knowledge together through creative acts of the mind." The African American teachers in this study, Janice Baines and Carmen Tisdale, were deeply committed to family and community practices, attending cultural/community events, attuning to the popular culture of children, and validating the language variation and play of children in their classrooms. Heath's research on the literacy repertoires of cultural communities (1982, 1983), González, Moll, and Amanti's attention to funds of knowledge (2005), and Long, Volk, Baines, and Tisdale's notion of critical syncretism (2013) together offer a more complete understanding of early literacies.

The issues outlined by Heath over three decades ago are still relevant in today's schools. Manyak's (2004) description of reading instruction in California critiques the ways that children's literacy learning was defined. Teachers trained children to be literate through discipline and control via curriculum, larger discourses, policies, and instruction. Educators valued individual performance over collaboration, and constantly compared and differentiated children's identities. In constructing their own literacy experiences, children were apt to follow the hidden curriculum of controlled bodies, dispositions, and attitudes rather than develop communicative competence. Clearly identities are both chosen and imposed. Children live out their lives in a landscape filled with multiple voices, linguistic and ideological diversity, and varied discourses. At times, these discourses are competing and contradictory, given the heteroglossic background of language in social worlds (Bakhtin 1981). Therefore, utterances are hardly exact replicas, but revoiced as different individuals take up words in ideologically charged social spaces, participating in "multiple, not always compatible, cultural worlds" (Dyson 2007, 118). Furthermore, the words spoken in one context do not have the same reverberations when spoken in another context. The more contexts an individual is a part of, the more linguistic flexibility s/he must maneuver to identify and be identified as an active member of that cultural community.

Children from immigrant communities illustrate this case in point. They are engaged in multiple communities or points of contact, specifically that of their cultural heritage with that of the dominant narrative. When constructing multicultural identities, children and their families confront competing and contradictory discourses that marginalize their home countries, languages, and practices. Martínez-Roldán and Malavé's (2011) case studies on immigrant families living in the borderlands between Arizona and Mexico illustrate the children's struggle to mediate their parents' cultural narratives with the narratives of others, particularly the narratives authored by their peers and by their school. Their search for identity is centered on "cultural and ideological struggles in homes, schools, and communities, and these multiple narratives and experiences are mediating children's sense of self" (Martínez-Roldán and Malavé 2011, 67).

Children who are bilingual and biliterate need opportunities and spaces to use hybrid language practices to convey these important cultural and familial identities. Often, such spaces are absent. For example, Juan, an Afro Latino bilingual second grader (second-generation Mexican immigrant) in New York City employed hybrid practices in recounting an interview with his father about how his father experienced the 9/11 attacks. He had conducted the interview as directed by his teacher; yet, because his father worked the night shift, he did not have the time to write anything down. He recounted the interview orally. In doing so, he displayed sophisticated hybrid linguistic practices. Here is a snippet of Juan's oral narrative:

> I felt the floor *moviendo violentamente* [moving violently (shaking)]. I thought I will always do what *mi papi* want. Always. *Mi papi me dijo que no sabe lo que está pasando . . . y me abrazó* [My dad told me he did not know what's going on . . . and hugged me.] I was so scared. We went outside. The building was falling, like collapsing. Hundreds of feet tall. Like falling, you know. Someone say "the plane hit the building." Papi said, "*No creo*" ["I can't believe it."] And people crying and screaming. And people saying they be good from now on, you know. Papi took me inside. We turn the tele [TV] on. It was happening. All before I come to school. (Souto-Manning and Martell 2016, 11)

Juan used information from the Internet (e.g., "hundreds of feet tall"), from a book that had been read by his teacher (e.g., "collapsing"), and TV interviews (e.g., "the plane hit the building"), in conjunction with his father's words to intertextually craft this narrative. He engaged in translanguaging, a powerful hybrid language practice, knowledgeably weaving together dominant

American English, Spanish, and African American language. Regrettably, such sophisticated language practices are often dismissed. Educators often meet hybrid language and literacy practices with much skepticism (Souto-Manning 2013a). In addition to language ideologies, which continue to position dominant languages as more powerful (dominant American English in the U.S.), promote linguistic hierarchies (as in the case of Spanishes), and deem languages to be problematic (such as the positioning that "'Black English' coarsens culture" [Johnson 2015]), Juan's linguistic remix may position him as not knowledgeable and fluent based on the lack of the interlocutor's familiarity with the semantics and syntax of the languages being employed. In addition, his realism may have been dismissed as not possible. Schools and schooling often fail to recognize rich linguistic repertoires and knowledgeable linguistic practices, such as those employed by Juan.

Going up to "God" with Jolene: Sponsors of Literacy

As highlighted by Heath (1983), communities have multiple and diverse cultural tools used to participate across settings and children draw on them to construct literacy-in-practice. That is, communities sponsor and provide spaces for the development of culturally situated literacies. Brandt (2001, 203) explicates this notion as "sponsors of literacy," which include people/groups that provide, restrict, or enhance a person's access to literate practices. Churches, community organizations, extended families, commercial spaces, and public facilities are examples of providers and "sponsors of literacy" that vary in practices that deem members communicatively competent.

The following conversation between Haeny Yoon and Jolene, within the context of Debbie White's kindergarten, illustrates this point:

> Jolene: Tomorrow is the weekend. It's not go-to-school day. Tomorrow, we can't go-to-school day. But tomorrow, I have another class that goes on weekends just.
> Haeny: Oh, really? What is it?
> Jolene: It's like, the same, but we speak a language.
> Haeny: Which language? [Jolene is Middle Eastern and goes to a mosque.]
> Jolene: Um, it's a different language.
> Haeny: Yea, what is it? What's it called?
> Jolene: If we speak that language and read and do everything, and we do anything, and I be good all day, the God [she points up] will bring us to him.
> Haeny: Oh.
> Jolene: That's why I have to do a great job.
> Haeny: What do you read?
> Jolene: We're reading a language that I do . . . a different language.

For Jolene, participation in a language community was ideological, set against the backdrop of religious activity. Language was not just a developmental skill, but it was part of her livelihood—a way of going to God. Consequently, school was not the only place sponsoring her literacy practices. Her literacy was inextricably tied to her linguistic, ethnic, and religious identity, influencing her own participation in school.

For example, it was clear that Jolene was trying to do what she viewed as good or the right thing. When she shared her one published story with the rest of the class, she made sure to string together a variety of ideas that would position her as a good writer:

> [She holds up her picture, see Figure 1.1] This is—it says Mrs. White. She's with me and it says, "Jolene," and then we're going to pick an apple, and all those are, um, the . . . tomatoes. This is the farm. And, I'm picking some apples to eat them. They're done growing, and there's some shapes and hearts and the . . . the rainbows, the rainbows are here. The sun is here with the rain, rainbows. And these are the flowers are already growed, and these are the corn, and these are the hearts all around. And, these are the hearts that I drawed, and I drawed some yellow hearts and some red hearts and those are the flowers. And this is the house behind them and this is the— this is the rainbow. It's coming really big this time, and these are the hearts,

FIGURE 1.1 Jolene's Writing Piece (Page 1)

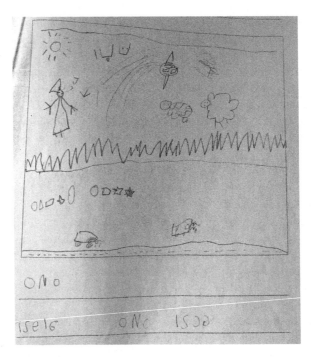

FIGURE 1.2 Jolene's Writing Piece (Page 2)

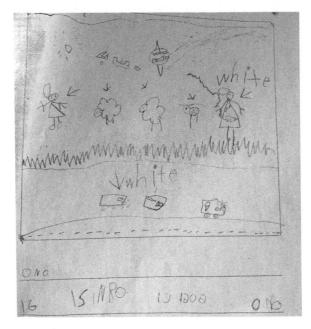

FIGURE 1.3 Jolene's Writing Piece (Page 3)

little tiny hearts, and these are the, um, corn again, and these are the clouds and these are the trees. And they're yummy, one bite, and we picked one tomato and then we put it on the—.

Debbie White had to graciously interrupt her with, "I hate to interrupt you but we have to get to all these stories. But children, did you look at all the details in her story? And she knew about every one of them."

Jolene was proud of herself as she smiled, took a bow (as Debbie taught them), and sat down. Her story documented and recounted the events of the past month at school: They went to an apple orchard, visited a farm, learned about different shapes in math (they were actually assessed on knowing five different shapes), and watched Debbie model a story about clouds and rain. Jolene, in an effort to please her teacher and parents (maybe even God), incorporated as many elements of writing a story that she could place on three pages (the length of her story). Jolene used literacy as a tool to identify herself as a good writer. She attributed good writing to being a good girl. In Jolene's world, these were highly important attributes that led ultimately to her entrance into God's world. While her story was "excessive" (in that she included everything that she interpreted as successful writing), her attention to detail and mechanics were applauded. Her ability and desire to follow the rules positioned her to be successful in school—specifically within literacy events, such as writing. Within this context, details and mechanics were perceived by the children to be more important than communicating and making meaning in public spaces; children like Jolene viewed writing pieces that were publishable under school terms as opposed to social terms—a clear emphasis during their informal, table group time.

Jolene also spent time regulating the actions of others, reminding them of rules she deemed unbreakable. Jolene valued rules, and while she imposed these rules on others, she did not come off bossy or mean. The rules she lived by were reappropriations of how she took up the suggestions of others as well as how she viewed the world. She placed herself within these bounded constructs because it gave her a sense of belonging in her communities: church, home, classroom, and the table. Her attempts to regulate others were attempts at defining the community's practices:

> "Coloring with crayons. Yes! Coloring with pencils? No!"
> "You didn't draw your name. You didn't draw your name. You have to draw your name. . . . Look, I draw my name on every page."
> "You need to finish your sheet. . . . Finish your piece."

Unsolicited by other children, Jolene offered others ways to regulate themselves, and it was up to those children to accept or refuse her suggestions. For Jolene, rules were comfortable. The structures allowed her to control her own actions and place them in categories appropriate for her worldview. Regulating writing workshop practices was not the goal of Debbie's instruction. However, Jolene equated good writing with good behavior. Others did not have to live by these rules or as Lou put it, "*You* finish *your* sheet, don't worry about *me!*" Lou obviously had his own ways of living in this context.

For many of her peers at this table (mainly Lou, Jaquan, and Tonea), literacy was clearly a social event that moved between writing each other into their stories, making inquiries into their social lives outside of school, debating the reality of television shows and playing around with ideas on and off the paper. Therefore, their complex literacies were not captured by their written products; their successful engagement with literacy was not fortified by accompanying written texts that deemed them capable by official standards. The children were clearly interested in each other's stories. In listening to the flurry of social activity at this table, we discover a great deal about children's family lives, their popular culture interests, their Halloween plans, and their friendships. Whether the stories were true or not, the children kept their relationships at the center of each writing workshop period, using writing as a way to document the social activity on any given day. Mrs. White's willingness to allow children's talk to transgress typical boundaries of silence and individualism gave credence to the social work of learning to write.

> Even within a climate where students' identities are increasingly circum-
> scribed, however, there continues to exist possibilities for productive disrup-
> tion of these normative definitions of what it means to be literate within
> classroom boundaries. (Vasudevan, Schultz, and Bateman 2010, 446)

As a social participant at her table, even the story Jolene shared shifted several times in the flow of conversation with her peers. However, in the official literacy event, Jolene treated storytelling as a performance—a way to show her own competence. Her demonstration of certain competencies (e.g., ability to copy the teacher, knowledge of shapes and letters, and details in her story) gave her a chance to make her identity as a "good writer" public. Her tablemates, who arguably helped her accomplish this work through dialogic interactions, were not recognized with the same level of competence (as evidenced by test scores and written texts). Therefore, while permeability in curriculum (Dyson, 1993) and classroom interactions is one part of rethinking literacies, the very definitions of enacting, performing, assessing, and measuring literacies must also be rethought. Inevitably, rethinking literacy to encompass the social work of children like Lou, Jaquan, and Tonea requires a reexamination of literate identities as multiple and complex rather than singular and simplistic.

Literate Identities: When Children's Agency Becomes the Standard

Children are cast into different positions depending on the limitations of literacy curricula. In Falchi, Axelrod, and Genishi's study (2014) of young children's writing enactments in school settings, the identity of being a "good student" correlated with compliance, while educators saw "bad students" as resistant. Narrow curricular constraints limit the potential for children to enact multifaceted identities as seen in Luisa, a pre-K child who stuck to following directions and carrying out the writing tasks assigned to her (see Falchi et al. 2014). On the other hand, another child, Miguel, resisted these constraints and expressed himself through drawing, design, and creative placement of writing and drawing on the page. However, his multimodal productions were not recognized or validated as valuable literacy attempts (Wortham 2004; Yelland et al. 2008). Privileging specific interactions with literacy creates explicit and implicit judgments about who is literate within classroom spaces. Therefore, it is important to open up curricular possibilities, moving from arbitrary skills as the standard to fostering children's agency as a worthwhile pursuit.

Making Rainbow Connections: Backing up to Table 1

Children, in relationship with one another, build practices, values, and traditions within local and situated contexts making literacy a social practice, "rooted in conceptions of knowledge, identity, and being" (Street 2003, 78). Social relationships underscore the importance of children's participation in literacy events since "stories are not private affairs; the individual imagination plays host to all the stimulation in the environment and causes ripples of ideas to encircle the listeners" (Paley 1990, 21). In Debbie White's classroom, the writing workshop was one of those curricular opportunities where children's play and literacy intertwined. Writing workshop lasted anywhere from forty-five minutes to one hour. She followed the typical protocol for a writing workshop: she began with a mini-lesson, moved into independent writing, and brought the children together to share at the end. During the independent writing time, she circulated around the room conferring with children about their writing (Calkins 1986; Graves 1983). The independent writing time was hardly silent, but likened to a collaborative office space where children chatted about their lives, discussed their writing intentions, or played around.

As was typical, some children were declaring their writing moves in real time.

> Lou said, "I'm making a rainbow," and he proceeded to draw a rainbow with red on the outside and blue on the inside. In response to Lou's declaration, Jaquan joined in the practice, and Jaquan started to make a rainbow too, and soon, Tonea followed. Tonea's was red on the outside, blue in the middle, and orange on the inside.
>
> Tonea commented, "It's rainbow colored. I went on rainbow connection." She then turned her attention to Jon and asked him, "Is you going to fancy it up?" meaning "Are you going to draw a rainbow too?"
>
> Jon responded with, "Will you just work on your own business?"

Lou drew a rainbow in that scene that would later become a trademark of all the children's stories at this table, including Jon's. In fact, while sharing their stories with the others in the classroom, each of them had what seemed like a precarious rainbow embedded into their stories. However, the social dramas in this table tell a larger story about the rainbow—it became a practice that was an emblem of their belonging. As seen earlier, Jolene described everything in her scene including the rainbow while sharing her published work.

Jon simply explained the rainbow away at the end, even though the rainbow really had very little to do with this plot line:

> These are the towers. Here's the motorcycle park right there. Here's the truck that's carrying the boxes. And me gonna drive it. The ice cream truck is right here. Here's me. I'm gonna get into it and make ice cream. . . . Here's a rainbow at the end.

Whether it made sense or not, Jon's rainbow was a textual response to Tonea as if to say, "I am going to draw a rainbow." Being left out of the rainbow enterprise was not consistent with the rest of his tablemates. The making of rainbows was a literacy event, an idea borrowed from one child to another, and a "verbal banner" (Paley 1990, 41) that became a symbol of this group's products. In this sense, identities and practices belong to individuals, but they also belong to the group in the enactment of social relationships.

Literacy is rooted in social practices, and a "particular literacy will be dependent on those particular contexts" (Street 2003, 78). Thus, literacies are always changing and a variety of literacies are taking shape through social movements locally and globally. For example, #hashtags and textspeak (e.g., LOL) are cultural practices, taken up by people as part of individual and group identity. Therefore, young children take up literacies in the same way—they draw from this larger social culture, their school practices, their peer interactions, and their family/ community life to enact their own symbolic "rainbows," or the practices that are important for their cultural and social identities. It is important and necessary to give children space to practice literacy flexibly, reconceptualizing early literacy from a didactic model of language teaching to a dialogic model of language conceptualizing, where possibilities for new and creative practices can take shape (Bakhtin 1981; Freire 1970).

Halloween Costumes and Horror Movies: The Twist and Turns of Conversation

On one occasion, Lou and Jaquan were arguing about the existence of Michael Myers, a figure from a satirical horror movie series (*Scream*). As Halloween was fast approaching, it was not uncommon for children to talk about Halloween costumes as well as scary movie plots. Their back-and-forth exchange included a fight about whether Michael Myers was real or fake, whether being on TV constituted nonexistence, and the insistence that wearing a mask shows that Michael Myers is a person, not a murderer. Within the argument were grandiose claims to support their opinions. Lou claimed to have seen Michael Myers in front of the local high school. Jaquan insisted that he saw him at a Halloween party, and he was (in fact) just a person with a mask. And while Lou's story got gorier with blood and chainsaws, Jaquan, Tonea, and Jon accused Lou of lying but repeatedly looked at Haeny for affirmation. In the end, they agreed to watch out for Chucky (the scary doll that comes to life):

> Jaquan: Chucky. No, Chucky, you don't mess with him. Don't mess with him.
> Lou: Yea, Chucky will kill you.

All the while, the children placed ideas on paper against the backdrop of scary stories. Their resulting stories were not pictures of chainsaws, bloody deaths, and killer dolls. Arguably, they knew how to navigate the official space of school, understanding what ideas were appropriate for their secret conversations and what ideas were appropriate for public sharing. Rainbows were embraced and killer dolls were discarded.

On other occasions, children were performing for each other rather than for the teacher, looking for peer affirmation on their literacy attempts. Jolene was testing out her skills by getting as close as she could to her paper and seeing if she could draw a star.

> Jolene: Hey guys. Hey guys. Look! When I put my hair down on the paper [She covers her paper with her hair falling forward and face right up to the paper with pencil in hand], I can do a star. Look. I put my head down and the star is really perfect. I still know how to draw a star.

Impressed by her accomplishments, Lou asked her to draw a special star for him as well while Jon commented, "That's for real. For reals," as he tested out his new verbal repository of phrases. Even Jolene, a consistent rule-follower, was prone to these lapses in writing, giving in to her inclination to play. Her demonstration of a newfound skill was not meant to be overlooked. She wanted her peers to be a part of her new discovery, and their response was expected. Thus, children's engagement within a writing workshop was not limited to impressing the teacher or completing the writing task set before them. Arguably, interactions revealed at this table make a case for the interplay of social interactions and writing, both necessary in accomplishing school-sanctioned events. Without the space to play, to talk, to question, and to inquire of each other, the goals of writing are mis-aligned with the social intentions and motivations of young children.

Jon was writing his name on the back of his paper and said out loud, "Writing workshop is so fun." However, we would venture to assume that he does not seem to be referring to the writing workshop from the curriculum's definition, but the writing workshop from a child's perspective. It was fun to play with the other children at the table and talk to each other about matters that concerned their immediate lives. The version of writing memorialized in the hallways and fancied up for publishing in the school world were not representations of the social and linguistic play occurring between the writers at this table—the teasing, the joking, the helping, the playing, etc. Some of these social acts were erased from their paper anyway, remnants of past experiences in historically situated times. The conversations around this table can be interpreted in one of two ways: as material to move their literacy intentions or as frivolous noise impeding "real" writing (e.g., the act of representing letters and words on paper). Luckily for them, Debbie White valued the sideways approach to writing and the roundabout ways in which writing appeared on paper. She knew that children were not always engaged in the physical act of writing, but she rarely saw the need to interrupt their "disruptions" (Yoon 2013). She, like master teacher Vivian Paley, welcomed different paths toward literacy because, more importantly, it was important to know who children were. She knew that

> Those who never disrupt may be withholding too much. Until they tell us more of what is on their minds they may not be able to listen to what *we* have to say. There is a tendency to look upon the noisy, repetitious fantasies of children as *noneducational*, but helicopters and kittens and superhero capes and Barbie dolls are storytelling aids and conversational tools. Without them, the range of what we listen to and talk about is arbitrarily circumscribed by the adult point of view. (Paley 1990, 38)

Identity Matters: The Moral and Ethical Obligations in Understanding Children as Agents

Childhood is a historically, socially, culturally, and politically situated period of time that belongs to specific persons in society. This distinct group (Table 1) engages in shared cultural practices as they produce and enact their own social, political, and cultural agendas. Discourses around childhood innocence, however, are often symbolic representations of adult nostalgia and utopian futures used to enforce singular family values, political/social agendas, government policies, and traditional cultural values (Bentley and Souto-Manning 2016; Jenkins 1998). The need to regulate childhood(s) leaves children from nontraditional backgrounds limited spaces to sustain their culture and narrowed choices in school: assimilate or resist—both of which have long-term and potentially dangerous consequences for children's identities in the world. In this section, we place importance on child agency as an ethical obligation and commitment to young children.

Uncovering Identities: Unlocking Children's Multiple Stories

> We cannot uncover every thought that influences a child. Nor is it necessary. The connections between one event and another will be made in the process of living, at home and at school. In both places the adult who listens and responds to what the children say can be an important guide. But the children themselves will unlock—or lock, if need be—the doors to their secrets as they play out their scenes; and the images in their minds will be adapted to the people and events around them. (Paley 1990, 130)

Vivian Paley's body of work is, undoubtedly, about uncovering and understanding children's identities. Rather than positioned as passive recipients of knowledge and practices, she views children as individuals who bring with them stories meant to be lived out with others—with an attention to relational literacies, which "are never produced singularly or in isolation but rather depend on interaction" (Licona and Chávez 2015, 96).

Young children are involved in their own "communities of practice" where they bring personal and cultural theories to classroom spaces in order to "develop, negotiate, and share them" (Wenger 1998, 48), simultaneously making sense of their world. This idea gives us a perspective of learning that is situated in the lived experiences of children as they participate with the materials, the circumstances, and the people within specific contexts. Embedded in this perspective is that learning is a social act, and as we participate and interact with each other, it shapes who we are, what we do, and how we interpret and come to understand what we do. Wenger's (1998) social theory underscores the intertwining of meaning, practice, community, and identity within participation:

- **Meaning:** Both individually and collectively, we make our worlds meaningful through experience.
- **Practice:** We use resources, frameworks, and perspectives to engage in action.
- **Community:** We learn through participating and belonging by being recognized and valued.
- **Identity:** We become who we are through participation.

It is important to think about issues of identity and belonging more than skills and information for young children as we rethink early literacy. Undeniably, schools in the U.S. are more focused on the former than they are on the latter. School should not only be about the content, which can arguably be learned from other places and may not be the most important aspect of education (as proposed by Freire 1970), but the opportunities that children have to cultivate and construct their social identities. Over time, the children in this chapter reflect practices that represent their own individual journeys into literacy as well as "a kind of community created over time by the sustained pursuit of a shared enterprise" (Wenger 1998, 45).

Cultural Literacy: The Fight for Diversity

E. D. Hirsch, the chair and founder of Core Knowledge (see www.coreknowledge
.org/ed-hirsch-jr), defined cultural literacy as a shared set of values and knowledge that should make up the repertoire of every child's background knowledge.
Consequently, he asserts that teachers need to explicitly impart children with
the "right" knowledge that makes up the fabric of American culture. However,
the definition of what is deemed "right" or universal for everyone to know is
often a question of power rather than an easily agreed upon list of attributes. The
Core Knowledge curriculum, as a result, claims to specify the kinds of knowledge
necessary for proficiency by prescribing the books, materials, activities, and conversations required between teachers and students. The problem with this kind
of thinking is rather clear—at some point, an individual or an institution needs
to decide which knowledge is valuable. For Hirsch, a White man who graduated
from an Ivy League college to determine cultural knowledge alone is problematic.
Furthermore, his belief that a single American identity needs to replace the mul-
tiplicity of cultural identities fuels comments like the one described earlier with
regard to the international flag of the U.S. mural in a kindergarten classroom in
New York City. For Hirsch, multicultural ideals threaten the social fabric of the
country, turning literacy into a political battle for cultural dominance. In his opin-
ion, multicultural education should not be allowed to "supplant or interfere with
our schools' responsibility to ensure our children's mastery of American literate
culture" (Hirsch Jr. 1987, 18).

Multiplicity of Identities: Table 1 on the Core Knowledge Block

Let us consider for a moment what this ideology looks like for young children,
like the ones introduced earlier, entering the space of school. For Tonea, her identity as an African American girl from a low-income community is located by
schools and schooling on a societal spectrum that deems her as less-privileged
and different. When girls like Tonea walk into the space of school, they are usually given interventions and specified curricula that tend to narrow the creative
options available for inquiry. Instead, the books provided, the content chosen, and
the strategies taught proliferate other people's cultures rather than cultivating her
own. Tonea is taught (via curriculum) that the "proper" or "appropriate" pathways
toward success are achieved through understanding and taking up Eurocentric
knowledge and ways of being (New and Mallory, 1994). Reminiscent in this
scenario is the vicious cycle of schooling:

> I see many students from "undesirable" class backgrounds become unable
> to complete their studies because the contradictions between the behavior
> necessary to "make it" in the academy and those that allowed them to be
> comfortable at home, with their families and friends, are just too great.
> (hooks 1994, 182)

Lou and Jaquan, despite their wild tales and adult-like exchanges of who is right or wrong, are often seen as problems and disruptions in need of compliance and docility. For Black boys, disruptions turn into fear, which in turn become justification for control and surveillance (Foucault 1977). While identities, as mentioned earlier, are deliberate choices that people take up, they are also influenced by the identities ascribed on us by other people, other communities, cultural institutions, and the larger society. Ascribed identities are especially important for Black boys growing up in America:

> To be seen as the "beast" with a "fearsome reputation" incites one not just to play the role but to see oneself that way. To be recognized that way is to be, as Fanon put it, "sealed into that crushing objecthood." The danger is in the desire for recognition, the subject of one's identification becomes the fantasmatic threatening figure of black masculinity. The act becomes reality. (Ferguson 2001, 125)

In other words, we start to embody and become who others expect us to be through acts of resistance and submission.

On the contrary, Jon, a White boy from a middle-class family enjoys the pleasures of sliding in and out of character. While he, at times, exhibited a rather short fuse and terse response to both his teachers and peers, his racial identity was not synonymous with fear. When Debbie White asked him a simple question like, "What are you working on? I'm curious about what's happening in your story," he looked at her dryly with eyebrows furrowed and said, "Give me a minute!" Debbie, in her usual way, responded, "That's what authors do sometimes, they want to take a minute." Although I suspect that Debbie would respond in clever ways to most of the students, there are teachers who consciously and unconsciously differentiate their attitudes in racialized ways. Jon, being identified as White, is afforded with privileges that are intangible to his peers of color. On one hand, Jon can move easily from "for reals" to "I'm gonna" without interventions to fix his perceived linguistic mistakes. On the other hand, children of color who speak language varieties are not given the same affordances and are immediately fixed and corrected (Dyson and Smitherman 2009).

And finally we turn to Jolene, a child who produced school-worthy written work and attempted to stay on task, although her ability to do this slipped in and out as she interacted with peers. However, she was also of Islamic faith and prone to stereotypical assumptions attached to those who use the language and participate in the practices related to that identity. Since the attacks on the World Trade Center, bombings orchestrated by al-Qaeda, and heavy-handed dogmatism led by Islamic extremists, educators could easily see her as a threat for no reason other than her religious affiliations and physical descriptors—important markers of her identity. Students like Jolene walk through our schools feeling alienated and forced to defend how they enact their identities. While children of other religions practice their faith openly, Jolene will likely have to justify her religious practices in front of others who are openly suspicious and hostile to her ideals.

Achieving One's Own Identity

We bring up these important social, cultural, and linguistic markers of personhood because literacy is not a neutral practice or a context-free endeavor. "Literacy is a social practice. . . . It is always embedded in socially constructed epistemological principles . . . rooted in conceptions of knowledge, identity, and being" (Street 2003, 77–78). Thus, claims that literacy can be reduced to a set of universal skills ignore the sociohistorical and cultural moments in which literacy exists. For instance, social media and other digital technologies have significantly changed what it means to participate in the cultural world. Moreover, those individuals traditionally viewed as competent communicators (e.g., book authors) may find themselves incompetent with social media (e.g., Twitter). Arguably, gathering Twitter followers and composing worthy tweets are skills that take practice and repeated participation over time. The changing nature of literacy is emphasized because proponents of "Core Knowledge" (e.g., Hirsch) and other reductive literacy curriculum programs view literacy as a stable set of objective skills whereas literacy in the social world is ever-changing, transforming before many of us catch up. Objectivity is hardly the goal of reading and writing and rightly so. Writing is "a dialogic practice, where words carry meanings that work to include and exclude others as well as spark conversations that transform ideas" (Yoon 2016, 3).

So, why do we discuss identity in relation to language learning for young children? The relevant and most important answer relates to issues of equity in institutions like school. Children from historically marginalized groups will find limited resources, labeling, inequitable assessment measures, and monocultural curriculum that is not only culturally confining, but intellectually sparse. The decontextualized language exercises that are bare bones and basics oriented fail to capture the complex weaving of children's stories, words, and social connections (Dyson 2013). Thus, the emphasis on basics proves unethical—children of color are not given as many opportunities (if at all) to engage in inquiry, to play deeply with their peers, to engage in critical discussions, to challenge hierarchies related to self and language, and to expand their cultural identities. The children who populate these pages offer multiple, complex narratives of literate identities where children deemed "below average" demonstrate an expansive literacy repertoire. It is obvious that "children are not first and foremost learners; they are first and foremost people living the complexities of their day-to-day lives" (Dyson 1995, 36).

We conclude this chapter by tying identity and literacy with the purpose of education. If schools are to provide windows and mirrors into the self and the world (Bishop 1990), we must foster productive spaces for children to thread together their social desires. We do not mean that children should not learn about the language of power nor should teachers refrain from teaching children basic skills related to reading and writing (Adger, Wolfram, and Christian 2007; Ladson-Billings and Tate 1995). However, it is important to ensure that language skills are embedded in authentic and relevant experiences that are meaningful for children's social lives. These spaces should embody the voices and actions of children who are actively inquiring and making decisions about the world around them. James Baldwin (1963) succinctly summarizes how one can expect to achieve their potential identity in his essay entitled, "A Talk to Teachers." He wrote:

> The purpose of education, finally, is to create in a person the ability to look at the world for himself, to make his own decisions, to say to himself this is black or this is white, to decide for himself whether there is a God in heaven or not. To ask questions of the universe, and then learn to live with those questions, is the way he achieves his own identity. (pp. 678–679)

With this purpose in mind, we take a sociopolitical approach as we redefine early literacy in the following chapter.

2

READING AND REWRITING WORLDS AND WORDS

Reading the world always precedes reading the word, and reading the word implies continually reading the world. . . . This movement from the world to the word is always present; even the spoken word flows from our reading of the world. In a way . . . reading the word is not preceded merely by reading the world, but by a certain form of writing it or rewriting it . . . of transforming it by means of conscious, practical work. . . . This dynamic movement is central to the literacy process. (Freire and Macedo 1987, 35)

Reading Words and/in Worlds

Young children start reading worlds much earlier than they read words. They read faces, author relationships, and communicate through coos, babbles, and cries. As young children recognize the faces of their parents or other caregivers, they identify and may start moving toward their source of nourishment before they read printed words. For example, an infant may start crying and burrowing into the mother's breast to express his or her need for milk. Infants may smile when they see a familiar face—of a caregiver or a sibling.

A few hours after giving birth, when Mariana stuck her tongue out at her newborn son, he stuck out his tongue back at her, engaging in a communicative act. Later, when he heard her voice, he would turn toward the sound. Some time later, when she picked him up from infant care, he would smile when he saw her face, clearly signaling identification, since he did not smile at other adults picking up other infants in the same locale. Mariana's son makes visible how young children author actions and interactions prior to voicing words, long before muttering a single intelligible syllable or utterance. Infants often move from extralinguistic interactions to coos and babbles, after which they may start communicating through semblances of words, through approximations.

Eight-month-old Antonio referred to his brother, Tomás, as *yaya*. While not consistent with the phonetics of Tomás and having a completely different meaning in another context (for example, γιαγιά means grandmother in Greek), *yaya* came to signify Tomás within the context of Antonio's family. Prior to speaking any words aside from mama and dada (for mommy and daddy), Antonio composed his first sentence, "*yaya ye yu?*" (with the intonation of Yaya, where are you?). When Antonio voiced "*yaya ye yu?*" loudly enough, if Tomás was home, he would come to Antonio. This reinforced the function of "*yaya ye yu?*" as an effective way of calling his sibling. When his sibling appeared, often voicing "Antonio!" or "I'm here!" Antonio giggled excitedly.

When adults do not understand actions such as the ones authored by Mariana's sons as reading and writing, as literacy broadly conceived, we see young children in terms of what they cannot do (in terms of deficits). This adult-centric view of literacy—of what counts as reading and writing—results in comparisons that impose adult timelines, practices, and outcomes onto children in inappropriate ways; in ways that frame young children as already being behind before they are born. However, a deeper examination of literacy as a social construction (introduced in Chapter 1) reveals the depth of practices that young children (even from infancy) exhibit as ways of asserting themselves in the world and connecting in relationship with those who inhabit it.

From early infancy, through coos, babbles, cries, smiles, gestures, and words, they author themselves in their worlds. They make sense and use symbols and grow to understand what Vygotsky (1978) described as a two-tiered symbol system. Whereas young children may start reading and labeling all vehicles similarly—and may even say "car" when they see a truck, a bus, or an airplane—they are already making sense of a symbol system, using one utterance to refer to actual vehicles. Eventually, they differentiate between the different kinds of vehicles, for example, using truck, car, and plane to signify different vehicles. Then, as they start reading and writing the words for truck, bus, and car, they use "language as a symbol or representation of something two steps away from the real thing . . . [involving] a second-order or twice-removed level of symbolization" (Meier 2004, 83). It is thus essential for early childhood educators and researchers to understand young children as literate beings, learning from their literacy practices—going from worlds to symbols, such as words—from infancy.

Young Children as Literate Beings

Young children's literacy processes differ from those of adults—that is, they are young authors whose writing practices differ in motivation and intent from that of adults (Ray and Glover 2008). They are symbol makers and symbol weavers, linking "play, pictures and print" (Dyson 1990, 50) to make meaning.

With our often narrow conceptualizations of what comprises literacy, we adults fail to see young children's brilliance when we do not recognize that learning how to read and write is a tiered process (Dyson 1982; Meier 2004; Vygotsky 1978) embedded in specific sociopolitical contexts (Freire 1970; Freire and Macedo 1987).

Many researchers have documented the processes of young children learning how to read and write symbols, what Vygotsky (1978) called "first-order" and "second-order" symbol systems. For example, when children are developing as writers they may start with marks on a page. Eventually, these marks become "mnemotechnic symbols," which are "indicatory signs for memory purposes" (Vygotsky 1978, 115). Through such seemingly simplistic acts, young children engage in developing (even if temporarily) their own sophisticated symbol system(s)—whether through scribbles, pictures, figures, or other symbols. In doing so, their:

> [W]ritten signs are entirely first-order symbols . . . directly denoting objects or actions, and the child has yet to reach second-order symbolism, which involves the creation of written signs for the spoken symbols of words. For this the child must make a basic discovery—namely that one can draw not only things but also speech. (Vygotsky 1978, 115)

While important as markers of reading and writing growth, a sole focus on symbolic representation ignores a central aspect of early literacy: reading, rereading, understanding, questioning, and rewriting worlds.

Young children develop as readers, writers, and speakers because reading, writing, and talking serve a sociofunctional purpose: to communicate (Halliday 1978). These also serve a political purpose: to speak up and advocate for fairness, to negotiate one's place in the world, and to challenge hierarchies of power. To understand that children are born literate, it is important to reconceptualize literacy in their terms, moving away from seeing vocabulary, phonological awareness and sensitivity, and print knowledge as requisite pieces of the early literacy puzzle (Dickinson et al. 2003; Dyson 2013). Instead, literacy learning needs to be acknowledged as a complex and expansive process, which often becomes reduced and oversimplified in colonizing ways. Such a reductionist and (over)simplistic approach to literacy becomes reified by policies and mandates linked to assessments and often to funding.

Within the context of the U.S., Siegel (2006, 75) verifies that "literacy is shrinking to fit federal and state educational policies that place severe limitations on what it means to be literate, and thus, on who can be literate." Yet, according to Halliday (1978, 57), reading and writing are fundamentally "an extension of the functional potential of language" and as such should not be tamed or reduced, but unleashed and expanded in ways that recognize the agency of young children.

On Play as Literacy

To realize the full functional potential of language in all of its forms (including literacy), we must acknowledge that young children develop language repertoires through authentic interactions and literacies in mediums that go much beyond pages or writeable surfaces. Young children are not merely readers of symbols, but readers of and interactors in social situations. This is very visible in children's play. In play, children not only play with oral language, but engage in resignification, using objects as symbols for others. For example, in Helena's Early Head Start classroom in Georgia, U.S., three-year-old Andreea grabbed a magnifying glass from the science center and took it over to the housekeeping area. That magnifying glass was first used as a spoon to stir a pot on top of the plastic stove. As her friend Nya approached her, asking, "I been calling you. Why ain't you answering?" the magnifying glass becomes a phone as Andreea holds it against the right side of her face. She alternates between saying "uh-huh" and "I know, I know" while nodding her head. Later that day, as Helena takes the children outside, the magnifying glass becomes a tray, on which Andreea serves (pretend) dessert, offered to teachers and peers alike. "Good morning, Ms. Helena! Some yummy dessert?" and later on as a way to look at bugs climbing up a plant. "There they go! There they go!" she says to Derrik, who's observing the bugs with her. As Andreea shows us, symbols such as magnifying glasses and other objects gain different meanings in different contexts . . . just as letters and letter chunks in written words and morphemes in orally spoken words. Through play, Andreea also shows us that she can plan, draft, and carry out different storylines. Play thus provides her space to develop actions not unlike those carried out by authors at a writing workshop (Calkins 1986), but in very child-centered ways.

Watching Andreea in light of the language components outlined by Lindfors (1987) and Genishi (1988), we see her engage with different components of oral language:

- Phonological (rules for combining sounds in a particular language—for example in English—*ng* comes at the end of a word; in Tagalog, it can come at the beginning: *ng-*)
- Semantic (combining morphemes to make words and sentences—e.g., combining the morphemes *walk* and *ing* to make *walking*)
- Syntactic (the rules that allow us to make sentences by combining morphemes)

Andreea combined and orchestrated these three components of oral language to communicate, speaking appropriately within the context of each situation. She combined morphemes to make up words, such as dessert- and -s to make desserts, displaying semantic knowledge. She put morphemes together to make meaning, "Some yummy desserts?" being clearly aware of the rules on how words can be combined to express meaning in English, despite variations within the

English language(s), and displayed her knowledge of syntax. While she muttered "uh-hum" and "I know, I know" while pretending to speak on the telephone, she issued a greeting and a question when serving desserts: "Good morning, Ms. Helena! Some yummy desserts?" That is, she also used pragmatics, or the rules of language use, to communicate differently when talking on the phone and when serving food. The understanding, development, and use of oral language and its components correlate with the components of written language and reading development: graphophonic, syntactic, semantic, and pragmatic (Souto-Manning and Martell 2016).

As we leave Helena's classroom and enter a kindergarten classroom in New York City, we see children copying letters and words. No housekeeping area is in sight. When asked about play, the teacher, Ms. Silva, regarded by the principal as an excellent teacher based on her students' reading growth according to a program entitled DRA (Developmental Reading Assessment), states, "We don't have time for that. I have to move them through reading levels." Such comments convey a dangerous assumption that play does not comprise learning and that play and literacy are separate. Contrary to Ms. Silva's perspective, we see play as literacy, if we just expand literacy to encompass all ways of making sense and making meaning in the world. Of course, reading and writing in traditional ways are part of that, but they do not comprise the entire definition of literacy.

Although children have an amazing capacity to develop language and an understanding of language rules by using language to communicate, more and more often classrooms like Ms. Silva's restrict the time and space children have to develop language as they interact socially through play. There is a mistaken understanding that teachers must show children how to engage in language and literacy practices. This is a misguided understanding that embraces a mythical, one-way, lockstep approach to learning. Genishi (1988, 2) explains that "children work through linguistic rules on their own because they use forms that adults never use, such as ... 'I see your feets.' ... Learning to talk requires time for development and practice in everyday situations. Constant correction of a child's speech is unproductive." Play offers fertile ground for language and literacy development and for children to figure out the rules and patterns of language. Play allows children to try out their emerging understandings in high-support, low-risk environments.

As master teacher Vivian Paley underscored, through play and story acting, young children are often in a quest for fairness through friendships, often involving fantasy—turning everyday spaces into the fantastic, turning reading rods into magic wands and blankets into capes. As young children play, they read situations around them and seek to disrupt those situations, reauthoring them more equitably. While we adults often think of authorship inherently involving the mechanics of writing, here we invite you to think of authoring and writing as two separate endeavors, albeit often enacted by the same person. For young children, however, the mechanics of writing can comprise an obstacle to their ability to communicate and diminish their ability to deploy language in sophisticated and complex ways. That is, children can author storylines without ever touching pencil (or other writing tool) to paper. They do this often—through play.

Through play, young children attend to storylines, settings, and characters. They bring to life conventional literacy concepts in unconventional ways (at least to adults). They competently plan their stories, draft them, revise storylines through multiple renderings, and develop complicated character plots. In the early years, play is literacy. And by this we do not mean that traditional literacy activities must substitute play, but that play is the grounds in which literacy skills develop. While we are aware that some would be hesitant to call for a definition of literacy which encompasses play, we make such a call as we strive to redefine literacy in expansive and inclusive ways, in ways that center on children's actions and in ways that position children competently.

Now that we have established play as literacy—not only in large strokes, as in making sense of and in the world, but also with regard to widely accepted literacy components, such as syntax and semantics—we turn to further exploring the content and common topic(s) of play in early childhood. To do so, we turn to the work of master teacher Vivian Paley.

On Fairness, Fantasy, and Friendship in Early Childhood

Fairness is a common theme in preschool classrooms, as documented by Vivian Paley (1988, 12). She identified fairness, fantasy, and friendship as "urgent matters" to preschool-aged children. She went on to explain: "When the issues were fantasy, friendship, and fairness (I called them the three F's), the speakers reached to their outer limits to explain and persuade. No one wanted to leave the circle until justice prevailed" (Paley 1988, 12). These were topics that mattered to her young students. Honoring young children's interests and foci, we recenter literacy on these urgent matters, so as to honor young children's voices and priorities, and redefine it in more inclusive and child-centered ways. Central to Paley's work is children's play as a necessary space to "frame meaningful conversations around equity and justice while simultaneously developing language" (Yoon 2014, 110).

In children's play, language is appropriated as children take up literate acts (reading, writing, talking, and gesturing) in order to sustain friendships, question ideas of fairness, and engage in fantasy storylines, through direct (and at times seemingly simplistic) statements, such as: "It's not fair!" For example, two-year-old Francisco loved *Peppa Pig* cartoons (about a talking pig with human characteristics and her adventures with family and friends, who are different kinds of animals). He read *Peppa Pig* actions and appropriated some of the linguistic features of the show. *Peppa Pig* used fairness-related language in some of its episodes as a way to relate to toddlers and preschoolers, who in particular are keen to issues of fairness. Peppa would mutter "Not fair!" when confronting something with which she disagreed, often authoring change. Noticing how muttering "Not fair!" positioned Peppa agentively (e.g., episodes 6: *Mysteries*, 14: *My Cousin Chloé*, and 33: *Piggy in the Middle*), Francisco decided to appropriate her phrase to (re)author his life. So, when Francisco was playing with a ball in preschool and another child got the ball and threw it away from Francisco, he muttered, "Not fair!" Initially, he got no response. Then, he walked over to his teacher, pointed to the ball, and said, "Not fair!" His teacher asked what happened. Francisco pointed to the boy and said, "He. He did this," while making the movement of throwing the ball away. The teacher called the other child to resolve the situation. They talked. The other child walked away, got the ball, handed it to Francisco, and said, "Sorry. Not fair." Francisco smiled.

This quest for fairness embraced by so many young children, as documented by Paley, is also illustrated by children's books, including one titled *It's Not Fair* (Rosenthal and Lichtenheld 2008), in which young children repeat "It's not fair!" after a number of questions and statements. Yet, it rarely delves into the racialized nature of fairness play in early childhood classrooms. That is, when issues of fairness address larger societal privileges, such as racism and xenophobia, they are often positioned outside the purview of early childhood education. This is signaled by realistic fiction books focusing on issues of social justice. For example, *That's Not Fair!/¡No Es Justo!: Emma Tenayuca's Struggle for Justice/La Lucha de Emma Tenayuca por la Justicia* (Tafolla and Teneyuca 2008) recounts the struggles for a fair wage by pecan shellers who worked twelve hours a day, seven days a week in San Antonio, Texas, when their already low wages were cut in half in 1938; its target audience is children in grades 2 through 6 (equivalent to ages 7–12), according to the *School Library Journal*. Another book, *When a Bully Is President: Truth and Creativity for Oppressive Times* (Gonzalez 2017), addresses issues of harassment, hate, and colonialism in light of the election of American president Donald J. Trump, who instigated hate incidents and signed hateful executive actions, which denied humanity to women, Muslims, Mexican Americans, and many other groups; it is geared toward children ages 7–10. Both of these—along with many social-justice focused children's books—exclude very young children, as if they were unable to grasp injustices; they are both geared at ages mostly outside of the early childhood range.

Recognizing that young children are navigating issues of fairness (what they will later relabel justice) from the earliest years, as we position play as early literacy and fairness as a central issue in early childhood play, we delve into issues of play and early literacy as racialized privileges, which deny children of color learning opportunities from early on. While this is a controversial issue, play can only be seen as central in early literacy if it is positioned as a right to all, as opposed to a racialized privilege to some (Souto-Manning 2017). And we can only position play as a right if we name the ways in which it is racialized today.

Play and Early Literacy as Racialized Privileges

Ironically, the opportunity to play is not fairly distributed among all children. We are fully aware that access to free play is a privileged practice, especially absent in the lives of Black boys, who are often situated as problems to be controlled rather than children who need to play. Their fantasy play is often viewed as dangerous, shrouded in the discourse of Black bodies in the political landscape. A clear example is the murder of twelve-year-old Tamir Rice, who was playing with a toy gun by a community center. Arguably, many of his White peers engage in similar play (e.g., superhero play, war games, good vs. evil), but Black boys are positioned as violent more often than their White counterparts. A Black boy can be seen as a "beast with a fearsome reputation" (Ferguson 2001, 125); even their pretend play is closely monitored and viewed as a threat, rendering dire, even fatal consequences. So is their behavior. This is evidenced by the disproportionate rates of suspension of Black and Brown boys in U.S. preschools, as documented by the U.S. Department of Education Office for Civil Rights (2014). Black children comprise 18 percent of U.S. preschoolers; yet, nearly 50 percent of out-of-school suspensions at the preschool level are suspensions of Black four-year-olds. Tunette Powell, whose sons were suspended multiple times throughout their preschool years, recounted her frustrations at a system and society that consistently punished her Black sons for actions that White boys got away with. Her point was not that misbehavior should go unpunished, but that there continues to be undeniable and underlying prejudices that lead to discrepancies in disciplinary policies.

Ladson-Billings (2011) has documented how African American boys are often seen as men, enduring harsher consequences for their actions. In response, she calls for the protection and preservation of the childhood of Black boys—a time when children should play, pretending with and against ideas from the cultural communities in which they belong. At times, children's play is ingenious and worthy of marvel; other times it is contradictory and disturbing. However, all children should have this right to explore and try out the complexities that come with "reading the world." Nevertheless, it is not uncommon to hear Black parents talk about the real dangers of their sons playing with toy guns—and the potentially high costs: their very lives. Thus, as a way of defining literacy in racially just ways, we acknowledge the importance of fantasy to childhood, while understanding fantasy as a racialized privilege in the early years.

But before turning to problematizing traditional definitions of literacy and redefining early literacy in racially just ways, we turn to the ways in which families of color have historically been authored as biologically inferior or as having impoverished cultural practices. Such readings of minoritized individuals and communities have infused the valuating of their literacy practices. As a result, their literacy practices are typically seen through a similar paradigmatic lens. Children of color have been positioned as needing to be saved from their own families and communities—by either divine intervention or by individuals whose cultural practices were deemed "appropriate." These paradigms also help us understand the roots of Whiteified and monocultural definitions of "appropriate," such as is the case of the set of guiding principles for early childhood education in the U.S., the National Association for the Education of Young Children's *Developmentally Appropriate Practice* guides issued in 1987, 1999, and 2013, firmly grounded on Eurocentric concepts and developmental timelines (Genishi and Goodwin 2008; New and Mallory 1994), without regarding the cultural nature of child development and the ways in which development is "biologically cultural" (Rogoff 2003). As we explore this racist history framing families of color and their children, we make visible the need to shift mindset, from faulting families and individuals for the child's failure to understanding the ways in which families have been minoritized and failed by (pre)schools and society.

How Families of Color, Their Languages, and Literacies Have Been Historically Positioned

Three paradigms grounded in particular sets of assumptions have framed the field's view of children of color, their families, their cultural practices, and the communities in which they belong. Goodwin, Cheruvu, and Genishi (2008, 3–4) explain how these paradigms (inferiority, cultural difference, and diversities) historically informed and influenced the field:

> The inferiority paradigm is grounded in the assumptions of the genetic or biological inferiority of those who differ racially and culturally from Whites; the culturally deprived paradigm compares racially, culturally, linguistically, and socioeconomically diverse peoples to a White, middle-class standard in order to illuminate the various ways in which they are deficient; the cultural difference paradigm shifts notably away from notions of inferiority or deprivation to an emphasis on the impact of cultural differences on the lives, experiences, and identities of diverse groups in ways that are not deviant but are unique and specific.

These paradigms also informed the way in which families' language and literacy practices are understood and framed. For example, some children are seen in (pre)school as not having the ability to learn, and thus are seen as inferior.

"He tries hard, but he just can't read. What a pity!" This illustrates how some children are seen as biologically inferior. This paradigm is visible in studies, such as those who proposed that the brains of White people had more mass than the brains of Black people (Morton 1839—a study that was later discredited, but which still shapes some people's beliefs about children of color). When not seen as inherently inferior, children of color are often seen as being culturally deprived. "His parents never read to him" and "his home has no language" are comments that illustrate the culturally deprived paradigm. The blame for children's poor academic performance falls onto the family. The cultural diversities paradigm posits that children of color are different from the norm, but unique, not deficient. "He's just so different" illustrates such a paradigm. While this is the most promising paradigm, it still needs reconceptualization as it frames children of color marginally.

These paradigms permeate the belief systems of adults and children as well, as illustrated by the interaction below, carried out by three four-year-old children—Santiago, Trevon, and Felicia—during choice time, within the context of Mr. William's Head Start classroom in Georgia. It serves as evidence of the discursive construction of difference as deficit.

> Santiago: ¡*Mira, mira*!
> [Trevon ignores Santiago.]
> Santiago: ¡Trevon, *mira*!
> Trevon: I don' know what he' sayin.'
> [Trevon and Felicia laugh.]
> Felicia: He don' speak no English.
>
> (Souto-Manning 2010c, 252)

Santiago's home language is Spanish. Trevon and Felicia's home language is African American Language (AAL). Perpetuating a hierarchy of languages, Felicia discounts Santiago's expertise by defining him as lacking English. By laughing, Trevon and Felicia construct Santiago as incapable of interacting and making himself understood. Trevon and Felicia were constructing Santiago in terms of deficits, in terms of what he could *not* do. It is clear that institutional discourses of exclusion and deficits permeate children's conversational narratives (Chouliaraki and Fairclough 1999; Souto-Manning 2014), at times even signaling internalized racism (Du Bois 1903). This illustrates how multiple paradigms continue to operate today; here, Trevon and Felicia mock Santiago for being linguistically deprived, for not knowing English. They read him ethnocentrically, scaling and rating his communicative practice against their own, as someone who is either incapable or has been deprived. This mindset frames not only how young children see their peers, but also how adults see children (not recognizing their brilliance).

This example illustrates the existence of linguistic hierarchies and differently valued literacy practices. It is a situated representation of the mindset that there is a language of power (that is, the language of those who have power, the normative language). The further one's communicative practices and repertoires are viewed from the normative language and privileged way of communicating, the less value they are attributed. This happens according to the perceived distance from the language of power, and not according to semantics, syntax, or any other linguistic feature. The communicative practices of children from linguistically, culturally, and racially minoritized backgrounds, albeit sophisticated, have historically been seen as inferior or full of errors. This requires children and families to have to contend with the schooling "discourse of sounding right" in contrast with their own communicative practices (Dyson and Smitherman 2009, 973).

Positioning African American Language as a Situated Representation of a Phenomenon

Here, we position AAL as a situated representation of commonly minoritized language practices held by (but not restricted to) individuals and communities of color. The phenomenon represented by AAL as a situated representation is that minoritized language practices are often seen as lesser than, as broken, and/or as incomplete in deeply racialized ways through the lens of raciolinguistics (Alim, Rickford, and Ball 2016). Yet, minoritized languages such as AAL often have rich histories and display great sociolinguistic complexity. With regard to AAL in particular, Dyson and Smitherman (2009, 973) invite us to carefully consider how, despite AAL's rich history, misconceptions and misguided policies have fostered "communicative disconnects between teachers and children during literacy instruction."

The idea of literacy "basics," which purportedly must be acquired by children so that they can advance to more complex literacy practices and understandings (as identified and problematized by Anne Haas Dyson [2013]) is erroneously imposed on the already complex and sophisticated language and literacy practices of children, families, and communities who have historically been minoritized and continues to marginalize them. The discourse of "basics" effectively positions children from minoritized backgrounds (and their communicative practices) as being "at risk" rather than "at promise." Such an idea of "basic" is grounded in the mindset that children lack the foundation required to develop rich literacy understandings and language practices. The concept focuses on "fix-its" (Dyson 2008; Dyson and Smitherman 2009)—reinforcing the idea that minoritized children's language practices are wrong and that their literacies are unworthy. This is despite the understanding that AAL is systematic and governed by rules, thus comprising a language.

AAL has phonological and grammatical features, as outlined by Rickford (1999). For example, it deletes certain suffixes and copula (*He walk* and *He here*) and employs multiple negation (*I didn't get none*), among other features. It has much more nuance than dominant American English; for example, with regard to the verb "to be," as AAL has the habitual be, which "marks a unique aspect referring to an intermittent activity" (Wolfram 2004, 118). Nevertheless, young children who are speakers of AAL are likely to experience communicative disconnects with their mostly White teachers (over 80 percent of early childhood teachers are White in the U.S.—U.S. Bureau of Labor Statistics 2014), who often position them as problems (Dyson and Smitherman 2009). As Dyson and Smitherman (2009, 974) state, "We question U.S. monolingualism and monodialectalism in a multilingual world demanding communicative flexibility," especially in light of pedagogical questions related to the development of early reading and writing, such as "Does it sound right?" We posit that this pedagogical question is at best incomplete, and urge educators to consider how sounding right is a culturally situated concept.

Dyson and Smitherman (2009, 979) posit that:

> Mastering the so-called proper way is not a precursor to learning to write. In fact, there is no evidence that explicitly correcting young children's language in and of itself is effective, even if one's goal is in fact to eliminate grammatical features from a young child's repertoire. . . . Conversely, there is evidence that children who speak nondominant vernaculars (including AAL) become bidialectal (or bilingual, in the case of AAL speakers) through interacting in diverse social situations with others who control varied ways with words, and through opportunities to exercise agency over language choices. . . . Such communicative flexibility would seem important in a world that is not standardized, a world in which daily life is increasingly negotiated by the style shifters, the code switchers, the multilingual composers. . . . But . . . there is more than linguistic research and pedagogic logic involved in how schools respond to young children; there is also ideology and politics.

Such ideologies and politics are present as hierarchies of language are used and enacted through official and unofficial means. Officially, they are enacted in learning standards such as the Common Core Learning Standards for kindergarten, which ignore children's rich and flexible communicative repertoires in favor of mastering the conventions of dominant American English, the so-called Standard English—www.corestandards.org/ELA-Literacy/L/K/. For example, the following Common Core Learning Standard sets such a linguistic hierarchy officially:

> CCSS.ELA-LITERACY.L.K.1. Demonstrate command of the conventions of standard English grammar and usage when writing or speaking.

Contrarily, Dyson and Smitherman (2009, 991) suggest an "alternative pedagogical story . . . [which] takes communicative flexibility, not mastering 'right writing,' as its goal." After all, there is no such a thing as a standard language. Language varies more than it stays the same. Officially and unofficially, teachers and peers are expected to correct AAL in favor of dominant American English, either seeing the use of AAL as signaling poor/broken language practices or indicating behavior problems (Souto-Manning 2009a). Dyson and Smitherman (2009, 991) propose that children and teachers "not be asked to filter others' voices through a 'proper' and fine-grained filter. Rather, through reading diverse literature, through talk, and through dramatic play, they would be encouraged to keep their ears wide open to the diversity of voices around them."

Boutte and Johnson (2013) explained how speakers of AAL are bilingual and their bilingualism must be understood and respected. Contrary to their call, AAL is too often seen as "broken English" (Baugh 2007). While many researchers have elucidated the richness of nondominant languages, such as AAL (John Baugh, Lisa

Delpit, Sonja Lanehart, John Rickford, Geneva Smitherman, and others), there is still a prevalent idea that AAL is an obstacle in and of itself, without the recognition that the problem is not the language practices and structures, but the linguicism, which relegates speakers of languages such as AAL to a lower status. Language is then positioned as a clear reminder and a wide frontier in the legacy of slavery, under the guise of paradigms of language inferiority and language deficit.

Regardless, the language practices of communities of color, such as is the case of AAL (although we recognize that AAL is not solely spoken by African Americans and not all African Americans speak AAL), should not be conceptualized as a "pass-through language, only to be used to get to Standard English" (Perry and Delpit, 1998, 15). Instead, such languages must be recognized as important to individuals' and communities' communicative repertoires. Education research, practice, and policy need to move to recognize the value of language diversities and of multilingualism, effectively rejecting "the monolingualism and monodia-lectalism of No Child Left Behind (and now of Every Student Succeeds Act) . . . the wrong educational philosophy" (Dyson and Smitherman 2009, 993).

Problematizing Traditional Understandings and Definitions of Reading

As is the case in education writ large, definitions of reading are Eurocentric. That is, they are built on (and therefore privilege) the practices of White, middle-class speakers of the dominant language in place (in the case of the U.S., Dominant American English—Paris, 2009[1]). To move to critical and emancipatory definitions of early literacy that center on fairness and relationships, we must problematize traditional definitions and understandings of literacy. In doing so, we build on the work of Grant and Sleeter (1996), who posited that it is impossible for curriculum to be acultural. Here, we posit that it is impossible for literacy to be acultural; it is *not* a neutral set of skills for young children to acquire. We also build on Freire's concept of education as a political endeavor (1970) and declare literacy a political endeavor, expanding reading and writing in more hopeful and inclusive ways. In order to engage in this problematization, we employ Freire and Macedo's unveil-ing of the purpose of academic literacy, which is (over)valued in early childhood classrooms throughout the world as essential for the advancement of individuals and societies. In doing so, we ask: What is the purpose of reading as traditionally defined? Who benefits from traditional literacies? Why? According to Freire and Macedo (1987), reading and writing are political tools used to sustain and cultivate the practices of the elite (e.g., classical works), perpetuating their dominance as the ruling class. On the contrary, reading and writing for everyone else is limited to decontextualized skills and decoding so that marginalized groups and individuals are only able to participate in a limited way, but never to overpower. This serves to "legitimize a dual approach to reading: one level for the ruling class and another for the dispossessed majority" (Freire and Macedo 1987, 101).

This traditional understanding of reading is "inherently alienating" (Freire and Macedo 1987, 101). It purports to be acultural (Grant and Sleeter 1996) and silences the experiences of young children, marginalizing their linguistic practices by placing emphasis on what Dyson (2013) refers to as the basics, such as "comprehension (literal and interpretative), vocabulary development, and word identification skills" (Freire and Macedo 1987, 101). If we reduce literacy to calling out words, developing vocabulary, and enhancing comprehension, then we strip literacy from its sociopolitical dimensions. In doing so, literacy serves to keep the status quo in place, reinscribing inequities in schooling and in society. That is, if literacy's sole function is "to reproduce dominant values and meaning," then it serves a colonialist purpose (Goodwin 2010).

As Freire and Macedo (1987, 101) proposed, if defined by its mechanical features, literacy "does not contribute in any meaningful way to the appropriation of working-class history, culture, and language." Thus, positioning literacy as social and political shifts power away from institutions that reproduce culturally dominant practices toward communities that transform and (re)produce language. While Freire's work (especially his definition of literacy) is seldom employed in early childhood education settings and is often not part of early literacy definitions, we contend that by seeing young children as fully capable humans, albeit different from adults, we can humanize their early literacy processes through Freire's emancipatory approach to literacy. After all, Freire's work invites us to reread literacy, troubling traditional definitions of literacy and moving toward the recognition of literacy as inherently political—historically and contemporarily.

The Political and Ideological Nature of Literacy

Literacy is political. According to Freire and Macedo (1987, 35–36), "Reading always involves critical perception, interpretation, and *rewriting* of what is read." Thus, literacy is an instrument for counterhegemony, for challenging, dismantling, and transforming current structures of power. In naming injustices and confronting what is, the status quo, literacy can serve as a tool to confront power and interrupt oppression. This perhaps explains why literacy is often oversimplified and stripped from its political nature—simply as a way to perpetuate hegemonic power structures.

Literacy is also ideological. It is rife with issues of power. That is, day in and day out children are failed, excluded, marginalized, and pushed out of (pre)schools. Such actions occur under the false pretense of limited reading skills; however, we posit that this happens by design. For example, the children at Eisenhower Elementary School, where Jaquan and his friends attended, were identified as literate by simplistic measures: letter recognition and sounds (see Yoon 2015). This attention to discrete tasks was not, and is not, unique to that particular school. However, the consequences of characterizing literacy this way continues to classify children based on race, class, and home language. "These categories were not simply about children's ability to recall letters and numbers, but soon, these labels began to serve as identity markers (e.g., the low ones) that eventually tracked students" (Yoon 2015, 382). Within the kindergarten classroom studied, the intersection between race, class, and test scores was undeniable yet unaddressed in any conversations about literacy teaching and learning. As Freire and Macedo (1987, 84) explain, a "large number of people who do not read or write and who were expelled from school do not represent a failure of the schooling class; their expulsion reveals the triumph of the schooling class. In fact, this misreading of responsibility reflects the schools' hidden curriculum." The hidden curriculum is one that consistently places the blame and burden on minoritized[2] children and their families for their lack of "readiness" (Graue 2006) to participate in school.

From this perspective, worthy reading practices and the definition of literacy are predicated on a matching game of sorts. That is, the language and literacy practices of those in power are labeled intellectual; the language and literacy practices of those who are minoritized (McCarty 2002) and nondominant in schools and society are deemed to be nonintellectual, without any further questioning or investigation. Intellectualism then becomes an excuse for historical status quo inequalities to be reinscribed contemporarily. For example, because Black people have generally held less power than White people in the U.S., the language and literacy practices of those in dominant positions will be deemed more sophisticated and intellectual than that of Blacks in a deterministic and overly simplistic manner. Such dominant practices dictate what counts as literacy and what is valued as language.

This is an important consideration, as too often the political dimension of education is invisiblized and negated in the early childhood classroom. Adults tend to blame children for their lack of readiness to discuss political issues, to engage in political work (Bentley and Souto-Manning 2016) while simultaneously hiding our own lack of comfort addressing political issues head on. Yet, as Morrell (2015) underscores, if we do not stand for justice, we stand for injustice. Seeking to exclude politics from the classroom merely signals a privileging of dominant literacies and models of learning, in colonizing ways (Goodwin 2010), as the (often unstated) norm. Freire and Macedo (1987, 122) posited, such apolitical definitions of literacy are "necessary to negate the political nature of pedagogy to give the superficial appearance that education serves everyone, thus assuring that it continues to function in the interest of the dominant class." These actions serve to keep the status quo (and its ensuing inequities) in place and halt much-needed efforts regarding transformation and reparations.

Not only is literacy political, but it is also relational, contextual, and situational. To reconceptualize literacies of power (Macedo 1994) as literacies that honor diversities, we must trouble traditional literacy approaches that rely heavily on positivist methods toward language development. By relying on rigor, mastery, and "scientifically proven" truths, we ignore the social, cultural, and political dimensions by which language is both located and enacted. Take, for instance, the following excerpt from a classroom lesson on phonemic awareness (see Yoon 2014, 109):

"UM," said Ms. Bailey, "Say it with me slowly, UUUMMM," overemphasizing the individual sounds.

"UUUMMM," repeated the students.

"Now add a druh [DR-]."

"Dr-uh-m," said the children.

"Good. Drum," said Ms. Bailey.

"Okay, now say U . . . SH."

"USH," repeat the children.

"Add cruh [CR-]."

"Cr-uh-shhh," said the students.

A few words later, Joe (a student) propped himself onto his knees to look at the teacher's manual resting on Ms. Bailey's lap and questioned, "Are we done with Heggerty yet?"

Michael Heggerty wrote a phonemic awareness program, adopted and mandated by the school district in the midwestern U.S. where Ms. Bailey taught. Knowing the "crushing" consequences of emphasizing decontextualizing language skills, Ms. Bailey attempted to keep these activities to a minimum, often cutting lessons short when children were becoming disengaged with the exercises (as illustrated by Joe). However, Michael Heggerty's phonics were also supplemented with various language activities that emphasized skills and an attention to mechanics, taking children away from the personal, social, and intellectual work of taking up language. Successful language users were those who practiced a set of standardized skills: letter formation, phonemic awareness, and sight word identification. Consequently, testing children on these discrete measures usually oversimplified the depth of their literacy repertoires. Instead, such assessments perpetuated the status quo by treating language as a culturally neutral, relegated skill rather than as a creative force to ask questions of their world(s).

Through the belief that the definition of literacy is universal, that literacy develops linearly and hierarchically (Gregory et al. 2004b), that schooling levels the playing field, inequities go unexamined, and students are blamed for the ways in which schooling fails them from the earliest years. They are positioned as responsible for discriminatory policies and practices that permeate and shape their schooling and very lives. This is how inequalities are kept in place. By recognizing the political nature of education and of literacy itself, it becomes clear that children are pushed out of schooling, given messages that they don't belong and that their literacy practices are unworthy, being ultimately failed by society. It becomes clear that they are not choosing to drop out or misbehave, but are inhabiting a space in which their survival is a matter of resistance.

Literacy as a Political Endeavor

Creating spaces for children to experience literacy education that has connections to their own languages (whether they are labeled by society as dialects, vernacular, and/or heritage), while providing access to the language of power (dominant American English) is an often ignored imperative (Adger, Wolfram, and Christian 2007; Ladson-Billings 2015). Understanding the language of power is crucial to navigating the politics of institutions, but even more important (as discussed in Chapter 1) are the cultural affinities that children develop as part of active social and cultural communities. Therefore, in a White, middle-class-dominated world, it is imperative for language politics to protect groups whose language and identities have been historically marginalized (Sleeter 2005). It is also crucial not to position or frame their language practices and repertoires simply as tools to acquire the language of power. They are full and valid in and of themselves.

Denying the political nature of languages and literacies can be paralleled with denying that #BlackLivesMatter, even in light of the Eurocentric and privileged comeback that "All lives matter." It is not a matter of whether all lives matter, and they do; but a matter of recognizing whose lives are constantly belittled, under attack, and marginalized. Clint Smith discusses, with clarity, the contentious political landscape in which Black boys currently grow up. He explains that his son's life is not worth more because of #BlackLivesMatter, but it is worthwhile in a political climate that views Black lives as dangerous and disposable:

> So when we say that Black lives matter, it's not because others don't, it's simply because we must affirm that we are worthy of existing without fear, when so many things tell us we are not. I want to live in a world where my son will not be presumed guilty the moment he is born, where a toy in his hand isn't mistaken for anything other than a toy. (Smith 2015)

For many children, (pre)schools can be inhospitable environments. Their literacy practices are often silenced, dismissed, and belittled. Such literacy practices often belong to those who have historically and contemporarily been colonized, stripped of power, minoritized, and positioned as nondominant. At times, not developing literacy is paradoxically empowering. It means refusing to read the world through Eurocentric and colonialist lenses. It means engaging in acts of self-affirmation and self-preservation. It is within this context that we locate literacy.

Thus, in a system of oppression and domination, where inequity reigns, literacy researchers must critically "question whether the current [literacy] framework ... is the most fruitful" (Street 1995, 24) and who it benefits. These very questions necessitate locating literacy historically and institutionally, allowing us to understand literacy socially and critically. "A sociocritical literacy historicizes everyday and institutional literacy practices and texts and reframes them as powerful tools oriented toward critical social thought" (Gutiérrez 2008, 148). Therefore, language is a sociocritical and sociopolitical tool used to call attention to contradictions in school literacies. As seen in the Michael Heggerty exercises described above, we problematize and seek to interrupt the narrow conceptions of literacy that are often used to disembody the practices of nondominant cultures. Instead, we propose the need for permeable spaces (Dyson 1993), where children merge official and unofficial practices, allowing for the social, political, and cultural enactment of literacy. For young children, these spaces are most often cultivated and experienced in play. Yet, play is a privilege granted to White children in wealthy communities and all-too-often denied from children of color and from children from low- and no-income homes. We must uphold play as a right for all; not as a privilege, but as the right of every child as proposed by the United Nations (Souto-Manning 2017; United Nations 1948). As such, play must be culturally relevant.

Culturally Relevant Rethinkings

Ladson-Billings (1992, 313) calls for literacy to be defined in ways that are culturally relevant. She highlights, "What people are taught to read is as significant as the fact that they read." Yet, she cautions the field against abandoning skills in favor of content, explaining that children must know how to read to develop independently and capably. A culturally relevant approach to literacy is predicated on the academic success of students of color. While academic literacy is defined by and privileges those in power, without mastering the language of power, one is unlikely to succeed in the current state of society. Ladson-Billings (1992, 314) goes on to propose culturally relevant teaching as holding promise for African American students, defining it as "a pedagogy of opposition. . . . The primary goal of culturally relevant teaching is to empower students to examine critically the society in which they live and to work for social change." In 1995 Ladson-Billings defined three foundational propositions of culturally relevant teaching: "(a) Students must experience academic success; (b) students must develop and/or maintain cultural competence; and (c) students must develop a critical consciousness through which they challenge the status quo of the current social order" (p. 160). These propositions must be considered centrally in any rethinking of literacy, so as to honor the practices, identities, and knowledges of minoritized and nondominant students, empowering them, their languages, and their cultures in the process.

As literacy researchers, it is thus essential that we identify the aims, purposes, and objectives of the dominant definition of early literacy in place so that we can critique and change the ways in which literacy functions to reinscribe dominant and colonialist practices, keeping a problematic status quo in place. This happens through insidious methods that determine how schools function and what counts as schooling success and who gets to be successful. Narrow definitions of literacy and learning also function to marginalize, silence, and negate the histories, cultures, and language practices (at least in the U.S.) of the majority of young children in today's classrooms. Despite being the numeric majority, their practices are summarily disregarded and devalued as a way to keep the current power structure in place. In early childhood classrooms, these definitions are closely tied to literacies of power (Collins and Blot 2003; Dyson and Smitherman 2009; Macedo 1994)—such as dominant American English, which becomes a measure of literacy success according to the Common Core State Standards for kindergarten.

Reading and Writing Words and Worlds: An Emancipatory Approach

Learning to read and write words happens within the context of one's world. Yet, in early childhood classrooms, standardized words, books, and programs are often used with diverse children. This aligns well with the traditional approach to literacy, which seeks to disempower and dehumanize nondominant and minoritized populations. To interrupt early literacy practices that dehumanize, we see the need to move from academic literacy—a commonplace yet problematic term and concept in today's classrooms and schools—to an emancipatory approach to literacy, which centrally considers issues of domination and colonialism, critically deconstructing them. We position the current epistemological stance, which frames rigor and knowledge as disembodied and acultural central pillars of the early childhood curriculum, as an attempt to maintain the status quo. Such a stance ignores sociopolitical structures and concerns of reading, schooling, and society writ large.

Rejecting such apolitical definitions of literacy, which pretend to be devoid of politics while reifying traditional power structures, we propose a revisioning of early literacy that is emancipatory. That is, the words and texts employed in classrooms serving young children must re-present diverse worlds, communicative practices, and cultural traditions. Teachers' communicative and cultural practices need to be positioned as situated cultural representations and not hold more power than the communicative and cultural practices of their students. That is, students need to engage in "learning, expressing their actual language, their anxieties, fears, demands, and dreams" (Freire and Macedo 1987, 35) by using their own words and/in worlds.

Such an approach to literacy requires that teachers be positioned humbly, learning from and with the children they teach, their families, and their communities (Freire 1998). It requires recognizing that literacy is not a set of specific basic skills, but an approach to living, learning, developing, understanding, questioning, and transforming. It sees literacies as ways of making sense in and of the world, reading what is and seeking to imagine what could be, rewriting futures more inclusively, justly, and hopefully. For example, one of the central aspects of (or practices associated with) reading is decoding. Yet, decoding is often seen merely as the act of reading letters and words. Here, we broaden decoding to include "*reading* the situations pictured" and imagining alternate pictures of how culture, human practices, and society are formed (Freire and Macedo 1987, 36).

For example, in Jessica Martell's second-grade dual-language (Spanish/English) classroom in New York City, children were able to explore issues of justice and injustice while meeting and surpassing mandated learning standards. Following the killings of many African American males by White police officers, many of the children had participated in Black Lives Matter marches (http://blacklivesmatter.com/) and were enraged by the exoneration of the White police officer who killed Eric Garner, a Black man who had been murdered not too far from their school in 2014. While they had engaged in a number of conversations about race and racism, especially after reading books such as *The Other Side* by Jacqueline Woodson (2001) and *Freedom on the Menu: The Greensboro Sit-Ins* by Carole Boston Weatherford (2005), this time it was different. They recognized that racism was a historical issue, but were experiencing how it was also contemporary (Souto-Manning and Martell 2016). Here is what happened:

> TJ walked in with a copy of the newspaper *AM New York* [a free newspaper distributed at New York City subway stations], displaying the headline "Grand Jury on Garner Death: No Charges." He looked at Jessica and said loudly: "No charges. Can you believe it?" Soon Amber said: "I saw a newspaper that said it was not a crime," referring to the *New York Post* front cover. Rashod, an African American boy, muttered: "Yeah. I guess Black lives don't matter." Ana, a Puerto Rican girl with light skin, said: "All lives matter. Not just Black lives."
>
> At this point Jessica stopped the regular morning routine, during which children typically read and talked over in-class breakfast, and called the class for a meeting. She wrote "No charges," "Not a crime," "Black lives matter," and "All lives matter" on the easel to capture the children's words as she invited them to problematize what they had said critically. She asked Ana to explain her statement. Ana based her explanation on some of Jessica's prior statements that all human beings are unique, and thus she deduced that all lives mattered. Then Jessica asked Rashod to explain his rationale. He looked at Ana and said: "I'm afraid I'm gonna get shot and die. They killin' people like me, not people like you." Ana looked at him silently. Rashod continued: "They killing Black people. Black men and Black boys. Like me." . . . After the silence, which seemed to have lasted an eternity in a classroom where children are never at a loss for words, Ana responded: "I guess you are right. You know, I hadn't thought of that." Without missing a beat, Rashod said: "You don't have to." The discussion progressed to an understanding of segregation, racism, unjust laws, racialization, and the immediate need for reparations.
>
> The children were very respectful of each other but pushed each other's understandings in significant ways. For more than an hour, the children developed not only their oral language, exposing arguments, basing their statements on documentation, and demonstrating many of the learning standards for second grade and beyond, but they also engaged in a much-needed examination of why Black Lives Matter cannot become All Lives Matter. As one of the children said: "It is not fair that people think that

you are bad because you are Black." Another added: "Yea. And some police are really violent with Black people. I don't think they would be with a White person."

Their comments displayed an understanding of the situation lacking in many adult circles. . . . They understood the need to have an honest and critical conversation about the marginalization of Blackness within schools and society. . . . They understood the need for reparations. They understood that Black lives matter. It was just fair! (pp. 76–77)

Within the context of Jessica's second grade, six-, seven-, and eight-year-old children had reaffirmed the centrality of fairness in their lives. As with Francisco's appropriation of the *Peppa Pig* expression "Not fair!" (see p. 33) and many examples captured by master teacher Vivian Paley, it becomes clear that no matter the topic, fairness is ever-present in children's worlds and thus must be accounted for in early literacy.

Reading skills, therefore, should lead to interpretations and reinterpretations of an inequitable world. Values and practices such as love, critical problem solving, solidarity, and social responsibility are often labeled as "soft" and "nonacademic." Yet, we posit that relational literacies are central to emancipatory redefinitions of early literacy—peer literacies, and family and community literacies. They have activist potential (Martin 2013, 119), and are "shifting, context-specific and contingent practices and ways of knowing that emerge as performative rhetorics and strategic responses to community needs, desires, fears, pleasures, dreams, and lived realities." Such values and practices are dismissed because they destabilize the core of educational inequity—coming to position young children from nondominant and minoritized backgrounds as subjects rather than objects (Freire and Macedo 1987; McCarty 2002; Paris 2009; Souto-Manning 2010b). Instead, we recognize and honor "the important relationship between language and the cultural capital of the people at whom the literacy program was aimed" (Freire and Macedo 1987, 157). In this way and from such a perspective, literacy becomes "one of the major vehicles by which 'oppressed' people are able to participate in the sociohistorical transformation of their society" (Freire and Macedo 1987, 157).

An emancipatory approach to early literacy recognizes the humanity, uniqueness, and value of young children, of their families' "funds of knowledge[3]" (Moll et al. 1992), and of their community resources (Souto-Manning, 2013b). It moves away from defining literacy as a collection of so-called basics (Dyson 2013) to also—and centrally—encompass a critical understanding of texts broadly conceived and/within the sociohistorical context in which they are located. Through emancipatory literacy, nondominant groups and minoritized individuals recognize the need to recover and cultivate "the historical and existential experiences that are devalued in everyday life by the dominant culture [which] must be recovered in order to be both validated and critically understood" (Giroux 2001, 228). From this perspective, learning to read and write inherently and centrally includes the critical reading, problematizing, and understanding of realities, of worlds. This requires moving away from literacy as conceptualized by progressive education, a practice that dehumanizes students and dismisses their language practices, expertise, and knowledge. Such a practice continues to use a society's dominant language (in the U.S., dominant American English) in the teaching of literacy, thereby colonizing and disempowering minoritized children, their families, and their communities.

It is in one's home language or language of the heart and the home that one commences to name his/her world. After all, it is unlikely that the dominant language will have the breadth and depth to acknowledge, name, and explain worlds beyond the one it privileges. Paris' work (2009) examines the use of AAL as structurally rich when youth built and employed shared lexicons as a way of speaking to others within cultural communities. These "multiethnic youth spaces" (p. 430) became intimate communities of practice where young people made intentional language choices to communicate emotions, integrate divisions, and form bonds cross-culturally. AAL signified a practice that the youth claimed as both an individual and collective identifier. Within these practices, they formed a type of "kinship" that went beyond familial bonds, but began with shared resistance against White-dominated society. As Miles (a participant in the study) said, "We all gotta stay together. We're the minorities" (Paris 2009, 443), speaking to the need for communities of color to stick together and sustain their voice.

Freire and Macedo (1987, 159) explain that "through the native language . . . students 'name their world' and begin to establish a dialectical relationship with the dominant class in the process of transforming the social and political structures that imprison them in their 'culture of silence.'" And "dominant class" refers to not only economically dominant, but to dominance in terms of race, culture, language, spirituality, gender, sexual orientation, and dis/ability. From this perspective, literacy is the ability and the extent to which one can use language for racial reparations, social reimaginings, and political de/reconstruction; to reimagine what is and envision more hopeful tomorrows.

Acknowledging the "historical roots and present-day consequences" of restrictive definitions of literacy under the guise of "academic rigor," Willis (1995) "argues for a reconceptualization of literacy that builds on [the] backgrounds and knowledges" of children of color, of children who have been historically and contemporarily minoritized. She proposes that "for school literacy to begin to move beyond its "neutral" conception of culture, educators at all levels must acknowledge the role and importance of more than one culture in defining school literacy" (47). As we expand definitions of literacy in school spaces, we come closer to dialectical encounters that productively interrogate the status quo (Freire 1970, 1985b).

Rethinking Literacies: Repositioning Texts, Power, and Identity

As we discussed earlier, literacies are not neutral, nor is teaching. As with literacies, teaching is inherently political. Understanding that teaching is political necessitates an understanding of the systems and institutions framing the ways in which texts and contexts are read and understood. It requires problematizing power relationships that press and oppress lives. In terms of languages and literacies, it becomes important to understand the intricate yet important relationship between language and power (Chouliaraki and Fairclough 1999; Fairclough 2003).

Thus, from a critical perspective, it is essential to rethink literacies, questioning what counts as texts, how they are positioned, how power intersects with particular kinds and definitions of literacy, and how identity is constructed through language and/in power. From this perspective, literacy encompasses both critical consciousness and resistance (Freire 1970). Critical models of early literacy trouble what is and invite us to problematize inequities. After all, according to Janks (2000, 178–179): "Deconstruction without reconstruction or design reduces human agency; diversity without access ghettoizes students. Domination without difference and diversity loses the ruptures that produce contestation and change."

Critical Approaches to Early Literacy

By definition, critical approaches are grounded in the need for transformation by questioning and challenging dominant policies and practices, which undermine and silence the beliefs and practices of those who were historically (and continue to be contemporarily) disempowered and marginalized. Given the colonialist nature of traditional approaches to early literacy, which continue to silence and marginalize the practices of minoritized children, their families, and communities, and "debates about what counts as literacy right now, as Western postindustrialized nations review their educational achievements, the addition of the word critical to literacy serves to complicate matters even further" (Comber 2001a, 301). But—what is critical literacy?

Lewison, Flint, and Van Sluys (2002, 382) propose four dimensions of critical literacy: "(1) disrupting the commonplace, (2) interrogating multiple viewpoints, (3) focusing on sociopolitical issues, and (4) taking action and promoting social justice." They propose that critical literacy is a way to problematize learning, content areas, and subjects of study; understand that knowledge is politically, socially, and historically situated (Luke and Freebody 1997; Shor 1987). Anderson and Irvine (1993) propose that critical literacy seeks to challenge and change uneven power relationships. Comber (2001a, 301) posits:

> Critical literacy resists any simplistic or generic definitions because its agenda is to examine the relationship between language practices, power relations, and identities—and this analysis involves grappling with local conditions.

In defining critical literacy, it is important to note that "the relationship between literacy and the politics of difference underlies critical literacy in theory and in practice" (Comber 2003, 260).

Positioning the relationship between literacies and politics centrally and critically, here we employ a Freirean framework to reread early literacy from a critical perspective, positioning a critical approach to early literacy against dominant ideologies, which permeate underlying purposes, messages, and aims (Souto-Manning 2005). Implicit in critical literacy frameworks is the agency of learners in constructing and deconstructing ideologies within words, texts, and ideas (Larson and Marsh 2005). To do so, we redefine early literacy basics, based on the critical pedagogy principles outlined in Souto-Manning (2005, 67).

The first basic principle is that when students enter (pre)schools, they already have knowledge of their own language(s), which must be recognized as worthy, being positioned at the center of teaching and learning. The second basic principle is that the student is the subject of his/her own learning, being capable of investigating and engaging in inquiry employing problem-posing, critical dialogue, and problem-solving. This negates basics being defined apart from the individual student—and thus rejects what Freire (1970) calls the banking approach to education, where knowledge is deposited in students' brains akin to the way in which money is deposited in banks. The third basic principle is that conflict, difference, and diversities are the basis for learning. That is, when old knowledge (often grounded in colonialist and status quo ideologies) collides with new understandings, perspectives, and points of view, students ask real and important questions, and learn dialogically (from and with each other), critically deconstructing and reconstructing their own knowledges. The fourth basic principle is that learning takes place collectively; it is not an individual endeavor—learning only happens collectively within a dialectical framework. The final basic principle is that academic practice is not spontaneous; it requires continuous inquiry and research. It requires the very redefinition of what counts as academic (apart from elitist aims, purposes, and definitions).

While recognizing the antithetical nature of fixed principles for a critical approach to early literacy and sharing a number of (re)inventions, below we share a situated representation (Dyson and Genishi 2005) of how critical literacy came to life in an early childhood classroom. The situated representation of a critical approach to early literacy unveils how first graders started recognizing the sorting function of schools, coming to name the racial segregation in school programs, namely pull-out programs for children labeled gifted and those for children labeled English learners (Souto-Manning 2009b), within a context in which the gifted program served mostly White children and the English Language Learners' (ELL) program served mostly children of color (explained in the following section).

Considering Multiple Perspectives in a U.S. First Grade

William: We don't need no medicine. No fixin'! My momma be takin' good care o' me.

Johnnie: What you mean?

William: It's all 'bout tryin' to make ev'ryone sames; but same's White; same's rich. I'm Black and I live in the project.

(Souto-Manning 2009b, 51)

William, a six-year old boy, troubled the deficit perspectives too commonly employed in U.S. public schools and society to frame children of color as lacking something, as being sick and thus needing medicine, or as needing to be fixed (Goodwin et al. 2008). This deficit perspective assumes that children of color and of minoritized backgrounds need to undergo remediation to adapt to the school culture, instead of seeing the need for schools and society to change in ways that more equitably position the practices and identities of individuals and communities of color, who have historically been minoritized. If a child's communicative practices and repertoire align with the school's privileged language (in this case, dominant American English), that child is likely to experience academic success and be labeled as gifted. However, if the child's language socialization processes differed from the one privileged by teachers, she/he is likely to be diagnosed as needing help, as "at-risk" from day one (Delpit 1998; Dyson 1999; Swadener and Lubeck 1995).

To counter such perspectives, the teacher paid close attention to process and tools. The process employed centered around interrogating multiple viewpoints, making differences visible (Harste et al. 2000), examining competing narratives and writing counternarratives to dominant discourses, such as the one identified by the children in the interaction above. The tools employed were children's books, first selected through a continuously generative process (Vasquez 2001), and later representing social issues (Lewison et al. 2002). Finally, critical dialogue served as a way for William's first grade class to uncover social issues in texts (words and worlds) and to further the conversation.

Specifically, to consider multiple perspectives, the teacher and her first-grade students read and discussed multiple versions of the same story—the three little pigs story, for example, from the wolf's perspective (Scieszka 1989) and more traditional versions from the pigs' perspective (Galdone 1970; Marshall 1989). In doing so, they carefully considered issues of perspective and point of view. Later, they read texts about the civil rights movement and its key figures, including Martin Luther King Jr. and Rosa Parks (Souto-Manning 2009b). These specific civil rights leaders were included in the state learning standards for first grade mandated by *No Child Left Behind*, U.S. federal legislation that purported the need for accountability in students' learning outcomes. In this case, teacher and students went beyond the unit of study presented in the school textbook and rejected the typically happy endings portrayed in most children's literature—even about slavery, as illustrated by books such as *A Fine Dessert* (Jenkins 2015), a book atrociously portraying how lovely slavery was while ignoring its myriad complexities, and *A Birthday Cake for George Washington* (Ganeshram 2016), which features slavery with a smile.

As the teacher, Mariana purposefully included media reports of racial discrimination in airports (Blacks being stopped more often at TSA security checkpoints), articles about unemployment rates being higher for people of color, the racial disproportionality in housing and educational opportunities, and multicultural children's literature featuring critical perspectives on civil rights and racism. The first graders explored multiple texts and versions of the civil rights movement and situated instances of racism.

Reading and rereading their own lives politically as texts, these first graders noticed racial segregation and disproportionality (akin to what was happening in housing, airports, and other contexts) in their own lives. They engaged in the following dialogue:

> William: Yeah. It's like when you don't know you goin' special ed, to resource, and you thin' you special. Then you know later that you really dumb. You all alone, ya' know. We all here in yo' class, but when we go to tha' other class, it's not everybody.
>
> Derrick: And how everyone who goes to Star [pseudonym for the county's gifted education program] is White.
>
> Kary: Wow . . .
>
> Shaniece: I don't know . . .
>
> Luz: But we go to the same school.
>
> Derrick: Just think . . .
>
> Johnnie: Yeah, Derrick. I'm not really sure.
>
> Erin: Well, there's a way. Let's find out.

Erin goes to the easel and grabs a marker. She writes the names of each of the teachers who teach in pull-out programs.

> Teacher: What are you going to do?
>
> Erin: I am going to find out how many go with each teacher.
>
> Teacher: How will this help you get to what you want to know?
>
> William: Yeah. How?
>
> Derrick: We can choose different color markers for boys and girls, and then . . .
>
> Madison: No, no, I know. If we are talking about Black and White, we need to get black and white markers.
>
> Ci'Erikka: White marker?
>
> Madison: Well, like we read, we are not really White. So, let's choose pink.

Erin then grabs a pink and a black marker.

> Jorge: Here is the brown.
> Erin: Oh yes, I forgot.
> Kary: We can't forget anyone.
>
> (Souto-Manning 2009b, 67)

After verifying segregation in their own school and lives, they continued:

> Taylor: But that's not fair!
> Kary: Fair? That's dead wrong!
> Tyron: We have to do something about it.
> Madison: Does everybody know?
> Teacher: What?
> Madison: That we have segregation?
> Ralph: We know, but what can we do?
> Derrick: I think we have to share what we know. I don't think it is right.
>
> (Souto-Manning 2009b, 50)

These excerpts portray a discussion which took place in a first-grade classroom in the southern U.S., just as students realized how racially and socioeconomically segregated pull-out educational programs were in their school. Pull-out programs consist of pulling individual children or small groups of children (e.g., those who qualify for gifted, ELL, special education services) out of their regular classrooms for focused enrichment or targeted remedial instruction. These enrichment programs, such as gifted services, typically served rich, White children. However, the recovery or remediation programs included those who came from low- and no-income families, and often culturally, linguistically, and racially minoritized families (Coutinho and Oswald 2000; Lee 2002; Lucas 2001).

In a localized manner, these first graders undertook "demographic analyses of school populations" (Comber 2001a, 302) and engaged in seeing communities from an anthropological perspective (inquiring into how people made sense of their lives and identifying their "funds of knowledge" [Moll et al. 1992]), developed linguistic knowledge to present and represent their findings and to question inequitable realities, revising what they knew and thus contributing to our reimagining of "what counts as literacy in new times" (Comber 2001a, 303). That is, to engage in critical literacy, it is not merely a matter of being critical. Critical literacy encompasses recognizing "that race, ethnicity, language, poverty, location, and gender impact . . . students' educational success and the ways in which they participate in authorized discursive practices available in educational institutions" (Comber 2001a, 306). It also involves opening up the definition of literacy, coming to redefine it in more just and inclusive ways. Key to doing so is recognizing multiple perspectives, voices, and stories—all while recognizing how power and/in society determine(s) their value.

These six- and seven-year-olds in a U.S. public school engaged with critical literacy to read worlds and words—in the process of problem posing, dialoguing, and promoting change. They also started critically reading their realities and naming injustices as they read picture books portraying stories of historical racism and segregation thereafter—such as *White Socks Only* by Evelyn Coleman and *The Other Side* by Jacqueline Woodson. Within this context, the children started asking questions about books being read in the classroom— Who wrote the book? Who is visible? Who is invisible? Why? Asking these questions led the children to pursue "complicated questions about language and power, about people and lifestyle, about morality and ethics, about who is advantaged by the way things are and who is disadvantaged" (Comber 2001a, 271). Again and again, the children engaged in unveiling inequities as they reread their own worlds critically. In doing so, they made visible young children's agency, ability, and capacity to read texts critically and to trouble an unjust status quo.

These first graders developed skills deemed to be basics in more traditional settings, such as comprehension (making connections between books and between books they read and their world), but moved to develop critical skills as well, which were leveraged to promote change in their very schooling and lives. They illustrate that reading words and worlds is a recursive process, and that critical literacy does not exclude traditional concepts and skills related to early literacy development—it merely goes beyond, leading to both the development of early literacy skills and of critical consciousness. Their journey shows us that learning and social action are not neatly separated, but can (and should) unfold together through critical literacy events.

Specifically, as they became aware of the segregation associated with ability and race in their school, these six- and seven-year-olds decided that something needed to be done. They decided to invite the principal to come in and talk, sharing what they had learned. The principal agreed that something had to be done. Eventually this led to the institution of push-in services. The children had not only critically read their world but they used their words to change it, making their world more equitable. Through their actions and words, they invite us to expand our concept of literacy to center on not only reading words, but reading, re-presenting, and rewriting worlds.

In this chapter, we explained how de facto traditional definitions of literacy marginalize children from minoritized identities and backgrounds. We reaffirmed our belief in literacy as a cultural and political endeavor. As such, we troubled and redefined what comprise the basics of literacy. In the following chapter, we explore the multiple contexts where these literacies are developed and practiced.

Notes

1. Paris (2009) employs the term "'Dominant American English' instead of the commonly used 'Standard English' to foreground unequal power relationships between the dominant variety of English and other varieties of English" (p. 445).
2. McCarty (2002) uses the term minoritized to acknowledge the power relations within so-called "minority" communities. "As a characterization of people, 'minority' is stigmatizing and often numerically inaccurate. . . . 'Minoritized' more accurately conveys the power relations and processes by which certain groups are socially, economically, and politically marginalized within the larger society. The term also implies human agency" (p. xv).
3. *Funds of knowledge* is defined by researchers Luis Moll, Cathy Amanti, Deborah Neff, and Norma Gonzalez (1992) as the "historically accumulated and culturally developed bodies of knowledge and skills essential for household or individual functioning and well-being" (p. 133).

3

MULTIPLE LITERACIES AND LANGUAGE COMPETENCIES ACROSS YOUNG CHILDREN'S SOCIAL CONTEXTS

Ways with printed words . . . are always integrally and inextricably integrated with ways of talking, thinking, believing, knowing, acting, interacting, valuing, and feeling. We cannot just take the "print bits" out and forget the rest. (Gee 2002, 30)

Young Children's Meaning Making Across Contexts

"Da-da-da," Logan points to his father. "Da-da-dá," Ana points to crackers. Children make meaning and make sense in a variety of contexts. In Logan's home in Brooklyn, New York, "Da-da-da" signifies dad. In Ana's home in Rio de Janeiro, Brazil, "Da-da-dá" signifies give me (and as she points to crackers, *dá*, from the Portuguese verb *dar*, comes to signify "give me"). Children's communicative repertoires are contextual, as illustrated by these two infants' communicative practices. Utterances gain meaning in social contexts, communicating very different intentions across cultural communities. As Bakhtin (1981, 262–263) pinpoints, there is "a diversity of social speech types (sometimes even diversity of languages) and a diversity of individual voices" and "languages that serve the specific sociopolitical purposes of the day, even of the hour." Therefore, the words we choose, the contexts in which we say those words, and the community of people we utter the words to are purposeful and experiential.

Young children are exposed to language in various contexts before entering school—homes, communities, peers, and the environment. They start reading their environment and authoring themselves in the world. For example, in New York City, young children may read Figure 3.1 as "subway," whereas children (and even adults) who grew up in other locales, may have difficulty identifying a subway station. Yet, the green iron structures on the city's sidewalks are easily identified by children growing up in New York City—they read them as signifying subway.

Even the word subway varies across contexts within the same community. For example, in New York, subway may be used to signify a train or a sandwich (Figure 3.2). After all, "each word tastes of the context and contexts in which it has lived its socially charged life; all words and forms are populated by intentions" (Bakhtin 1981, 293).

In addition to language varying across larger contexts, it also varies across communities and within communities across interlocutors. For instance, it is very likely that we communicate differently with someone interviewing us for a professional position compared to a significant other. Similar to adults, young children deploy distinct communicative practices when playing with peers and communicating with a parent or teacher. Within contexts, they may engage in language variation as they take on different roles in play or when they are

FIGURE 3.1   Subway Station
© iStock

FIGURE 3.2   Subway: Sandwich or Train?
© iStock

creating storylines with dolls who signify differing roles (for example, mother and daughter). Wolfram, Adger, and Christian (1999, 1) label such variation dialect, "a variety of a language associated with a regionally or socially defined group of people." In such a vein, we can understand that the so-called "Standard English [and any 'standard' language] . . . is a collection of the socially preferred dialects from various parts of the United States and other English-speaking countries" (Wolfram, Adger, and Christian 1999, 17). Yet, specific communicative practices and dialects are valued differently within and across communities and communicative contexts in society. With this recognition, Adger, Wolfram, and Christian (2007, 1) posited: "Every language differs to some degree from place to place and from group to group."

> They use the term *language variation* to refer to the fact that a language is not uniform. Instead, it varies according to social characteristics of groups of people, such as their cultural background, geographical location, social class, gender, or age. Language variation may also refer to differences in the way that language is used in different settings, such as in the home, the community, and the school, and on different occasions, such as telling a friend about a trip or planning a trip with a travel agent. (Adger, Wolfram, and Christian 2007, 1)

Adger, Wolfram, and Christian go on to explain that "groups that contrast linguistically and culturally with mainstream society have been identified [according to]: the deficit position and the difference position" (2007, 17). Many—in (pre)schools and in society—still believe that language variation is an ailment and "speakers of dialects with vernacular forms have a handicap—socially and cognitively" (Adger, Wolfram, and Christian 2007, 17). Members of dominant groups in society "often believe that members of the stigmatized groups must change in order to be accepted" (Adger, Wolfram, and Christian 2007, 17). We strongly disagree with this perspective. To be sure, the language of power is not semantically or syntactically superior; it is the language of those who have power (Delpit 1988). Although (over)valued in society, it is not always the most appropriate way of communicating. Seeking to trouble existing language hierarchies, here we use the term *language variation* instead of dialect to underscore that linguistic and communicative differences do not comprise deficits. Adger, Wolfram, and Christian reaffirm that "no variety of a language is inherently better than another in terms of how languages are organized. No speakers have a diminished ability to function cognitively and expressively as a result of the variety of the language that they acquire" (2007, 17).

Young children's language usage is purposeful; their communicative repertoires serve as tools to engage with others in their immediate contexts—to interact with adults, to connect with other children, and to participate in sociocultural activities. They learn language to communicate. They speak because it serves a purpose. They do not learn about language; they learn through language. They draw on their language universe to make meaning—navigating within and across boundaries established by adults, some of which we call languages. They make use of their entire communicative repertoires to make meaning—drawing from what adults often see as different languages, such as English and Spanish. As Genishi and Dyson (1984, 1) remind us: "At a time of life when we credit them with little intelligence, children master a most complex and sophisticated system of sounds and meanings." In making meaning, young children establish identities through active participation in their social and cultural communities using language as a mediating tool.

Literacy as Reading the Word and the World

Literacy is much broader than reading and writing symbols; it includes reading words and worlds (Freire and Macedo 1987). The movement from world to word is always present. Yet, context and prior experiences re-presented in classroom materials (books, posters) and curricula tend to advantage those who are members of and fluent in the culture of power (Delpit 1988). It is from such a perspective that in this chapter we explore the social, cultural, and political contexts that influence children's language interactions, and move toward critically redefining what it means to be "literate." Through a variety of examples, we explain how being literate in one social context, especially in the digital, contemporary age, does not always translate into "literate" in another context (Marsh 2005a, 2005b). Print literacy is just one mode of literacy, often (over)valued and largely communicated in the context of school. However, children come to school with the "communicative and linguistic practices of their cultural communities, popular culture [practices] in conjunction with media and peers, and the cultural norms that validate and make available specific resources for multimodal production" (Yoon 2016, 4). Thus, their literacy practices are not restricted to print.

Literacy: Challenging Adult Definitions, Honoring the Brilliance of Young Children

Children learn the rules of their language through communicating, before ever entering school or having a formal lesson. "By the time they start kindergarten, children know most of the fundamentals of their language, so that they are able to converse easily with someone who speaks as they do (that is, in their dialect)" (Genishi 1988, 2). Yet they are often seen through deficit lenses, measured against adult definitions of language and literacy (which are often very restrictive). They are regarded as not knowing much, needing literacy, and not being "ready" (Graue 1992).

Bakhtin (1981, 259) reminded us that:

> The study of verbal art can and must overcome the divorce between an abstract "formal" approach and an equally abstract "ideological" approach. Form and content in discourse are one, once we understand that verbal discourse is a social phenomenon—social throughout its entire range and in each and every of its factors, from the sound image to the furthest reaches of abstract meaning.

For example, in Figure 3.3, a three-year-old child engaged in a written conversation, clearly attending to the way print looks. He used a number of wiggly lines to signify "chicken." Through the process of authoring multiple wiggly lines, he demonstrated his knowledge that in English, print is read from left to right, top to bottom. These are part of what Marie Clay (1993, 2000) titled *Concepts About Print*. This three-year-old child showed in this written conversation that he knew much about how written language works.

Genishi (1988, 2) explains that human beings are born to communicate; "they have an innate gift for figuring out the rules of the language used in their environment." They become literate within a certain context. The context is a very important factor. Children learn language through interactions with those around them. Yet, they may display their learnings in ways that don't signify much to us adults. For example, learning about animal behavior from firsthand observation,

FIGURE 3.3   Hello. What is Your Favorite Food? Chicken.

(pre)schooler Travyon sketched notes comprised of symbolic representations (Figure 3.4). Although these notes did not make sense to adults and did not make sense to him after a few hours had elapsed, they are part of the process of his development as a writer. He understands that print (written language) serves specific purposes; he used written symbols to make meaning. He shows us how writing letters is not necessarily a precursor to written communication.

As Owocki and Goodman (2002, 81) explained, although Travyon had not "yet discovered conventional letter forms," he was "attending to the way print looks." They proposed:

> Although children's early forms of cursive and print aren't readable to adults, and aren't even readable to the writers soon after they've written, we call this writing because it is intended to communicate meaning . . . [through] circles, squiggles, lines, crosses, and letterlike forms. (Owocki and Goodman 2002, 81–82)

In addition to observing and participating in particular contexts, children engage in figuring out and testing language and literacy rules. They read from signs and pictures. They may associate the McDonald's golden arches with french fries based on their prior experiences. They may repeat what adults say. But beyond that, they figure out the rules and variations within their home language(s). For example, children may repeat "I went high" when recounting their adventure on

FIGURE 3.4 Making Meaning Through Symbols

the playground's swing or author their own: "I go high" or "I goed high," experimenting with syntactic rules by initially engaging in the overuse of generalized conventions in one or more languages, using the conventions of one language in another (for example, using *y* in Spanish to connect sentences in English), and eventually becoming strategic language users and code-switchers employing the syntactic rules governing a specific language and abiding to adult expectations of language use.

In her TED talk, Kuhl (2010) declares that babies are linguistic geniuses. That is, they have infinite capacity to learn languages—and to produce sounds that adults later become unable to muster. Based on brain research, she affirms that: "Babies and children are geniuses until they turn seven, and then there's a systematic decline." She goes on to declare that infants are "citizens of the world." Differently from adults, who have difficulty hearing specific sounds (for example, it is not uncommon for native Spanish speakers to have difficulty with tonal languages and for native Japanese speakers to differentiate between the /r/ and /l/ sounds), most hearing babies "can discriminate all the sounds of all languages, no matter what country we're testing and what language we're using, and that's remarkable because you and I can't do that. We're culture-bound listeners. We can discriminate the sounds of our own language, but not those of foreign languages." She urges us to recognize the genius in every infant; after all, their small brains can undertake complex processes often absent in adults. While we do not fully agree with the deterministic and linear nature of the process described by Kuhl and do not subscribe to the idea of fixed "critical periods," as we recognize that children move along unique timelines for learning and growth, we learn from her work about the infinite linguistic capacity of infants, even while reaffirming our opposition to lockstep, linear, and uniform learning processes.

Language acquisition is a sophisticated and complex process. Throughout time, the field has moved from the understanding put forth by B. F. Skinner in *Verbal Behavior* (1957), which posited that language acquisition is similar to the acquisition of other observable behaviors with an emphasis on "the importance of the environment, rather than a person's thought processes in shaping learning," and purported that "people learn largely through responding to stimuli" (Genishi and Dyson 1984, 5). Then, with Noam Chomsky's 1959 critique of Skinner, which rated Skinner's theory to be at once simplistic and empty, there was a call for the study of the formal properties of a grammar to learn how "human beings are specially designed" (p. 57) to learn language. Chomsky (1957) proposed that human beings have a "built-in structure," which accounts for our ability to mean, to communicate, to author words and sentences in a short amount of time despite relatively impoverished linguistic input. Not too long after Chomsky's theory of *universal grammar*, developmentalists critiqued his theory for not taking development into account. It was then that Piaget and Inhelder (1969) proposed that children's language develops as they interact with their environment. Later, scholars attempted to explain how children acquire language from a constructivist approach (Genishi and Dyson 1984; Olah 2000) proposing that children learn language through interactions with the people and places where they belong. Since then, scholars sought to understand how complex the process of language acquisition is—exploring pragmatic factors and cross-linguistic differences, for example. This complexity has been called "cumulative complexity," to refer to the process whereby as "children's utterances increase in length, the rules they must unconsciously know to form them increase in both number and difficulty" (Genishi and Dyson 1984, 5). That is, their use of language and "what they can do with language becomes more complex" (pp. 5–6), going beyond the complexity of sentences to encompass complexity of communication (bringing together multiple ideas, for example).

From such understandings, a constructivist or interactive approach to language development emerged, positioning children as active participants in their own language acquisition and learning, with a sociolinguistic focus on context. This is predicated on the tenet that "the social situation can have powerful effects on the kind of language a child produces. To learn how children use language we need to see them in a variety of contexts, using a range of sociolinguistic abilities" (Genishi and Dyson 1984, 2–3), and not only within the context of laboratories, which have punctuated studies in early childhood throughout time (such as Bronfenbrenner's).

Through a comparative study of literacy practices, Heath (1982, 49) underscored "the inadequacy of unilinear models of child language development and dichotomies between types of cognitive styles." Further, she called on researchers to study and seek to understand "the development of language use in relation to written materials in home and community" employing "a broad framework of sociocultural analysis" (Heath 1982, 49). From a sociocultural theoretical perspective, literacies and literacy practices are complex, interactive, and interpretative actions located in specific social and cultural realms.

> As educators, we have long paid attention to the social context in which children learn and develop. But, to many, the phrase "social context" may suggest no more than the societal setting in which events occur—in this case, the various surroundings at home, at school, and in the community in which children learn to talk, read and write. In recent years, however, a much more radical understanding of the importance of the social context of development has emerged as the result of a convergence of theoretical and empirical research in a variety of disciplines. According to this new understanding of social context, human infants are not only influenced by the social context in which they develop, but their very development as humans is dependent on opportunities to participate with others, notably parents, family members, peers and teachers, in the activities that constitute the culture in which they are growing up. Children's development is thus as much a social as an individual achievement. (Wells 2009, 271)

That is, through interactions in sociocultural contexts, children learn by communicating with others. This is the approach we employ here. Yet, we move beyond such a constructivist approach, in positioning young children agentively, not only acquiring language, but also (re)writing and (re)authoring interactions and contexts (as exemplified in Chapter 1). A relational literacies approach "compels a consideration of agency as an always contingent and contextualized relational practice as well as a possibility for action" (Licona and Chávez 2015, 98).

Children develop print awareness as they play with language through materials and resources (e.g., puppets), authoring imaginary worlds. Through engagement in pretend play (Genishi and Dyson 2009), children test out hypotheses about language and try on different voices and interactional sequences. They understand "how language is used in particular social contexts, or . . . how social structure is related to linguistic structure" (Genishi and Dyson 1984, 7). In doing so, they develop and enact rich and diverse communicative repertoires.

In Phillip Baumgarten's Head Start classroom in Georgia, U.S., children use print to make meaning (attending to the way that print looks). The room is filled with food packages, catalogs, restaurant menus, receipts, phone books, coupons, maps, pads of paper, Post-its, and other materials, which allow children to authentically engage with print in culturally relevant and contextually situated ways. Through "familiar literacy events," such as "bedtime stories, reading cereal boxes, stop signs, and television ads, and interpreting instructions for commercial games and toys," children learn to "follow socially established rules for verbalizing what they know from and about the written material" (Heath 1982, 50). These artifacts gain meaning as children engage in repurposing and remixing them.

For example, after noticing that his friend Asia was not feeling well, Jameel held her hand, walked her to the reading area, and told her: "You sit here, I'ma take care of you." He grabbed a marker and brushed it across her forehead. "You real hot, girl. I'ma write some medicine for you to feel good." Then, he grabbed an orange crayon and a small notepad and proceeded to write down wiggly lines

FIGURE 3.5 Writing with Purpose

(Figure 3.5), as he voiced: "You gotta take two of them. You's gonna be better." Asia, who was looking at the floor the entire time, head hanging, peered at Jameel and smiled. At the bottom of his prescription, he made a very big and dark marking. Looking up at Asia, he declared: "My signature. So they know iz legit. So they give you the medicines." Within the social context of play, Jameel was engaging in a familiar literacy event. He attended to the way written and oral language were used within the social context of a medical doctor's office. He appropriated literacies and enacted specific practices and identities through play.

On the Purpose of Literacy

As young children negotiate literate identities, their purpose is to communicate and interact with other human beings (Wells 1986). Regardless of how print looks (or whether words are spelled conventionally), children advance their understandings and practices of weaving symbols through practice with the intent of communicating. M. A. K. Halliday (1973, 1975), referring specifically to oral language, and more interested in communicative functions than in word acquisition, proposes that children have difficulty learning to read because of the way(s) reading is taught and the materials employed. That is, reading "bear[s] little resemblance to what the child has learned about the function of oral language" (Taylor and Vawter 1978, 943).

Halliday (1975) identified seven different functions of oral language:

- Instrumental: When language is used to communicate preferences, choices, wants, or needs ("Give me a . . ."). Often employed in classrooms for problem solving, gathering materials, role playing, and persuading.
- Personal: When language is used to express individuality ("I am . . ."). Employed by young children as they engage in making their feelings public and negotiate interactions with others.
- Interactional: When language is used to interact and plan, develop, or maintain a play, group activity, or social relationship ("I'll be the mom, you'll be . . ."). Seen in classrooms where children engage in play, dialogue, and discussions, and talking in groups.
- Regulatory: When language is used to control ("You need to do . . ."). This function of language comes into play as children engage in making rules for games and play and explaining how to do something.
- Representational: When language is used to explain ("I'll tell you what my momma said . . ."). Young children engage with the representational function of language when they convey messages, share something about the real world, or express a proposition.
- Heuristic: When language is used to find things out, wonder, or hypothesize ("What if?" and "Why?"). Young children engage with the heuristic function of language when they answer questions, engage in inquiry and research.

- Imaginative: When language is used to create, explore, and entertain ("Let's just pretend that . . ." or "Last night, my bed turned into chocolate . . ."). Young children engage the imaginative function of language when they act out stories, play with rhymes, and engage in other kinds of word play.

It is important to make room in the classroom for children to explore the multiple functions of oral language. After all, these oral language functions shed light onto written language. As Halliday stated, children learn an oral language because it serves a function: to communicate! A parallel can be made here to reading and writing—to written language more broadly.

As James Gee (2002, 31) explained:

> Sociocultural practices that embed "ways with printed words" almost always involve human beings both coordinating and getting coordinated by other people, as well as other forms of language, nonverbal images and symbols, objects, tools, technologies, sites and times. . . . Such practices are a "dance" in which people are simultaneously active (coordinating) and passive (getting coordinated), a dance in which they get "in synch" with other people.

For example, in the birthday card below (Figure 3.6), a five-year-old child in Pre-K, Nico, wrote a birthday message for his teacher. Although for those outside of education, this may simply seem to be a note, Nico's actions tell us much about his literacy understandings and practices. He understands the interactional and relational functions of writing; he writes for a communicative purpose. Nico wanted to deliver a message to his teacher, to communicate with her. He employed approximations, used upper- and lowercase letters to make meaning, and his meaning was clear. Familiar with the genre of birthday cards, he used big letters on a page to wish her happy birthday. Then, he declared that she was the best teacher. His exclamation mark makes such declaration clear. He wrote

FIGURE 3.6   Happy Birth Day! You Are The Bist Techr! I LOVE You!

LOVE in bold capital letters, making a smiley face out of the letter O and a heart out of the letter V. The paper, pencil, and letters (symbols) were deployed by Nico to convey a very particular meaning, being used as specific mediating devices (Wertsch 1998) to get in synch with his teacher, to communicate. Specifically, he was trying to establish an affective connection with his teacher, making a birthday card as a way to engage in a private interaction with his teacher, within a context in which collective communication is the norm. He engaged with literacy as a social practice, actively and purposefully. His literacy learning was palpable as his participation in his classroom community changed (Rogoff 2003). But to realize the power and potential of Nico's literacy practice, we must not only move beyond reductive theories, but also beyond reductive applications of theories, what Rose (1988) calls "cognitive reductionism."

For example, not to engage in cognitive reductionism of young children's cultural processes, we must recognize that their "participation in the practices of dynamic cultural communities can be distinguished from membership in ethnic groups, which often is treated in an all-or-none, static fashion" (Gutiérrez and Rogoff 2003, 21). After all, as Cole and Engeström (1993, 15) argue, culture "is experienced in local, face-to-face interactions that are locally constrained and heterogeneous with respect to both 'culture as a whole' and the parts of the entire toolkit experienced by any given individual."

The way that children negotiate meaning, becoming literate beings and being "symbol makers, symbol weavers" (Dyson 1990), is one of the most impressive achievements of humanity. Because children are cultural beings, literacies develop differently, based on social, cultural, historical, and political processes and interactions in different classrooms, (pre)schools, communities, and societies. Young children learn and grow within the context of cultural communities, "coordinated group[s] of people with some traditions and understandings in common, extending across several generations, with varied roles and practices and continual change among participants as well as transformation in the community's practices" (Gutiérrez and Rogoff 2003, 21). Individually and collectively, they develop the capacity to link play, interactions, pictures, and print in sophisticated ways. Reflecting on what this means with regard to the example presented earlier, we can see that Nico took on an agentive role, coordinating tools (deploying paper and marker to write), and authoring symbols, to engage in communication with his teacher.

Social Contexts of Children's Literacy Practices

Gordon Wells (1986) writes about multiple social contexts and underscores that social contexts extend beyond the contexts where literacy practices occur. There are multiple social contexts within schools, homes, and communities. It is in such contexts that children learn how to make meaning—through spoken utterances, written words, and gestures. A child's individual literacy practices are deeply influenced by the context(s) in which they take place. So, to understand early literacy, we must consider individual practices as well as societal practices. As we enter Phillip's Head Start classroom, we learn from Tamikka and Brianna about the social contexts shaping their literacy practices and enactments.

Three-year-old Tamikka and four-year-old Brianna created imaginary worlds in a pretend grocery store (Figure 3.7). Brianna played the mother. Tamikka played the daughter. As they were in the middle of grocery shopping, shopping list in hand (comprised of symbols such as scribbles and drawings), Tamikka answered the telephone with a smile and a pleasant voice: "Hey guuurl, how you doin'?" After a few seconds, she continued, "I know that's right. I know that's right," as she laughed with gusto. As she put a plastic vegetable in her basket, Brianna tugged on her shirt, saying "Moooooommaaaa" loudly. Tamikka's demeanor immediately changed as she firmly looked at Brianna (embodying the behavior culturally known as "giving her the look"), pointed to a chair, and said: "You hush, chile." She crossed off an item Brianna had added to the list. Brianna made a sad face and looked down. Within the space of seconds, Tamikka's communicative practices and roles shifted—all within the same physical context, but in shifting interactional terrains and social contexts. Tamikka's linguistic registers[1]—or "social languages" as Gee (1996, 2002) proposes—shifted.

Tamikka's performance helps us understand that language use is not generic. It is specific and situated. Gee (2002, 31) proposes: "Social languages are varieties of a language that are associated with specific socially situated identities ('who is talking/writing/acting') and specific socially-situated activities ('what is being done')." In the scenario above, Tamikka embodied two distinct socially situated identities—as someone's sista and as Brianna's momma. Although both social languages in use are employed within the context of pretend (through play), Tamikka displayed awareness of social language in use related to specific socially situated activities. Social languages both reflect and construct the identities Tamikka enacted during each of the particular times and particular interactions—even though she remained in the same physical space. Tamikka drew on grammatical resources differently in each of the interactions described earlier. Such social languages and the grammatical elements deployed are relevant not only for oral but for written language as well.

> This ability to organize and express inner feelings and experiences through shared gestural, visual, and verbal symbols is a part of children's human heritage; meaning making, like eating and sleeping, is an inherent part of being alive. (Dyson 1990, 50–51)

As we frame children as capable literate beings, we come to see that Tamikka and Brianna's shopping list is "no longer seen as evidence of children's immature understanding of the world . . . Rather, they are viewed as evidence of children's creative capacity for discerning links between a symbolic meaning . . . and some thing" (Dyson 1990, 51). It's easy to see how play has a key role in children's growth and development as symbol makers and symbol weavers.

FIGURE 3.7 Negotiating Literacies Across Interactional Contexts

Play is a space where they can take risks and engage with a broad variety of symbols authentically.

It is within a variety of social contexts that children learn language and negotiate literacies through their use. Before entering (pre)school, they may have developed literacy as defined by traditional benchmarks, such as accuracy, fluency, and comprehension, as they read a variety of symbols and communicate. Through authentic interactions, they negotiate literate identities, communicating meanings across contexts. Literacies emanate from the "dynamic relationship between individual and collective practices and sociohistorical change" (Brandt 2001, 201). Often, we adults are the ones who do not see how children already have such skills and practices. We position ourselves as "sponsors" of literacy; that is, we "provide, enhance, or deny opportunities for literacy learning" (Brandt 2001, 203). Brandt (2001, 201) underscores: "In an information economy, reading and writing serve as both instruments and products by which surplus wealth gets produced and competitive advantages get won." Literacy becomes quantified as an economic tool. From such a perspective, instead of learning about children's literacies, we adults are often too quick to judge children's literacy practices against our own individual (often restrictive) definitions of literacy: reading books and writing words.

Literacy learning happens in the context of classrooms and communities, where students' "linguistic and cultural-historical repertoires" (Gutiérrez and Rogoff 2003, 22) can be positioned as curricular resources. After all, children learn through participation in communities of practice (Rogoff 2003). Regrettably, young children who have been socialized into literacy practices that do not have power in schools (as book reading and writing letters do) tend to be disadvantaged. Those whose home communicative practices align with the interactional norms of schools are advantaged; their home communicative practices are valued—not necessarily because they have more complex syntax, but because they meet what is expected in and by schools. That is, "[a] person's unconscious knowledge of both linguistic and social rules . . . enable her to use language appropriately in different social contexts. When a speaker applies these rules in talking or interacting, she is engaged in communicative performance" (Genishi and Dyson 1984, 5). This is illustrated by Souto-Manning's (2013) study that looked closely at language misalignment, academic achievement, and participation in affinity groups (in this study, those children with knowledge of and interest in Bakugan and Little Pet Shop), which can be defined as communities of individuals with a shared affinity-identity (Gee 2001). In this case, the closer a child's language was to the dominant language used in schooling, the more likely the child was to be seen as competent by his/her teachers and peers—socially and academically.

The Sociocultural Nature of Early Literacy

As we reenter Phillip's Head Start classroom, we see how cultural practices get reenacted day in and day out. For example, one day, in the housekeeping area, Tiffany pretended to be a baby doll's momma, reading *The Three Bears* to the baby (Figure 3.8). She was clearly familiar with the behaviors associated with reading. She knew that print carried a message as she swooped her right thumb underneath the words printed in the book. She knew that books carried messages—or told stories—and was familiar with the concept of audience. Even though the book she was reading was titled *Colors* and not *The Three Bears* as she had announced, she displayed many emergent reading behaviors. Where had she learned them? "From my grandmomma," she responded, explaining that when they go to church her grandmother swoops her finger under the words in the Bible. She also shared that her grandmother read to put her baby sibling to sleep. Yet, her grandmother was not formally literate (could not read and write in the traditional sense, decoding and encoding words)—she was engaging in reading behaviors, on the discourse of storybook reading. Gee (2002) proposes that literacy is a socioculturally situated practice. As Tiffany was socialized into book reading through her interactions with her grandmother, she acquired other cultural models—about reading and about the world (such as women being primary caregivers for babies).

Tiffany also displayed her awareness of social language and literacy practices (Gee 2002), displaying her knowledge of different genres as she switched between reading the book and talking to the baby doll. She engaged in greeting rituals, which tend to be more fixed and predictable, asking the baby, "You okay?" and "You liking the story, huh?" She also engaged in storybook reading, introducing the book to the baby doll, looking at the cover of the book, telling the title, reading the story, offering a closing event, and then commenting on it. This is a practice her grandmother had engaged in, modeling it again and again. While she

FIGURE 3.8 Enacting Concepts about Print

pretended to decode words, her knowledge of a child's storybook structure was sophisticated as displayed by the structure employed in her reading of the book.

As we seek to understand the implications of social languages and genres (as evident in the scenarios featuring Tamikka, Brianna, and Tiffany), it is important to understand that "social languages and genres are not a product of a human biological capacity; rather, they are creatures of history and culture" (Gee 2002, 35). This understanding urges us to reconsider the traditional definition of early literacy as learning to read. It begs us to challenge it, seeking to understand the brilliance of young children as they negotiate a variety of social practices, social languages, and genres—within and across (pre)school, home, and communities. Early literacy thus encompasses blazing multiple pathways to and with words— oral or written—alongside lots more!

But, how are social languages and genres (such as those displayed by Tamikka, Brianna, and Tiffany) acquired? According to Gee (2002, 35), "through processes of socialization. . . . When people learn new social languages and genres—at the level of being able to produce them and not just consume them—they are being socialized into . . . Discourses with a big 'D.'"

Discourses as the Production of Social Languages and Literate Identities

Discourses with a big D involve more than language. "Social languages are embedded within Discourses and only have relevance and meaning within them" (Gee 2002, 35). So, Tamikka, Brianna, and Tiffany could perform specific social languages because they were fluent in the Discourses associated with talking with a close friend, disciplining a child, and reading a storybook. "A Discourse integrates ways of talking, listening, writing, reading, acting, interacting, believing, valuing, and feeling (using various objects, symbols, images, tools and technologies) in the service of enacting meaningful socially situated identities and activities" (Gee 2002, 35). Gee (1996, 2002) invites us to consider Discourses as identity kits, which allow individuals to enact specific identities and engage in activities related to that identity. As they are socialized into particular Discourses, individuals acquire "cultural models" (Holland, Lachicotte, Skinner, and Cain 2001) or theories about the world (Gee 2002). Such cultural models define what counts as "normal" and "typical" in classrooms and in society.

Cultural models also shape larger professional practices and guidelines in exclusive and situated ways, such as the case of the Developmentally Appropriate Practice guide in early childhood education (Copple and Bredekamp 2009). Cultural models are situated and informed by particular perspectives and points of view. They are not right or wrong as absolute constructs. Cultural models influence our ideas of the world in general and of early literacy in particular. As such, notions of what is deemed to be "appropriate" and/or "best" in early childhood education must be acknowledged within a context in which ethnocentrism reigns. That is, it is important to acknowledge and question what counts as best and appropriate. After all, as New and Mallory (1994) posited, the word *appropriate* is inherently cultural. Thus, such notions must be troubled as they are ethnocentric constructs (Souto-Manning 2010a), ideas and concepts based on the understanding and belief that one's own group or culture is better or more important than others and should serve as the standard against which all other practices are rated.

Literacy as Reading and Writing the World, as a Political Endeavor

Freire (1970) proposes that education is inherently political, and so is literacy. "It should serve as a starting point and not an end in itself" (Souto-Manning 2010b, 8). Literacy is at once historical, theoretical, social, and political. But it often gets stripped of such components, becoming a tool for colonization and (at times) an insurmountable obstacle to access. "Reading does not consist merely of decoding the written word or language; rather, it is preceded by and intertwined with knowledge of the world. Language and reality are dynamically interconnected" (Freire and Macedo 1998, 8).

Literacy is realized as human beings read worlds and words—and author them. Thus, literacy is not merely depositing literacy strategies and tools into students' brains (via the banking concept of education), but a critical co-construction of the world. The banking concept of education disempowers and colonizes. As Freire (2000) explains, "[t]he dominant elites utilize the banking concept to encourage passivity in the oppressed, corresponding with the latter's 'submerged' state of consciousness, and take advantage of that passivity to 'fill' that consciousness with slogans which create even more fear of freedom" (p. 95). This is simply not how teaching and learning (complex processes) happen.

The pedagogy of literacy is also political—whether it is by sanctioning texts for read alouds that fail to serve as mirrors for children from minoritized backgrounds (Bishop 1990), by covertly deeming one register to be correct (the dominant language of/in schooling), or by engaging in teaching actions and interactions that honor some families' ways of communicating while invisiblizing others. "Many political and educational plans have failed because their authors designed them according to their own personal views of reality, never once taking into account . . . [those for] whom their program was ostensibly directed" (Freire 1996, 75). Even pedagogical practices such as picture reading, which some posit emanated from show ways (quilts used by formerly enslaved Africans migrating North) were appropriated without credit, claimed by Whiteified practices (see Woodson, 2005). Additionally, interactional patterns commonly employed in classrooms reflect socialization in a particular Discourse (Gee 1996). Thus, teaching, learning, literacy, and curriculum are inherently political.

As children who are members of minoritized communities navigate within and across multiple communicative practices within and across contexts, they are often taught that their language is wrong and needs to be fixed. Also, the communicative competence that children display by moving back and forth between dialects, vernaculars, and registers gets ignored in monolingual classrooms. For example, words such as *parkeastes*, which employ Spanish-language verb conjugation conventions to English verbs (e.g., park) in sophisticated ways are too often seen as deficits, as signaling lack of knowledge, instead of according to the resourcefulness and creativity employed.

With regard to talk (classroom discourse), Cazden (2001) documents how IRE (initiation-response-evaluation) is commonly used in classrooms, labeling it "the language of teaching and learning." She explained: "Patterns of language use affect what counts as 'knowledge,' and what occurs as learning" and asked: "How do these patterns affect the equality, or inequality, or students' educational opportunities?" (p. 3). The answer is: in multiple ways! Dyson and Smitherman (2009) explain how "sounding right" in the classroom is based on the assumption that dominant American English and its communicative patterns are what count as right. Regarding AAL, Dyson and Smitherman (2009, 973) explain that it:

> [H]as a rich history of scholarship that both documents its historical evolution and sociolinguistic complexity and reveals the persistent lack of knowledge about AAL in our schools and the continuing negative stereotypes about its speakers. Currently, federal funds for early schooling target the literacy learning of low-income children, who are disproportionately children of

color; these programs, though, assume, as a literacy "basic," a singular correct way of using language.

Within such a context, there are misalignments and disconnects between students' practices and the aims and goals of schools and schooling. They go on to explain that sounding

> "[R]ight" to young children will vary for developmental, situational, and, as emphasized herein, sociocultural reasons . . . [and] illustrate how, in the course of teacher-student interaction, young children's major resources for learning to write—their very voices—may become a source of problems. (Dyson and Smitherman 2009, 973)

Educators often frame these as problems of the individual, under the guise of readiness and remediation. Here, we engage with the notion of *re-mediation* (Gutiérrez et al. 2009) as we see a need for reorganizing classroom spaces, curriculum, and resources in ways that honor and build on children's languages and literacies as assets.

Differences in communicative patterns can have dire consequences for young children. For example, a U.S. kindergartner, George, had been sent to detention more than half of his school days due to his use of AAL (Souto-Manning 2009a). His communicative practice was read by his teacher as problematic, signaling a behavior problem. For example, his White middle-class kindergarten teacher, thinking that she was being polite, would use "George, would you like to . . .?" preceding a direction (such as "Sit down."). George understood such indirect clauses cloaked as questions to truly signal a question for him to consider and answer. His teacher used questions and indirectness as markers of politeness. Because she was in a position of power, her communicative practices held more weight; she ethnocentrically scaled and rated George's communication against hers. So, instead of learning about his home communicative practices, she deemed them wrong and denied George access to learning. As with George, many children are not socialized in dominant American English patterns prior to entering schooling. In fact, young children may feel that it is silly to respond to questions that the teacher already has the answer to—not seeing the function of this type of communication. This diadvantages them.

Literacy "provides a referent . . . to further interrogate and reflect upon questions" (Giroux 1987, 6). In reading and critically rereading realities, one can engage in the counter-hegemonic act (Gramsci 1971) of rewriting what was read, authoring more hopeful and just tomorrows. Bartolomé (1996, 235) proposes that through literacy, teachers "can either maintain the status quo, or they can work to transform the sociocultural reality at the classroom and school level so that the culture at this micro-level does not reflect macro-level inequalities." Here, we introduce three ways of transforming unjust sociocultural realities: embodied literacy, racial literacy, and critical literacy. We do so as we seek to challenge the idea that reading is simply calling out words (Freire 1985a).

Embodied Literacy

Play is an embodied literacy (see Chapter 2): "Its multimodal facility for manipulating meanings and contexts powerfully shapes children's learning and participation in classrooms" (Wohlwend 2008, 128). Going beyond printed symbols and serving purposes external to communication, play allows teachers to see children as fully capable and to expand our conception of communicative repertoires and of literacy itself.

Heath (1982, 93) defines literacy events as "any occasion in which a piece of writing is integral to the nature of the participants' interactions and their interpretive processes." Here, we recognize that while writing is a particular enactment of literacy, it is not the only one, and we call for a more inclusive and child-centric definition of what counts as a literacy event to be any event where meaning is negotiated in a social context. We draw on Moje's (2000, 655) definition of literacy practices as "socially situated beliefs, values, and purposes that shape how and why people use literacy" and on Thiel's (2015, 46) call for us to acknowledge that:

> Literacy is not bound in manuscripts, coiled up in composition notebooks, and encased in mark making utensils, nor is literacy merely a communication tool. Literacies are leaky, seeping deep into our bodies and unfurled through our movements, perceptions, and reactions to other bodies.

While storybook reading and bedtime stories are literacy events, so is play. In play, children bring together multiple meanings, embodying semiotic signs and signifying in multiple ways. Wohlwend (2008, 128) posits that "Children emphasize or combine particular modes to strategically amplify their intended meanings as they play: (1) to try out social practices, (2) to explore the multimodal potential of material resources, and (3) to construct spaces for peer culture within classrooms." Through play, children negotiate their membership in specific communities, take up a number of (real and imagined) identities, and have opportunities to perform literate identities and make sense of texts (Wohlwend 2007, 2008). Through play, children create affinity groups around shared interests as "activities or routines, artifacts, values, and concerns that children produce and share in interaction with peers" (Corsaro and Eder 1990, 197).

This is political because once a common staple in early education (Paley 1992), play has been pushed out of early childhood classrooms in the name of academic standards, in favor of teachers imparting knowledge and strategies and enacting a banking approach to education. Making room for play (especially the child-led messy play which offers so many spaces for learning) has become a revolutionary act (Souto-Manning 2017). Further, conceptualizing play as an embodied literacy is a political stance. After all, it involves rereading our own conceptualizations of literacy, often restrictive and adult-centric to understand the ways in which children creatively author through the creative use of materials (Kress 2003).

In Phillip's Head Start classroom, children engaged in multimodal authoring through embodied literacies as meaning makers—using objects, gestures, sounds, images, and more. Within the context of this Head Start classroom, play was reconceptualized because "multimodal literacy re-centers play in school curriculum as a valuable semiotic system in its own right and revalues play as essential to 'new basics'" (Wohlwend 2008, 135). Three-, four-, and five-year-old children authored stories, resignified objects and signs, and engaged in flexible and creative meaning making. They expressed their ideas and employed authentic communication. For example, it was not uncommon for children to undertake authoring stories by repurposing cloth and other materials (as shown in Figure 3.9). They transformed the carpet into a bed, for example, as they enacted specific roles and an intricate storyline. As Wohlwend and Hall (2016, 155) explain, "Young children's

FIGURE 3.9 Embodied Literacy

engagements with literacy occur as immersive and embodied interactions," filled with "emotional investments" (p. 166). When we recognize embodied literacies, we also "recognize children as knowledgeable cultural participants and creative cultural producers" (p. 167).

Yet, as adults, we are often (even if unknowingly) "bound by cultural convention, correctness of form, and ready-made signs of written language, [whereas] children are freer to invent their own signs with whatever materials, modes, and semiotic systems (including play) are suited to the immediate purpose" (Wohlwend 2008, 128). Cultural conventions can stifle young children's learning processes as we often hold these conventions as norms against which to rate children's creative engagements. As we recognize the political nature of literacy—what is present, absent, which stories are told, whose communicative practices are included or excluded—we must move toward revisioning what counts as early literacy. We take up the task of expanding literacies, honoring embodiment and emotionality, exploring it further in Chapter 6: Languages and Literacies in Peer Culture, reconceptualizing childhood cultures as spaces for children's construction of language and literacy repertoires (Corsaro 2003; Paley 1992; Wohlwend 2011; Yoon 2014).

Racial Literacy

What does literacy have to do with race? And why identify "racial literacy?" This is a question considered by Guinier (2003, 2004), who calls for educators and educational researchers to move from racial liberalism to racial literacy, proposing, "In order to change the way race is understood, race has to be directly addressed rather than ignored" (Guinier 2003, 207). Guinier (2004, 114) invites us to "rethink race as an instrument of social, geographic and economic control" and proposes that "racial literacy offers a more dynamic framework for understanding American racism." According to Guinier (2004, 202), a racially literate person uses "race as a diagnostic device, an analytic tool, and an instrument of process." Employing Guinier's framework in an early childhood setting, Rogers and Mosley (2006, 465) succinctly explain:

> First, racial literacy defines racism as a structural problem rather than as an individual one. Second, racial literacy locates debates about public process, which are often cloaked in the subtext of race, within an explicitly democratic context that is forward looking. Third, the process dimension to racial literacy can be used to guide participatory problem solving.

In Phillip's Head Start classroom, racial literacy allowed young children to refute internalized racism as displayed by their loved ones. For example, Rashon (Figure 3.10) dreamed of having dreadlocks. His father communicated that he thought dreadlocks had a negative connotation. Discussing how others see students and how students see themselves through racialized lenses and honoring children's conflicts and questions, Phillip engaged the class in a discussion of who is bad and why, unveiling the racialization of "being bad," even by children of color.

The construction of who is good and who is bad had previously and problematically been "cloaked in the subtext of race" (Rogers and Mosley 2006, 465). Then, Phillip asked, "Do you really believe this?" and "Why?" They worked to uncover why their image of "being bad" was racialized. They shared their personal experiences. They talked about loved ones. Together, they understood the association of dreadlocks with "being bad" as a structural idea, and not as an individual belief. Phillip guided the class in participatory problem solving, problematizing racial texts and subtexts. Through such a process, Rashon then felt comfortable resignifying a shirt from the housekeeping area of the classroom as his "thinking dreads," which signaled that he was ready to work (see Figure 3.10). Dreadlocks were resignified from "being bad" to "being ready to think," begging us to trouble traditional constructs and notions—such as readiness.

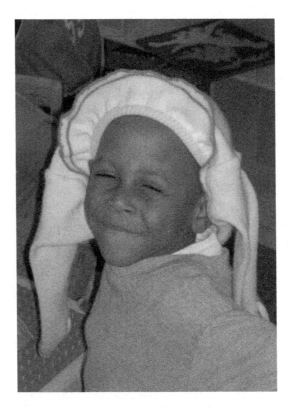

FIGURE 3.10 Performing Counterstories, Authoring Selves

Critical Literacy

Critical literacy practices originated from critical pedagogy, bringing to life the many sociocultural, historical, and political meanings behind texts and contexts (Comber 2003, Vasquez 2014). Critical pedagogy premises that individual human beings are agents of change, linking critical theory and classroom practices (Freire 1970). Through critical pedagogy, teachers transform their classrooms into spaces where students can engage in critical conversations and take action around issues of power, privilege, literacy, diversity, and social action. According to McLaren (1999, 50),

> [A] pedagogy of critical literacy becomes the primary vehicle for the development of "critical consciousness". . . . Literacy . . . becomes that common "process" of participation open to all individuals. The problem of "critical consciousness" cannot be posed in abstraction from the significant historical contexts in which knowledge is produced, engaged, and appropriated.

Critical literacy practices come to life through everyday classroom practices in unique ways within and across contexts and "involve people using language to exercise power, to enhance everyday life in schools and communities, and to question practices of privilege and injustice" (Comber 2001b, 1). Underlying critical literacy frameworks is Freire and Macedo's (1987, viii) notion that critical literacy is about "reading the word, and the world" and seeing the world from particular frames. A central aim of critical literacy is to "use texts as social tools in ways that allow for a reconstruction of these same worlds" (Luke 2000, 453). This framework draws attention to what is included in and what is left out of a text and pushes us to identify the ideological underpinnings of texts (Luke 2000).

In Phillip's Head Start classroom, critical literacies were negotiated day in and day out, as children read injustices in their classroom and in the world and sought to promote change. At times, they brought such issues into classroom community meetings, other times students addressed issues through writing (e.g., writing letters, seeking to promote change, and fostering more just practices). There were many critical literacy actions taken up by Phillip's students as they sought to transform their worlds.

Literacies in Multiple Social Worlds: Understanding Social Literacy Practices

In this chapter, we examined how literacy is practiced in nuanced ways across different cultural communities. Through a number of examples, we made visible how young children navigated multiple social worlds (Gutiérrez 2008) organized by sets of rules, interactions, and social practices, which can be challenged and changed (Vasquez 2014). After all,

[O]nly when we understand a child's multiple literacies (i.e., different ways with words embedded in different social practices and Discourses) in a . . . specific and situated way . . . can we really understand and appropriately assess a child's language and literacy development. This most certainly means understanding children's specific "ways with words" that, while rooted in home or community-based Discourses, are not "school aligned" (and, in fact, children from all cultural groups have these, though some have more than others). It means, as well, questioning the rather general way in which literacy is treated in school, much academic research, and in assessing children. (Gee 2002, 41)

In Part II (Chapters 4, 5, and 6), we seek to understand relational literacies, "practices through which we learn to exist differently and simultaneously" (Martin 2013, 137), sites of production of third spaces, enacted with the people who are present in young children's lives and anchored in the spaces young children belong. In doing so, we delve into literacies in families and homes (Chapter 4), in neighborhoods and communities (Chapter 5), and within the context of peers and peer culture (Chapter 6).

Note

1. According to Schiffman and Spooner (2012), a linguistic register refers to: "A set of specialized vocabulary and preferred (or dispreferred) syntactic and rhetorical devices/structures, used by specific socio-professional groups for special purposes" (p. 22).

PART II

Spaces of Belonging: Relational Literacies

Literacies are negotiated through actions and interactions. They are often deployed across relational contexts—the multiple and overlapping spaces where children belong. Grounded in the belief that young children navigate within and across a variety of relational spaces—peer groups, families, schools, and communities—the chapters in Part II reaffirm children as active and capable members of multiple communities.

In *Chapter 4: Languages and Literacies in Families and Homes*, we explain how actions and interactions as well as cultural practices in such settings can be centrally repositioned in early education. We position families and homes as central parts of children's lives much before they enter (pre)schools. Theorizing from practice, we explain how Moll and González (1994) identify children's cultural practices as "funds of knowledge," asserting that within every family there are existing social, cultural, and linguistic practices that children develop in order to belong and participate. We expand on the literacy resources that families possess through oral traditions, cultural practices, and familial practices. Through examples, we situate these home literacies (Gregory, Long, and Volk 2004; Souto-Manning 2010a) as integral in understanding the resourcefulness of cultural communities, especially those that have been traditionally viewed as deficient or inferior (Goodwin, Cheruvu, and Genishi 2008; Valdés 1996). In doing so, we call on early childhood teachers to open "curricular closets in regulated times" (Dyson 2010, p. 307). We conclude by situating families and homes within the context of neighborhoods and communities (Haight and Carter-Black 2004).

Chapter 5: Languages and Literacies in Neighborhoods and Communities positions children as active members of multiple communities with a particular attention to children's literacy environments. In Chapter 5, we explore the myriad communicative practices embedded in ethnic enclaves, community institutions (e.g. Brandt's idea of "sponsors of literacy," 2001), and non-traditional spaces for literacy learning. In doing so, we move away from innocent and romanticized ideas of young children as helpless and powerless (introduced and challenged in Chapter 1), seeing them as capable and active members of communities. As we do so, we review how scholars examine participatory literacies where youth are engaged in co-constructing unique forms of interaction including spoken word, activism, and writing (Fisher 2007; Jenkins et. al. 2009; Paris 2012). Similarly, we position young children as active and knowledgeable participants in their own right, within and around their neighborhoods and communities. We provide examples of young children fully and capably engaged in communities. As we theorize these examples, we make visible the ways in which literacies are sponsored in spaces outside of the school historically, socially, and politically (Freire 1970; Long, Volk, Baines, and Tisdale 2003; Souto-Manning 2010a, 2010b).

In *Chapter 6: Languages and Literacies in Peer Culture*, we explore childhood cultures as spaces for children's construction of language and literacy repertoires. Within play spaces, engagement with popular culture, and interactions around digital platforms, children create their own set of literacy practices as a way to engage with their peers (Corsaro 2003; Paley 1987; Wohlwend 2011; Yoon 2014). These engagements come through shared knowledge and understandings. Furthermore, peer cultures allow us to see how young children form affinity groups, foster membership, and appropriate identities. In this chapter, we extend the concept of funds of knowledge to include cultural practices found in peer groups, popular culture, and digital platforms (Dyson 1997; Marsh and Bishop 2014; Vasquez and Felderman 2012). Children's cultural spaces, therefore, are multiple; and children accumulate practices in participation within these communities.

4

LANGUAGES AND LITERACIES IN FAMILIES AND HOMES

As a young child in a working-class family where no one had even graduated
from high school, I do not remember any books or reading activities taking place
in our apartment. . . . I do not recall reading anything before starting first grade.
But this does not mean that we had no experiences with literacy. (Nieto 2010, 38)

Multiple languages and literacies are at play within the context of young children's
families and homes. At times, they are called family literacy practices, other
times, home literacies. These are cultural practices specific to families. They "are
numerous, varied and frequent" (Barton 1996, 52). Sonia Nieto, in the quote that
opens this chapter, reflected on her own upbringing and the home literacies present in her home; they go beyond books and reading activities. Magnetic letters,
books, and writing tools are not necessary. They are literacy practices of schools
and schooling.

Rather, family literacy practices may include singing hymns from memory as
an intergenerational practice, engaging in call-and-response, playing the dozens
(especially amongst siblings and/or cousins), using expressions such as "You a hot
mess" to express affection, and expressing the meaning of song lyrics—such as
those by Marvin Gaye and Stevie Wonder—through dancing and gestures. They
happen through actions and interactions. They are relational; "multimodal, participatory, and embodied meaning-making practices and performances" (Licona and
Chávez 2015, 96). While family literacy practices at times may involve printed
materials, such as in the case of recipes, print is not necessarily focal in all home
literacies; relational literacies honor a "relational style of processing information"
and making meaning associated with Afrocentric ways of teaching and learning
(Irvine 1991, 118). In fact, the very concept of relational literacies moves away
from defining literacy singularly and linking it closely to alphabetic knowledge,

thus recognizing literacies as "multimodal, technological, embodied, imagined, and/or performed" (Irvine 1991, 96). Relational literacies position "community histories as meaningful" and purposefully aim to "make people and places knowable and understandable" (Licona and Russell 2013, 2) to identify, communicate, and unleash the power of collectives. Furthermore, relational literacies bring to focus the literacies and collective practices of those whose voices and perspectives were historically marginalized.

While rich and present within and across diverse homes, only a small set of family literacies are recognized by (pre)schools . . . those coherent with the culture of power or with the culture of those who have power (Delpit 1988). Often, the cultural practices of families from minoritized backgrounds are not deemed as worthy as those aligned with the culture of power. Practices of families from dominant and majoritized backgrounds—such as book reading, question and answer, IRE, and bedtime stories—are associated with objectivism and seen as acultural or as normal. Here, we posit that seeing some cultural practices (read family literacies) as official, and others as marginal, is a way to communicate to children that their families are not worthy. By embracing the literacy norms established by dominant communities, educators, schools, and society impose this false norm onto all.

Remediating Family Literacies

Although family literacy has traditionally been defined as the ways in which print is used in home contexts, as you can surmise (based on your reading of Part I of this book), we engage in expanding the concept of home literacies to the ways in which language and communicative practices come to life in homes and across interactions with family members, anchored in cultural practices.

For example, Head Start teachers J. W. and Marilyn (Souto-Manning 2010a, 165) noticed that the three- to five-year-old children they taught (mostly African American) spoke as if "cutting someone's turn" or "entering an unwelcome conversation." Instead of judging the children's communicative practices against their own (as two White teachers teaching mostly African American children), they came to understand that the children were collaboratively and simultaneously coconstructing meaningful narratives and negotiating actions, albeit in ways that were initially unfamiliar to the teachers. The interaction below serves as an example of children's narrative coconstructions grounded in home language practices (i.e., overlapping speech, indicated by =):

> Keisha [to Xavier]: She be mindin' my business. She need to mind her business or come help me.
> Tyra [to Keisha]: What you want me to do? You want me=
> Xavier: =Don't you be pretendin' you don't know nothin'. You been watchin'. Find somethin'.

Tyra: Okay. Cleaning up.
Keisha: This a mess! You know we need help cleaning up.
Xavier: You know what=
Tyra: =Gon need be done.
Xavier [to Keisha]: She know what need be done.
Keisha: Uh-hum. I hear you. She betta get her behind busy. She goin' or not?

Such communicative practices draw on African American communicative patterns, including call and response and collective improvisation (as evidenced in jazz, for example). Ignoring the power of such practices in the classroom would mean placing students at a disadvantage as White middle-class turn-taking in the classroom diverged from the culturally situated rules governing home and community interactions. In this example, we can see how the children employ five key features of African American Language syntax along with two features of African American Language phonology (Alim 2003, 46):

1. Habitual be: indicates actions that are continuing or ongoing, e.g., in "She be mindin' my business."
2. Copula absence: absence of is and are in some present tense forms, e.g., in "This a mess!"
3. Stressed been: denotes the remote past, e.g., in "You been watchin'."
4. Gon: indicates future tense, e.g., in "Gon need be done."
5. Double negative: e.g., in "Don't you be pretendin' you don't know nothin'.
6. Postvocalic-r: the r after the vowel is absent, e.g., in "She betta get her behind busy."
7. Dropping the g: e.g., in "Don't you be pretendin' you don't know nothin'."

Communicatively, the children are displaying membership in a community of African American Language speakers; they were strategically constructing their identities. Not only were they aligning with the language of their families, but with the language of much of the music they hummed throughout the day in their preschool classroom. They were recycling expressions they'd heard from adults in their lives, such as "She betta get her behind busy." Thus, they took up different roles in their play. Dialectically, they are following the rules of AAL; they are communicating effectively through an expansive communicative repertoire.

Recognizing the richness of the communicative practices the young children they taught brought from home, J. W. and Marilyn redefined literacy, taking a more oral turn—including sophisticated hymns and intricate recipes orally recalled—as opposed to being restricted to print decoding and book reading. For example, the children sang, "He's got the whole world in his hands," through call and response during transitions spontaneously. One child would sing, "He's got the whole world," and others would answer, "in his hands," and then a child would chime in, "He's got his brothers and his sisters," and the group would respond, "in his hands." While singing, children moved their bodies to the rhythm of the song, clapping, and performing in a way similar to those taking place in many African American churches. "It's incredible how they can remember these entirely," said J. W. He purchased a book by Kadir Nelson portraying the song, providing links between their own literacies and the literacy practices (over)valued in schools, namely reading and writing. In such instances, the children started seeing their communicative practices competently, and drew on their full communicative repertoires as they made meaning of and constructed meaning in their classroom and preschool.

By acknowledging their literacy privileges as shaped by an ethnocentric approach to academic success and learning, J. W. and Marilyn got a glimpse of the authentic and meaningful practices taking place in the children's homes and communities. The short quote below (from a conversation between J. W. and Marilyn), while not exemplifying the complexities of all learning processes, does exemplify how Marilyn and J. W. learned about children, their families, and communities. Reflecting on the process, Marilyn stated:

> I see literacy in a whole new way now. . . . Before . . . if someone would ask like, what's literacy mean to you, I would've been like, reading books to children, and having, you know, print on the mirror. . . . But I think now I realize, oh, it's so much more than that, than just books and words around the classroom. . . . For example, dramatic play and the whole . . . pretending to talk on the phone while cooking the meal, like that, is totally early literacy.

As they paid close attention to and learned from the children they taught (instead of judging them), there was a clear shift in stance—from teaching children to learning with them, their families, and their communities. Not in the way that so many people propose—by pathologizing and "helping" them—but by truly seeing the learning in meaningful ways. Here, it is important to recognize the learning of teachers who engaged in redefining literacy practices. While this process might initially appear easy and simplistic, it involved letting go of the cultural deprivation paradigm that has characterized some Head Start programs as well as early childhood education as a whole (Goodwin et al. 2008), and move to identify, leverage, and support the rich literacy practices children bring from home.

To shift "away from notions of inferiority or deprivation," they had to purposefully and intentionally put "emphasis on the impact of cultural differences on the lives, experiences, and identities of diverse groups in ways that are not deviant but are unique" (Goodwin et al. 2008, 4). It involved embracing a fluid identity of teacher and learner simultaneously—teaching one literacy system while learning others—from and with the children who were members of the classroom community and their families. Here is what they said about home literacies as Mariana interviewed them (= indicates overlapping speech):

> Mariana: So . . . how did home literacies change children's participation in the classroom?
>
> Marilyn: Like, they could draw and then tell complicated stories, but if we wanted them to write, they got lost in the process and didn't like it.
>
> J. W.: Yes, and the stories [they told] were so sophisticated and complex. Many adults, many of our college students could not tell [or even keep track] of all the layers.
>
> Marilyn: So, their drawings told the story, and they had so much on the page. Sometimes it didn't make sense to look at and they didn't even look nice =
>
> J. W.: = Aesthetically =
>
> Marilyn: = Yeah, but when we listened to them, it was all about the relationships, which are so hard to picture anyway.
>
> J. W.: So it's important for us to understand what they mean on their own terms—without going, "ooh, this is not how you do this!" Not judging it against how I always thought of literacy, against how I grew up knowing interactions work. (Souto-Manning 2010a, 171)

J. W. and Marilyn positioned children as coconstructors of curriculum, as unique contributors. Within these Head Start classrooms, the children and the teachers negotiated ways to (re)define texts to include practices that meant much to the children. Often, in responding to texts being read, children performed their responses as opposed to simply verbalizing them, a practice adopted due to the extent that children performed to communicate in their homes and communities, as documented by J. W. and Marilyn. So many of the children were used to dancing to music and letting their feelings emerge through movement; their performative responses were more complex than their oral reactions to texts and situations. Expecting children to connect to a text verbally while sitting quietly on carpet squares conflicted with how many of the children expressed feelings and experiences in their own homes and communities. Thus, J. W. and Marilyn encouraged children to engage in music and performance as ways of authoring and responding. It was amazing to hear some of their drum performances "speak" more eloquently than any of us could. They engaged in call and response and in very complex rhythmic patterns requiring attention, repetition, and extension (with complicated mathematical permutations situated well beyond the curricular scope of Head Start) as they drummed and composed together. For example, if one student started with two beats, another student could repeat the two beats in the same rhythm, add something, and toss it back to the initial drummer, adding complexity yet coconstructing patterns at every turn.

Family Literacies: Looking Back and Moving Forward

In contrast to the powerful family literacy practices negotiated in J. W. and Marilyn's Head Start classroom, people of color and their languages and literacy practices are often seen through an inferiority or a deficit lens. As discussed in Chapter 2, this has been the case historically and continues to be the case contemporarily. Such perceptions frame children whose identities have historically been minoritized in terms of deficits needing to be fixed. Instead of admitting that this is a process of colonization and marginalization, we call it literacy and schooling. Departing from such a deficit-ridden and problematic perspective, in this chapter, we take up the notion of re-mediation, affirming that what needs fixing are not children's communicative repertoires, but the very definition of literacy, which needs to go from singular to plural, encompassing families' cultural practices and the ways in which young children make sense of their lives and worlds through a variety of means. This is because "the notion of re-mediation . . . disrupts the ideology of pathology linked with most approaches to remediation. Instead of emphasizing basic skills—problems of the individual—re-mediation involves a reorganization of the entire ecology for learning" (Gutiérrez, Morales, and Martinez 2009, 227).

To show the power of family literacy practices to literacy learning, in this chapter, we share examples of how teachers access and pedagogically reposition home literacies as funds of knowledge (Moll et al. 1992). We see this repositioning as necessary as funds of knowledge aim to "develop innovations in teaching that draw upon the knowledge and skills of local households" (Moll et al. 1992, 132); that is, that draw on family literacies. Moll and colleagues (1992, 132) affirm that "by capitalizing on household and other community resources, we can organize classroom instruction that far exceeds in quality the rote-like instruction" children from minoritized backgrounds encounter in classrooms such as Ms. Silva's (see Chapter 3).

We propose that the very definition of literacies must be expanded and reenvisioned more inclusively to encompass not only what has been traditionally sanctioned in (pre)schools, whether it includes play or not (as explained in Chapter 2), but also the ways in which young children, families, and communities read and write their worlds. After all, "teachers need to build on what the children *do have*, rather than lament what they do *not have*" (Nieto 2010, 38). It must include oral and written communication alongside gestures and signing (including those who communicate through languages such as American Sign Language) and many other family-generated cultural practices (ways of making sense in and of the world). We see diverse practices, homes, and families as assets, which significantly enrich the education of all children.

Through a number of examples from our work and a review of the work of other researchers, we seek to unveil the rich and sophisticated practices, which occur within families in children's homes, the people and places where children belong. In doing so, we unpack home literacies as cultural practices grounded in the concept of belonging. We also explain how cultural practices in family and home contexts can be centrally repositioned in early education, leading us to understand the need for questioning restrictive definitions of literacy and moving toward more inclusive understandings. This is an imperative in a diverse world. We specifically position ourselves against the existing "time warp in which children who embody certain kinds of diversity have become the problem, and standardization has become the 'fix'" (Genishi and Dyson 2009, 10). But before we do so, we briefly review traditional definitions of family literacy, which purport that (pre)schools and teachers must teach families how to engage their children in literacy activities and that school materials must be inserted into homes so that children are "ready" for school (Graue 1992, 2006).

On the Trouble of Family Literacy as Traditional Models of Emergent Literacy

"Family literacy, as a term, today tends to refer to the many and varied projects being proposed or currently operating that are designed to enhance literacy within the home," and is framed as "a problem" (Purcell-Gates 1993, 670). Most examples of home or family literacy practices are in fact school-to-home literacy practices; impositions of (pre)school discourses onto the narratives enacted in the context of the home. They focus on book reading, storytelling, and written language. For example, family literacy programs often focus on how parents and families can help their child(ren) read. They model to parents practices such as bedtime story behaviors, tell parents to read to their children, to tell them stories, to foster phonemic awareness, teach phonics (letter names and sounds), to talk to their children, to label objects and ask questions to which they already know the answers (Shanahan 2015). Families are often positioned as audience, volunteer, or paraprofessional; rarely are parents positioned as resources or as decision makers (Greenwood and Hickman 1991). Here, while we acknowledge these programs in extending the reach of the (pre)school agenda, we do not regard them as home literacies. Instead, we invite you to pay close attention to the sophistication of home literacies in their own right, without scaling and rating them according to school-sanctioned definitions or seeing how they permeate (pre)school practices (Marsh 2010).

Emergent literacy has been "traditionally defined as the acquisition of skills necessary for reading and/or using family literacy practices as transitory 'stepping stones' to be left behind when more traditional literacy practices [have] developed" (Souto-Manning 2010a, 154). Some of these skills have been labeled "concepts about print" (Clay 1993). Others have become their own programs, in decontextualized and meaningless ways for young children: such is the case of phonemic awareness and phonologic knowledge, which have been labeled phonics and become instantiated in early childhood classrooms through a variety of commercialized programs. Regardless, early literacy scholars, such as Holdaway (1979) and Clay (1991), underscore the need for enhancing children's exposure to print and expanding their vocabularies by promoting regular and systematic interactions with oral and written language. Doake (1981) indicates that when parents/families and young children participate in traditional literacy practices in the home (e.g., book reading), children become more proficient and successful. Such recommendations have led to a quest to develop literacy skills faster and faster, without respect for children's own timelines and rhythms (Genishi and Dyson 2009; Genishi and Dyson 2012), emphasizing a panoptical approach to time (Lesko 2012) and enacting the assumed superiority of adults.

Phonics and word recognition have become well-disseminated "basics" of early literacy without much regard for the multiple pathways to literacy learning and development in ethnocentric ways (Souto-Manning 2010a). That is, there are specific bodies of knowledge that are regarded as prerequisites to acquiring others. This presupposes that literacy develops in a part-to-whole fashion, in material ways, similar to a wall, in which bricks have to be layered between concrete in order for greater heights to be achieved. This approach disregards the brilliance of young children. It also disregards the fact that children develop pragmatic, semantic, and syntactic understandings and practices through play, actions, and interactions much before they engage with graphophonics (letter-sound correspondence, or what many title "phonics"). Taking on such a simplistic and misguided approach to the development of literacy, many publishers have developed commercial programs in these two areas, boxed sets often detached from the meaning-making processes and worlds of young children in (pre)school classrooms—regarding children as empty vaults or presupposing processes of silencing or erasure of children's communicative repertoires. This is substantiated by studies that link preschool and kindergarten literacy skills to later academic success, which fail to account for immaterial conditions and processes.

Dickinson and Sprague (2001, 273) note: "The receptive vocabulary scores children received near the end of kindergarten were strongly related to children's subsequent literacy development. In addition, data from the end of seventh grade also suggest that kindergarten status plays a role in predicting later reading comprehension." But—what else? What additional conditions are in place during the early childhood years which lead to literacy success in seventh grade? Furthermore, are vocabulary scores a measure or are they a symptom of other factors, which may influence academic success? Similarly, Catherine Snow and her colleagues Burns and Griffin (1998, 188) identify letter recognition, phonological awareness, phonics, concepts about print, book knowledge, and oral comprehension and vocabulary as "basics" of early literacy, declaring: "Enhancing children's letter knowledge and phonological awareness skills should be a priority goal in the kindergarten classroom." Taken together, these declarations make up the literacy basics—a commonly adopted way of categorizing young children as literate. Again, we must ask, are these conditions building blocks (or "basics") of literacy or are they semiotic representations of other conditions that allow children to advance academically—such as White privilege, family income, social supports, etc.?

Studies such as Durkin's (1966) link specific practices in the home-to-schooling success, verifying that children who were schooled in school-aligned and privileged literacy practices in the home, prior to entering school, did better academically. This comes as no surprise to us. As Dorothy Strickland (2004, 86) confirmed decades later, "Children from homes where parents model the uses of literacy and engage children in activities that promote basic understandings about literacy and its uses are better prepared for school." But since when are parents responsible for "preparing" their children for schools? And whose definition of literacy is privileged in schools? Since schools are designed to privilege the language and literacy practices of dominant groups, they reward such practices. Yet, this seemingly uncritical study with unsurprising findings (at least to us) initiated races to acquire literacy skills earlier and earlier and to advance reading levels faster and faster (Souto-Manning and Martell 2016).

Strickland (2004, 87) explains the traditional approach to early literacy development, predicated on three understandings:

> First, children reared in families where parents provide rich language and literacy do better in school than those who do not. Language-poor families are likely to use fewer "different" words in their everyday conversations, and the language environment is more likely to be controlling and punitive (Hart & Risely 1995) [sic]. Second, exposure to less common, more sophisticated vocabulary (i.e., rare words) at home relates directly to children's vocabulary acquisition (Dickinson & Tabors 2001). Third, there is a strong relationship between vocabulary development and reading achievement.

We take issue with this statement as we do not believe in the concept of "language-poor" families. We believe that their practices are simply minoritized, disregarded, disprivileged, and devalued. Additionally, we do not deem the communicative styles present in many Black households in the U.S., which display more directness, as controlling or punitive. Finally, we question what counts as "different" words versus wrong words, thus troubling colonialist notions of sophisticated vocabularies, communicative practices, and literacies. Instead, we embrace Shirley Brice Heath's (1982, 1983, 1990) explanations of the languages and literacies in which young children engage—within and across communities—as equally worthy, even if they are not valued in (pre)schools today.

But this deficit view of children's diverse ways with words is not isolated. In fact, it informs much for what counts as literacy, literacy achievement, and literacy success in early childhood classrooms today (as we explored in Chapters 2 and 3).

In the U.S., even the statement jointly issued by two major professional organizations in the teaching of reading and in the teaching of young children (respectively), the International Reading Association and the National Association for the Education of Young Children (1998, 6), reinforced a readiness approach to literacy, stating, "Failing to give children literacy experiences until they are school age can severely limit the reading and writing levels they ultimately attain." Such stances continue to add to the language (and literacy) debt which society owes to its youngest children who are members of minoritized populations. As Genishi and Dyson (2012, 20) eloquently explain:

> We imagine the classroom stage, not as a race, but as a dance hall, where teachers and children adapt to each other, even as they sometimes move to a rhythm all their own. The teacher responds, leads, and sometimes lets go to observe more carefully the rhythms of children in motion. Then teachers and children come together and, rather than racing to a top, spread their skilled, responsive movement across times and spaces, dancing their way into the future.

Understanding Young Children's Literacy Practices

Early literacy researchers posit that young children develop literacy through their participation in literacy events (Dyson 1989; Ferreiro and Teberosky 1982; Purcell-Gates 1996). These happen within the context of families way before they happen in (pre)schools. They learn how oral and written language work and how "print, as a language signifier, maps onto speech" (Purcell-Gates 1996, 409). Purcell-Gates and Dahl (1991) documented the ethnocentric nature of school literacy (what counts as literacy) and its overreliance on written language in a two-year study documenting the literacy development of thirty-five low-income children. They found that the children "who entered kindergarten knowing more about print and its functions in the world were generally more successful with the formal literacy instruction they encountered at school, performed higher on achievement tests, and were judged as more advanced readers and writers by their teachers" (Purcell-Gates 1996, 409). That is, literacy as defined by schools legitimized certain family literacies while delegitimizing others. From an intersectional perspective (focusing on the overlapping and intersecting forms of oppression experienced by minoritized individuals and communities [Crenshaw 1991]) delegitimized literacies are largely associated with and enacted by racially, culturally, and socioeconomically minoritized communities and individuals. That is, literacy practices—at least school-worthy literacy practices—are framed by a matrix of domination (Hill Collins 2000, 2009), portraying the organization of intersecting oppressions. Thus, power must figure centrally in (re)defining family literacy practices.

Because some families' cultural practices are being imposed on other families and children in the name of family literacy practices and children's academic success, we end up with an impoverished definition of what counts as literacy. Acknowledging that family literacies exist before programs or projects are proposed and implemented by educators and policymakers, here, we employ Rudine Sims Bishop's (1990) metaphor of windows, mirrors, and sliding glass doors to explain how literacies must reflect a child's own family literacy practices and communicative repertoires, serve as windows into new and unfamiliar family literacy practices, and provide sliding glass doors whereby children can expand their own worlds and enter other worlds, developing new communicative and cultural competencies.

We take up Teale's (1986, 192) call for a "reconsideration of traditional wisdom which has it that children from low-SES backgrounds come to school with a dearth of literacy experience." Such calls for more inclusive and diverse definitions of literacies are beneficial to all. This is important not only for children who have been historically minoritized, but also for those who have always found mirrors in the literacies present in classrooms and (pre)schools (Bishop 2015). Keeping in mind the ways in which literacies must serve as windows, mirrors, and sliding glass doors helps us re-mediate home and school contexts. This is because too many children do not see their homes and families in the literacy practices traditionally deployed in (pre)schools, nor in the materials used.

Instead of judging the language repertoires and literacy practices children acquire at home against our own ideas of language and literacy, it is important to identify, document, and learn from them. Taking a critical anthropological approach is essential as we seek to understand the function of certain practices for household functioning, e.g., the mother of a second grader in Jessica Martell's made and sold tamales (further discussed in Chapter 4). She had learned tamale making intergenerationally. Not only did she know how to cook them, but how to price them just right, so that she would make a profit and so that her customers could afford to purchase tamales.

Yet, it is important that we recognize that we can only learn about others' cultural practices when we recognize our own practices as culturally located and ourselves as cultural beings (Souto-Manning 2013b). Otherwise, we will always see our practices as "normal" and others, in contrast, as "abnormal," thus believing that children lack "the ability to use language in complex ways and . . . [have] few literacy resources and little support at home" (Gregory et al. 2004b, 1). Without this recognition, teachers may see this work as an "add on" and may as a result—even unintentionally—focus on shallow understandings of children's cultural practices. As a field, all too often, in a quest to define literacy, historically minoritized "children's literacy practices were invisible and excluded from these accounts. Likewise 'invisible' were the mediators or unofficial 'teachers' in these children's lives—their siblings, grandparents, friends and other community members" (Gregory et al. 2004b, 2).

Knowing that the field has recognized that "literacy learning does not begin when children enter kindergarten and first grade; rather, it is the result of many and varied experiences with print from the time they are born into a family that utilizes print as a mediator for life's many demands and activities" (Gregory et al. 2004b, 670–671), we call for a more inclusive understanding of literacy that goes beyond the utilization of print for communication. This is especially important because oral storytelling traditions are foundational cultural practices for a number of communities. For example, researchers have documented that many Native Americans in the Pacific Northwest and African Americans pass down important moral and spiritual concepts from generation to generation through oral story-telling, having robust oral traditions (Banks-Wallace 2002; Hymes 2004). Thus, by restricting family literacy to written language, we cast inequities and make invisible many families' ways with words.

What We Know

Over the past four decades, much research has been done to better understand young children's language and literacy development in homes and schools (Dyson 1989; Heath 1983; Purcell-Gates 1996), documenting the development of literacy concepts in both of these settings. Here, we focus specifically on home literacies, as children experience a number of sophisticated literacy practices prior to enter-ing classrooms. Much of this learning happens implicitly, in situated ways.

Young children play with and experience reading a variety of symbols (whether written or enacted). They become members of literacy communities, and learn to make meaning, to communicate. Because they read symbols in/and the world prior to entering schools (as explored in Chapters 2 and 3), we do not define home literacies as the permeability of school literacy practices into homes, but as home-based practices and funds of knowledge. In doing so, we agree with Eugene García's (2012) call for more of the home into schools and less of schools into children's homes. This necessitates teachers blurring the role of teacher and learner and continuously learning from families as a matter of curriculum design. That is, regarding family literacies as cultural practices, teachers must engage ethnographically, learning from and documenting the cultural practices of the families who make up the (extended) classroom community. To document and learn from these cultural practices, educators must engage in

> [G]enuine attempts to understand a culture from an insider's perspective. This is possible only to the extent that the researcher assumes a . . . nonjudgmental stance, resisting cultural arrogance and an "interventionist" attitude. This is clearly difficult, though, and it is only by confronting these issues honestly that we can hope to achieve such a stance. (Purcell-Gates 1993, 675)

Building on the work of researchers who have unveiled the sophistication of family literacy practices and how teachers can leverage them to unleash pow-erful learning, such as Shirley Brice Heath (1982, 1983, 1990), Luis Moll and colleagues (1992), Norma González and colleagues (2005), Victoria Purcell-Gates (1993, 1996), Lisa Delpit (1995), Gloria Ladson-Billings (1994), and Eve Gregory and colleagues (2004a, 2004b), we reaffirm the value of home literacies—even when these cultural practices challenge the field's previous definitions of literacy. We do so because we recognize the Eurocentric nature of such definitions and see the need to learn so that we can grow as educators. We acknowledge that the very notion of home literacies may "undermine commonly accepted stages of early literacy learning as well as question the popular vision of parental involvement in literacy activities embodied in [traditional notions of early literacy such as] the bedtime story" (Gregory et al. 2004a, 1). Many damaging myths serve as a matrix of colonization (Hill Collins 2000, 2009), keeping intersectional oppressions in place and upholding a status quo of inequities.

One of the biggest and most damaging myths regarding languages and litera-cies is that "children must forget all they know about their home language (if the home language is not the language of power in schools and schooling) in order to learn to read, as if written language and the activity of reading had no relationship to real language functioning" (Ferreiro and Teberosky 1982, 274). Presumptions like this assume that children arrive at school with "no language," and that families who do not engage in schooling practices at home—such as book reading—fail their children. These myths ignore the fact that language and literacy practices develop before schooling, within the context of families and homes (Ferreiro and Teberosky 1982). As explained in Part I of this book (Chapters 1, 2, and 3), chil-dren make meaning and make sense of the world within the context of their fam-ilies and communities, a context punctuated by relationships and often marked by love and care (Heath 2012). After all, as Rogers (2002, 251) reminds us: "Literacy is increasingly conceptualized as a social practice . . . as a set of processes that shape and are shaped by social institutions."

It is thus important to understand that family literacy practices "are more than just ways of using literacy and language in the home" and encompass "a wide range of literacy practices [which] exist in families and communities" (Rogers 2002, 251). Taking up this understanding and acknowledging that family litera-cies are culturally situated practices, this chapter examines the social practices of families that are shaped and refined in the context of diverse homes with diverse communicative repertoires, often given different values by schools and society.

Communicative and linguistic differences have been documented for decades—as have the different values they are given in a society where "race continues to be a significant factor in determining inequity" (Ladson-Billings and Tate 1995, 48). Simply put, race matters in the valuation of communicative repertoires and literacy practices. For example, in 1982, Shirley Brice Heath documented "ways of talking" (p. 49) during bedtime stories across three communities: Maintown (mainstream, middle-class, school-oriented communicative patterns and culture), Roadville (White mill community), and Trackton (Black mill community). She found that in both Roadville and Trackton, communicative patterns did not align with the linguistic patterns in use in schools, thus disadvantaging those children in school. On the other hand, children in Maintown were socialized in communicative practices closely aligned with schooling practices, and thus were seen as capable and smart. Maintown practices included bedtime stories, read-alouds, and question-and-answer sessions. Children from Maintown were familiar with the curricular structures of schools as they had been schooled "through modeling and specific instruction, ways of talking from books which seem natural in schools and in numerous institutional settings such as banks, post offices, businesses, or government offices" (Heath 1982, 50). They knew how to behave and participate not because they were inherently more capable, but because the home literacies in which they were socialized aligned with school literacies. They belonged. As Gee (2015a, 1) explained, they did not need to negotiate the acquisition of a secondary discourse ("the ways in which people enact and recognize socially and historically significant identities or 'kinds of people' through well-integrated combinations of language, actions, interactions, objects, tools, technologies, beliefs, and values") as they entered this new setting. They were already fluent in the schooling discourse; it was their primary discourse.

Such dominant practices and discourses were largely absent from households in Trackton, where "The ways of school are merely an overlay on the home-taught ways and may be in conflict with them" (Heath 1982, 50). As Heath explained, "Family literacy events for mainstream preschool children are bedtime stories, reading cereal boxes, stop signs, and television ads, and interpreting instructions for commercial games and toys" (Heath 1982, 50) and Trackton family members did "not believe that they have a tutoring role in this learning" (Heath 1982, 66). Trackton's adults, as Heath (1990, 501) describes, "did not have special routines of question-and-answer displays or baby games, and they did not offer the labels for items of the environment to their children." Yet, they had sophisticated communicative practices, having great knowledge of teasing and verbal retorts. They commanded attention from spectators and swirled "multi-party talk, shifting roles, and widely distributed functions of child caring" (Heath 1990, 501). Amongst themselves, children "entered their games and banter, talked to themselves replaying conversations about them, and acted out fussin' routines" (Heath 1990, 502). From infancy, they went to church services with adults, later joining church choirs.

Adults in Trackton's households did not oversimplify their language but exposed their children to sophisticated and complex vocabulary, differently from the interactions between parents and children in Maintown and Roadville.

> Trackton children must be aggressive in inserting their stories into an ongoing stream of discourse. . . . When Trackton children go to school, they face unfamiliar types of questions which ask for what-explanations. They are asked as individuals to identify items by name, and to label features such as shape, color, number. (Heath 1982, 68–69)

Although Trackton children may display great pragmatics, semantics, and syntax in their oral stories, they would likely score the lowest in readiness tests. In fact, it has been widely accepted "that whatever it is that mainstream school-oriented homes have, these other homes do not have it; thus these children are not from the literate tradition and do not belong in school" (Heath 1982, 50). In Trackton, Heath (1982, 65) reported, "[t]here are no reading materials especially for children (with the exception of children's Sunday School materials), and adults do not sit and read to children."

Rejecting such an exclusionist definition of literacy, we invite you to recognize how in Trackton children acquired important and sophisticated skills. Heath (1982, 70) explains:

> Print in isolation bears little authority in their world. The kinds of questions asked of reading books are unfamiliar. The children's abilities to metaphorically link two events or situations and to recreate scenes are not tapped in the school; in fact, these abilities often cause difficulties, because they enable children to see parallels teachers did not intend, and indeed, may not recognize until the children point them out.

Trackton children's knowledge and use of oral language far surpassed their understanding and use of written language.

It is not only the children who have been underrepresented and minoritized who need to see their home languages and literacies in the classroom, but children who always see their communicative styles and practices reflected in classrooms and schools also need to see diverse languages and literacies (Bishop 2015). Otherwise, they "get an exaggerated sense of their own self worth and a false sense of what the world is like, because it is becoming more and more colorful and diverse as time goes on" (Bishop 2015). Thus, instead of seeing literacy as neutral (which we rejected in Chapter 2), we see literacy practices as situated within the context of families and located within a power-laden sociopolitical terrain. We see funds of knowledge, the "historically accumulated and culturally developed bodies of knowledge and skills essential for household functioning and well-being" (Moll et al. 1992, 133)—such as carpentry, folk medicine, and crop planting—even if they are not essential for our own household functioning, as family literacies.

Funds of Knowledge as Family Literacies

Moll and colleagues (1992) and González and colleagues (2005) proposed that funds of knowledge are based on the premise that all human beings are competent and have knowledge. Funds of knowledge comprise an approach to learning about and understanding families and households qualitatively, learning from them through the documentation of their cultural practices (Moll et al. 1992).

Moll et al.(1992, 133) "use the term 'funds of knowledge' to refer to historically accumulated and culturally developed bodies of knowledge and skills essential for household or individual functioning and well-being." They explain that using funds of knowledge for teaching involves learning and documenting such knowledges and skills. It

> [A]lso involves studying how household members use their funds of knowledge in dealing with changing, and often difficult, social and economic circumstances . . . how families develop social networks that interconnect them with their social environments (most importantly with other households), and how these social relationships facilitate the development and exchange of resources, including knowledge, skills, and labor, that enhance the households' ability to survive or thrive. (Moll et al. 1992, 33)

Theorizing from families' rich practices, we explain our belief that within every family are existing social, cultural, and linguistic practices that children develop to belong and participate. This includes expanding the literacy resources that families possess through oral traditions, cultural practices, and familial practices. We do so as we seek to challenge and change how "in contrast to the households and their social networks, the classrooms seem encapsulated" (Moll et al. 1992, 134). If we are to create inclusive and equitable literacy practices, classrooms cannot be positioned as encapsulated, disconnected from larger sociopolitical issues, and pose as acultural. We must genuinely value their practices and communicate respect. Doing so necessitates understanding that teaching and learning must be

> [M]otivated by the children's interests and questions . . . [after all] knowledge is obtained by the children, not imposed by the adults. This totality of experiences, the cultural structuring of the households, whether related to work or play, whether they take place individually, with peers, or under the supervision of adults, helps constitute the funds of knowledge children bring to school. (Moll et al. 1992, 134)

But—how can teaching be grounded in family funds of knowledge? How can teachers access them? First and foremost, a symmetrical relationship must be established between teachers and family members. While this is essential, it is also difficult, especially in those families for whom teacher deference is a core value. Teachers will need to unveil the amazingly rich funds of knowledge existent within the family and reposition them centrally in the classroom. We posit that this can only happen when an authentic relationship, which acknowledges and challenges power differentials, has been developed. This relationship can become the basis for the exchange of funds of knowledge and is likely to contribute to "reducing the insularity of classrooms, and contributing to the academic content and lessons" (Moll et al. 1992, 139).

In Jessica Martell's dual-language second grade in New York City, funds of knowledge were routinely identified and positioned centrally in the curriculum. For example, in teaching procedural writing in Spanish, she invited a mother who made tamales for a living to come and share her process with the young children she taught. The children not only understood the importance of accuracy in a procedural text (after all, if procedures were not accurate, children would not have a tamale at the end), they were reminded of the value of Spanish as a language and rethought their image of people who spoke Spanish. Before this experience, many of the children regarded those who spoke Spanish as a first language simply—and problematically—by their limited or lacking English skills. They had a single story (Adichie 2009), a stereotype of Latinxs as poorly educated, even though most of them identified as Latinxs. This engagement with a family fund of knowledge allowed them to read the world with new eyes and revise their definitions and assumptions of Latinxs. The invited parent was able to leverage family funds of knowledge to challenge stereotypes and single stories about Latinxs while at the same time addressing mandated learning standards. This is further explained in Souto-Manning and Martell (2016).

In that same classroom, multiple opportunities for funds of knowledge to make curriculum and teaching more inclusive took place. Jessica Martell knew that there were many ways to identify and document funds of knowledge, all of which include humility. As she got to know families through formal and informal interactions (which often took place at drop-off, pick-up, and during after-school hours as family members came to pick up their children from the after-school program), Martell made a list of the multiple funds of knowledge students and their families had. She always added to the list as she got to know students and their family members throughout the year, similar to the work of Mary Cowhey (2006). Cowhey (a second-grade teacher in Northampton, Massachusetts) engaged in home visits as she sought to identify and document funds of knowledge. In these home visits, Cowhey learned from and about the families, their practices, and expertise. Instead of entering their homes as an expert, she entered their homes as a respectful guest, who had much to learn from the families. And learn she did. For example, she learned that one of the parents worked on a farm and immediately knew that this would enhance her students' understanding of the life cycle. She learned that one of the parents sewed and another was a quilter (practices passed down generationally within the context of a mill town), and she called on them to make vests for the students' teddy bears (Souto-Manning 2013b). Knowing the established learning standards well and identifying and documenting family literacies allowed her not only to enhance students' access to learning, but also to reposition families as experts from whom her students could learn. Like Cowhey, teachers such as Martell saw their roles in their relationships with families not as "attempting to convey educational information, as valuable as that may be, but as learners, as researchers with a theoretical perspective that seeks to understand the ways in which people make sense of their everyday lives" (González, et al. 2005, xi). Below, we share an example from Martell's second-grade classroom in New York City.

Kite Making: Learning from Marcel's Grandfather

Marcel, an African American second grader, relished the time he spent with his grandfather. Each day, as Jessica Martell dismissed her second graders by the school's playground, she saw how Marcel was always excited to see his grandfather when he picked Marcel up from school. Because she took time to talk with her students and get to know them, she learned that Marcel had a very close relationship with his grandfather. What she did not know was that he was a kite maker, who made money selling kites. But one day, as Martell was about to read the book *The Three Questions* by Jon J. Muth (2002), Marcel saw a red kite on the cover. He proceeded to tell the class about how his grandfather made kites and how his special kite was red too. Listening and learning from Marcel, Martell immediately asked him if we could invite his grandfather in to make kites. "But he don't know how to write," Marcel answered. "Not a problem," Martell answered, "he can tell us so much about kite making; more than people like me, who can write." Although initially unsure, Marcel grew excited to have his grandfather come. Instead of judging Marcel's grandfather according to literacies (over)valued in schools, Martell seized the opportunity to have Marcel's grandfather teach the class about kite making, linking an amazingly rich learning experience to learning standards in listening and speaking, mathematics, and science. She had not only identified one of Marcel's grandfather's funds of knowledge, but had connected this rich opportunity for learning to mandated content and standards. Marcel's grandfather was extremely knowledgeable about the materials, weight, measurements, and procedures for kite making. He shared his fund of knowledge with the children.

As Marcel's grandfather demonstrated how to make kites and guided children through the process of kite making, introducing important considerations and concepts such as the role of size, weight, wind, and materials to height and speed, the children asked questions and learned a great deal from Marcel's grandfather. "Wow. He knows so much," Amalia, one of the students in Martell's class whispered while making a kite. The fact that Marcel's grandfather did not know how to write did not come up; his kite-making literacy was impressive and the children learned much from what he knew, while never focusing on what he didn't know.

As evident in the example above and as proposed by Norma González (1995, 6), if we are to integrally value the funds of knowledge present in the homes and communities of the children we teach, we "must redefine households as being rich in resources for educational purposes, and schools must validate the knowledge with which students come equipped." We can no longer afford to define knowledge in ethnocentric ways—or in ways that have been historically (over)valued in schools—or we will continue to fail children from historically minoritized communities, thus pushing them out of school and effectively positioning them at the margins of society.

Even if families and households do not have monetary funds, they are still rich in funds of knowledge. The very concept of funds of knowledge is premised on rejecting deficit and inferiority paradigms (explored in Part I of this book). They are examples of how firsthand experiences with families within the context of homes and communities allow educators to identify and document their competence and knowledge. Knowledge of family funds of knowledge can afford positive pedagogical actions and implications. This was the case of the household where seven-year-old Irma lives with her parents, grandmother, and two siblings in New York City. It was also the case of four-year-old Kai's household in Georgia in the U.S.

Three generations lived in a single-room occupancy (SRO) dwelling in New York City. In Irma's household, Vicks VapoRub served to cure most ailments—if someone had a cold, Vicks would resolve it. Irma's grandmother, Ana, said that "*vaporu*" was good for sore throats, acne, headaches, and sore muscles. In Irma's family, it was well-known that Vicks was a catch-all cure for many diseases. "*Cura todo*" [cures everything], Ana smiled as she held a can of Vicks VapoRub. "*Tenía hongo en las uñas de los pies y poniéndome vaporu en un mes se me quito*" [I had fungus on my toenails and by putting Vicks VapoRub on, in a month, it went away]. As the elder in the family, Ana took on the role of *curandera* (the family healer, who used folk remedies) and offered remedies such as Vicks to younger family members. Natural remedies were a common part of her childhood growing up in a rural area of Mexico, with no medical doctors. As the family immigrated to the U.S. but was not able to afford prescription medicine, insurance, or doctor visits, her family-healer expertise became an invaluable fund of knowledge for her family. As Irma watched her *abuelita* Ana, she learned about the medicinal power of herbs as well as the miracle of Vicks VapoRub. As a cultural practice, her knowledge of healing through natural remedies was an important family literacy.

In Kai's home in rural Georgia, prayers were seen as remedies, and his grandmomma asked God to heal them when they were sick. The practice of talking to God through prayers, making bids for health and well-being, were an important fund of knowledge of his family. His great-great-great-great-grandmother was born into slavery and there wasn't much she could do but pray. Over time, the practice of praying had been taken up by generations of family members. The prayers were authored much like letters, but in oral format. Any time something was out of their hands, they prayed. "Dear God," Kai bowed his head. They also prayed to thank God for graces received, for meals (saying grace), and for life and living ("praise the Lord!"). As a cultural practice, four-year-old Kai learned spiritual and cultural traditions from his grandmomma. He also learned to self-regulate and to persevere through prayer. After all, as his grandmomma said, "He's got the whole world in His hands." In terms of school-related literacies, he learned how to author thank you messages and persuasive notes, and developed an understanding of genres. All through prayer.

While interesting, cultural practices such as the ones employed by Kai's and Irma's grandmother and great-great-great-great-grandmother and passed down intergenerationally may not be framed as traditional literacy practices. Here, we affirm that they are. Additionally, teachers may not be able to access them as they are positioned outside of the purview of schools and schooling; yet, they are central to the functioning of these households.

Funds of knowledge are household-situated cultural practices. They are ways in which families make sense of and in the world, drawing on their histories and building on their assets. Because they emanate from families, they allow for the expansion of what Vygotsky (1978) called the zone of proximal development, the zone between what the child can do independently and with support from a more knowledgeable peer or teacher. Instead of regarding the teacher as the only one providing scaffolding, family members can do so if teaching is grounded in their knowledge and practices. Funds of knowledge are situated within the context of families; they are not universal. Some examples of funds of knowledge are: construction, carpentry, architecture, herbal and folk medicines, baptisms, cooking, childcare, negotiating (*rematar*), border crossings, songwriting, farming, quilting, horses, equipment operation, among others (González et al. 2005; Moll et al. 1992). There is much knowledge to tap into and to build on if we expand our definition of early literacy.

Accessing Funds of Knowledge and Learning About Home Literacies

"I'm here! Tell me your funds of knowledge!" This is certainly not how teachers identify, access, and document funds of knowledge. Imposing on families and expecting families to be comfortable as curriculum codesigners is not the way to gain entry into funds of knowledge as home literacies. In fact, when teachers ask families about their funds of knowledge, it is likely that only the most privileged families will feel comfortable sharing; after all, over time, minoritized families have received the message that their language(s), cultural practices, and identities either do not matter or are not as valuable as White lives and dominant knowledge.

Accessing funds of knowledge involves learning about the history of the region where families live, the analysis of "the social histories of the households, their origins and development, and most prominently . . . the labor history of the families, which reveals the accumulated bodies of knowledge of the households" (Moll et al. 1992, 133). It takes time. It varies according to family. It hinges on the development of authentic relationships. For example, while home visits may be a possibility for some, for others, home visits would feel uncomfortable at best. A New York City public school teacher, Abigail Salas Maguire, stated, "I can't impose onto families, especially not in New York City, where you have families taking turns sleeping in the basement of rat-infested flower shops. I have to give them dignity and respect. I don't want to use my power as their child's teacher to impose on them."

She meets with families at a local playground and at a local public library instead. She brings her own niece with her, making herself vulnerable in the process. As she develops relationships in these in-between spaces, she gains access to more personal locales and information. "It takes time," she reminds us.

Regardless, funds of knowledge are identified and accessed as teachers form authentic relationships with families, predicated on mutual trust and respect, both of which take time to develop. Because home literacies are only unveiled in relational ways, teachers may find "that building on children's home literacy experiences was much more difficult than they had originally believed" (Gregory et al. 2004b, 3). It takes effort. A lot more than opening a curriculum guide and reading from it. It demands hours beyond the regular schedule. As New York City teacher Martell says, "It's hard work, but it's worthy work. I am teaching human beings. I need to know who they are and the people to whom they belong. Only then can I teach them." It is also important to remember that teachers cannot "simply assume that children shared their own literacy lives" (Gregory et al. 2004b, 3). After all, they are immersed in the cultural practices and funds of knowledge of their own families. While at times children may share their family literacy practices, as educators we cannot solely rely on them as informants. We must position ourselves as researchers—learning from and about their families in ways that get beyond superficiality.

For example, an elementary (PreK-5th grade) ESOL (English for Speakers of Other Languages) teacher in Georgia, Mary Martin, documented the funds of knowledge of a Mexican-American immigrant family, which cut across generations, going to the flea market on the outskirts of town. Instead of making judgments about their practices or the choices they made, she documented the cultural practices at play within the context of a flea market. She learned how the "families more purposefully engaged children in *remates*, calculations, and other academically aligned activities in a real-life scenario" (Souto-Manning 2016, 269). She also learned how it was confusing to the children how she referred to the one-dollar bill as "a dollar" when within the context of the flea market, children knew the same bill by the name of "*un peso*," the name for the Mexican currency. She realized that beyond language differences, there were communicative repertoires associated with family funds of knowledge that she needed to be familiar with if she was going to build on the strengths and knowledge of the children she taught.

Every Sunday, families filled their cars with items and headed to the county's flea market. They got there before the sun rose. Children spent more than twelve hours in the flea market, from set-up to take down. They did not have a private space to read or complete homework. They were expected to participate in the transactions taking place, being full participants of that community of practice. Their learning was evident through their changing participation in the tasks at hand. For example, when Martin started spending Sundays at the county flea market, six-year-old Santiago did not do much more than observe, fetch items, and support adults by running small errands. He never negotiated or handled money. Over the course of a year, his role grew, as can be observed in the following interaction with an adult.

Within the flea market, children knew how to make change and engage in quick calculations. Instead of subtracting, they added on, from the value of the good being sold to the value of the bill they were handed, all while engaging in conversations with their customers. Here is an example of how *rematar* happened within the context of the flea market:

> Adult: ¿*Cuanto* [How much]? [points at a pot]
> Santiago: *Cinco* [Five]. [holding his right hand up]
> [Adult walks away]
> Santiago: *Cuatro, cuatro* [Four, four].
> Adult: *Dos* [Two].
> Santiago: *No. No puedes comprar esto por dos pesos* [No. You cannot buy this for two pesos].
> [Adult walks away]
> Santiago: *Tres* [Three].
> Adult: *Vale* [Okay].

The adult hands Santiago a five-dollar bill. Santiago says "*tres*," grabs a dollar bill and says "*cuatro*," and then grabs another dollar bill and says "*cinco*." He hands the adult two dollars back. Although Santiago's father was watching him, Santiago, a six-year-old who often displayed difficulty with single-digit addition and subtraction at school, could quickly engage in mathematical calculations in a real context—within the flea market. These interactions were repeated multiple times within each hour on busy days. As Martin realized how much the children knew about negotiating and calculating with money, she found read-alouds that would bring their expertise to the center of the curriculum and teaching, thus expanding the zone of proximal development through the repositioning of funds of knowledge.

Martha Floyd Tenery (2005) wrote about her experience learning about funds of knowledge through home visits in Arizona. Although this is not the only way to document funds of knowledge and learn about home literacies, it is an approach successfully employed by many teacher-researchers. This approach requires a reframing of home visits, whereby teachers learn from families instead of teaching them so-called evidence-based ways to enhance their children's literacy. Tenery (2005) explains how there is great anxiety associated with the first visits, but how subsequent visits are much more comfortable. She explains how entering her students' homes allowed her to create bridges between students' home literacies and school-sanctioned literacy practices. In visiting one Mexican-American family, she learned about cooking and home remedies used by family members. She explains this sociohistorically; the "reliance on home remedies prior to medical care suggests that the family may have developed this domain of knowledge in response to subsistence living" (Tenery 2005, 124). Physical and social geography were part of the family's everyday repertoire through transnational domains of knowledge. That is, "extensive knowledge of U.S.-Mexico international commerce, tourism, and taxes [were] . . . demonstrated by the uncle and the father" (Tenery 2005, 124). She suggests that these knowledge domains "can serve as the foundation for learning modules or thematic units developed by teachers" (Tenery 2005, 125).

In addition to domains of knowledge, Tenery explained her learnings regarding interactional patterns, rich albeit distinct from preferred interactional patterns in classrooms and (pre)schools. She attributes patterns of interaction to "adaptive responses and sociocultural processes" (Tenery 2005, 125). That is, the presence of extended families as a cultural fixture combined with socioeconomic situations, resulting in members of multiple households living under the same roof, allowed children to interact with individuals of multiple ages. It also made it so that children played important roles in sustaining the household, being expected to take on roles such as "cooking, cleaning, babysitting, translating, and carrying out cultural rituals such as baptismal celebrations" (Tenery 2005, 125). Finally, with regard to cultural practices, Tenery learned that knowing Spanish was essential for maintaining a link to Mexican relatives—whether physically distant or in their own households. Spanish was not an asset, an add-on, but a necessity for survival. Religion also played

> [A]n eminent role in the families by helping them cope during difficult
> times, by providing family members with a sense of commonality and a sense
> of connection to tradition through rituals and ceremonies, and by producing
> a sense of belonging in the larger scheme of life." (Tenery 2005, 126)

She learned that all families she visited immigrated to the U.S. to provide a better future for their children. Although many of them had to withstand temporary hardships, the purpose of their journeys was clear.

These learnings led Tenery to see her role with new eyes, and position herself as a mediator, re-mediating multiple contexts and the roles of teacher and learner (as a researcher of the funds of knowledges of the families of the children she taught). It also dispelled prevalent myths and stereotypes attributed to families of Mexican origin—"such as lacking morality, having broken families, nor valuing education, and demonstrating low skill levels" (Tenery 2005, 129). What Tenery learned through home visits allowed her to unveil "rich resources for learning, as skill domains of knowledge and cultural practices may be utilized in classroom to conceptualize mathematics, comprehension, and composition lessons" (Tenery 2005, 129). One example directly related to literacies is the role of oral histories and narratives coauthored by families, which combined with "expressions of cultural identity and solidarity," allowing teachers to see "students within a cultural and historical framework" and Mexican immigrant families "as resourceful, connected, and full of life experiences" (Tenery 2005, 129).

In New York City, teacher Jessica Martell did not enter children's homes before developing a relationship with their families; and even then she did not make home visits foundational to her practice. Having grown up in a small apartment in East Harlem, she knew how terrified her grandma (the person who raised her) would have been to have a teacher visit. So, respecting cultural traditions, which uphold the teacher on a pedestal (as her grandmother had done), she was not too keen on home visits. She did get to know families and accessed funds of knowledge in other ways.

Foundational to Martell's practice was that she always made a point of developing relationships. She made herself available to families via email and cell phone. She was always happy to schedule a time to talk. Her excitement for family cultural practices was contagious. Parents and family members knew that she regarded them as invaluable resources, as curriculum coconstructors. Instead of interviewing family members in their homes individually, she invited families to the classroom and engaged her students as coresearchers, as interviewers. Children asked questions, made connections, and provided valuable information and examples. They were invited to suspend judgment and to learn from and about the cultural practices of each family as worthy and unique. In doing so, they expanded their worlds, perspectives, and literacy repertoires.

It all started with Martell's request for families to come share the story of the day their child was born. "You want me to do what?" one of the mothers asked. "Yes, you are the only one who knows this very special story; the story of the day your child was born. I don't know it, and I would love to learn from you," she responded. "But I wasn't there when she was born," a mother whose daughter had been adopted from Tanzania explained (Figure 4.1). Martell responded, "You can tell about the day Kai was born within your family." No one was excluded.

FIGURE 4.1   On the Day You Were Born: Family Stories as Entryways

All stories were different. They told the class about the child and the family, about the particular day the child was born, but also shed light onto the cultural values and practices embraced by each of the families.

Communicating her stance of a learner in authentic ways and making family stories and perspectives foundational to her teaching was essential. While initially nervous, families came to verify how valued their stories were (Souto-Manning and Martell 2016). It was from children's birth stories that Martell taught her class about historical timelines (a topic of the social studies curriculum) and about original source research (meeting English Language Arts learning standards for second grade).

Martell often spoke of her own family, bringing family members to more informal school functions, and made a point to get to know her students' families. She asked them with genuine interest about their lives and interests. She would ask questions such as, "Today Marcel shared with us that you make kites. Can you tell me more? I was so interested." Or "Ana tells me that you write children's books. I would love to have the chance to read your books. Where can I buy them?" she asked a Boricua father who was a children's author. Once she got a sense of the depth of the practice, verifying that it was not simply a hobby, but a cultural practice, a fund of knowledge essential for household functioning, she'd find a way to make it part of the curriculum, centering her teaching on it. Instead of passing judgment, she used interactions with families (even if they happened because the child did not get picked up on time) as opportunities for learning.

So, when she found out that Martin's mother made tamales for a living, she decided to invite her to share this fund of knowledge with the whole class (Figure 4.2). Not only would it make Martin more confident (he was not very confident in his ability and identity as a learner), but it would also communicate

FIGURE 4.2 Tamale Making, a Fund of Knowledge

to the class the value of Spanish for learning and communicating (this was a dual-language classroom within a sociopolitical context that (over)valued English), and allow the class to learn about a Common Core learning standard (a mandate) through culturally grounded ways. Through tamale making, students would learn about procedural texts (Souto-Manning and Martell 2016). Initially being regarded as someone whose child said, "I thought my mom didn't know anything," merely because she was a Spanish speaker who had not had opportunities to develop traditional literacy skills, namely reading and writing, Martin's mother was reframed from an assets perspective; as someone who knew a lot.

Documenting Family Literacies

In order to reposition home literacies in classrooms, it is important to learn about and from family literacy practices—in action, across contexts. This necessitates considering the importance of boundary crossing as teachers position themselves as cultural workers (Freire 1998). In such a way, teachers can position themselves as learners and researchers, documenting children's home literacies. Or they can position themselves as action researchers who collect information in and out of the classroom, making sense of the data inductively and codifying common themes in classroom activities (redesigning home literacies in the context of the classroom and/or school).

Many times, children serve as informants, initially identifying particular funds of knowledge for their teachers. It is up to the teacher to follow up and to seek additional information. In addition to serving as informants, children can be positioned as coresearchers who learn about their families' cultural practices with new eyes, adding value to what they had previously taken for granted. Children can be engaged in member checks to add validity to the work being done by teachers (Souto-Manning 2010a, 2010b). Further, young children are often the ones to redefine and refine classroom practices based on home literacies, making them more complex and culturally relevant. Such a process can usefully inform teachers seeking to better educate a new generation.

Home literacies cannot be assumed. They have to be learned and documented—as valuable resources and whole practices. In Head Start (as in the case of J. W.'s and Marilyn's classrooms), reconceptualizing the role of home visits as opportunities for learning while challenging privileged, ethnocentric literacies and positioning children as curriculum makers became a necessity—as a generative literacy curriculum was fashioned from the fabric of children's lives. In doing so, it was important to understand how language in use and various contexts affected each other. Rymes (2016) offers a powerful framework to analyze classroom events in the early childhood setting, which considers the following three dimensions: (1) social context (larger factors affecting the interaction), (2) interactional context (what is appropriate and expected in an interaction), and (3) individual agency (the influence an individual has on how interactions are signified and understood). While these dimensions can only be teased apart analytically, doing so allows the multidimensionality of interactions with families to be considered and investigated more thoroughly.

Reyes et al. (2015) conducted a study with early childhood preservice teachers, and they concluded that for teachers to reframe their approach to teaching, they must engage in ongoing exploration, actively pursuing "viable opportunities to directly interact and develop relationships with families," becoming "active participants in family and community literacy events, situated inside and outside the school context" (Reyes et al. 2015, 29). How? There are many ways to develop authentic relationships with families. For teachers to develop relationships as learners, it is important to ground the relationship in respect and trust. Thus far we have witnessed varied ways in which teachers developed authentic relationships with families. For example, Tenery made home visits to understand and learn from families, Martell brought families in as experts in their lives and the learning within the classroom, and Martin made an effort to document the weekend flea market. There is no formula to developing such relationships, although it is clear that respect and trust are foundational. In each of these cases, teachers embraced the role of learners, documenting family literacies and bringing them back to the classroom, using them as levers for transforming learning. Although not a formula (we do not believe in one-size-fits-all approaches to teaching and learning), we hope that these examples can shed light onto possibilities for getting started. Below is yet another example, coming from Cowhey.

Cowhey, a teacher at Jackson Street School in Northampton, Massachusetts, considered these three dimensions—social context, interactional context, and individual agency (Rymes 2016)—by engaging in an inventory of the human resources available in the extended classroom community (involving family members). Through home visits, she got to know the families of the students in her classroom community and documented home literacies and community resources, leveraging those resources to support children's inquiries and to engage in deeper learning (through interviews, community visits, etc.). Whether sewing, quilting, gardening, or speaking a language other than English, Cowhey communicated her value for what went on at home by positioning family literacies at the center of teaching—not as an overlay, but as foundational to access content mandated by learning standards in authentic and community-grounded ways. For example, in teaching about the life cycle, she tapped into the expertise of family members who worked on a local farm. As reported in Souto-Manning (2013b, 45), to teach like Cowhey is to, first and foremost, embrace the stance and have:

> [T]he courage to admit that you don't know it all—and that you will be learning from and with your students. It is the act of embracing a humble stance that blurs the roles of teacher and learner. In doing so, you help students understand that the books present in your classroom portray incomplete accounts and that there are human resources beyond the classroom walls

that can further the learning journey of that specific community. In doing so, you will help your students see that their learning community extends beyond the classroom walls. . . . Welcome the opportunity to learn with the children who are members of your classroom communities and make room for multiple voices, perspectives, and points of view to be considered.

In Martell's second-grade classroom in New York, home literacies were often located within a larger sociocultural and political context. She always knew that her interactions with families were framed by external factors, whether or not she sponsored values coherent with societal norms, policies, and discourses. For example, her interactions with one particular mother were framed by a larger social context of fear regarding immigration and deportation. Martell realized that speaking to the parent in Spanish (her first language) was a way to communicate respect and to protect her from monolingual English speakers. The mother knew a lot about *remesas*, pathways to special education services, and navigating an undocumented world. Martell framed the interactional context so that the mother was positioned agentively. She explained to the mother how little she knew about documentation as she herself was Boricua and had been born in New York. Her family had never needed to navigate immigration pathways, as Puerto Rico's citizens are American citizens, even though it holds the status of a territory with limited rights as compared to states. Finally, she validated the mother by asking if she could serve as a resource to other parents navigating documentation battles, repositioning this literacy from clandestine to official, worthy, and recognized. She was only able to document these literacies because she honored the mother's language background and made herself vulnerable, explaining that she did not know much about immigration processes. Forming relationships and alliances with other families, this mother eventually ran for and became part of the school's PTA, calling for translation in all PTA meetings, not as a crutch for particular parents, but as a regular practice. She also pushed for PTA-sponsored sessions with immigration lawyers in light of DACA[1] and other relevant topics.

While Martell did not fully document the literacies shared by the mother, she repositioned the mother as an expert as she developed curriculum around issues of documentation under the guise of an author study of René Colato Laínez, which in addition to studying his author's craft, led the class to read and discuss books such as *From North to South* (about the deportation of a child's mother from California to Mexico) and *Waiting for Papá* (about Beto, a child who immigrates from El Salvador to the U.S. with his mother, leaving his father behind for years due to visa issues). Some of the children in her class, who were in a free after-school program for immigrant children focused on language and literacy, were able to interview their parents about their immigration journey, and despite differences in pathways, documentations, etc., all found out that their families had emigrated to the U.S. for a better life. In the following section, we explore additional ways of repositioning family literacies in curriculum and teaching so as to leverage learning goals.

Linking Family Literacies to Curriculum, Leveraging Learning Goals

Although family literacies are valuable in and of themselves, they can also be leveraged to access learning goals. After all, as Gee (1996) explains, schools too often embrace discourses (ways of being, behaving, interacting) that honor the ways of communicating among White, middle-class families. In such a way, children whose families' communicative practices differ from the language privileged in schooling are effectively acquiring a secondary discourse, which may have been unfamiliar to them prior to schooling. It is thus important to not only document family literacy practices, learning from them, but to "envision, plan, and build bridges between students' interests, expertise, experiences and individualities, and curricular goals" (Souto-Manning and Martell 2016, 83). This includes identifying family funds of knowledge, making connections between them and curricular goals and standards, enacting an agentive pedagogical stance, which seeks to "avoid the standardization of teaching and learning by placing children front and center in curriculum and teaching" (Souto-Manning and Martell 2016, 83). That is, unlike anthropologists who may document cultural practices as an end in themselves, teachers engage in applied cultural anthropology, documenting practices as a means to support teaching and learning.

Amanti (2005) invites teachers to reject static notions of culture and to embrace the role of cultural anthropologists, engaging in ethnography whereby teachers learn from the culture of the young children they teach as enacted within the context of their families and communities. This involves visiting with families "to gain firsthand knowledge of our students and their families rather than accepting the second- or thirdhand accounts of researchers" (Amanti 2005, 132). Teaching, then, can center on students' home literacies and funds of knowledge, repositioning their lives and interests. This is "the reverse of the typical Anglo-centric curriculum developed by education specialists usually located at a great distance, spatially and conceptually, from the classroom" (Amanti 2005, 132). As she visited her students' homes one year, Amanti (2005) found that many of them had experiences with horses; thus, she positioned horses at the center of her teaching, valuing and honoring their expertise. She was not surprised by their expertise given the historical importance of horses in the southwestern U.S. She also found that home literacies were at times located transnationally, as some of her students' expertise with horses came from relatives who lived in rural areas of northern Mexico. Thus, she embraced an expansive understanding of home. She engaged in a funds-of-knowledge project—"not about replicating what students have learned at home, but about using students' knowledge and prior experiences as a scaffold for new learning" (Amanti 2005, 135). Together, Amanti and her students coplanned and cogenerated curriculum. She explained how this sets her students up for success as it builds on something they already know, building on familiar knowledge to foster learning. Amanti (2005) explains that although studying horses allowed her students to be positioned as capable one specific year, curricula and teaching grounded in students' funds of knowledge and home literacies "cannot be packaged or standardized for export" (Amanti 2005, 138); instead, teachers must learn about students' home literacies as ethnographers who work to unveil expertise and to communicate that students' home literacies "are academically valid" (Amanti 2005, 138), in practice rejecting paradigms that position the knowledge and practices of historically minoritized families as inferior and/or deficient (Goodwin et al. 2008).

As a result of identifying, documenting, and repositioning students' home literacies and funds of knowledge in her teaching, Amanti (2005, 138) invites us to reject "the one size fits all approach" and reflects:

> [C]ritically on whose knowledge should control classroom practice—mine, or that of others in more powerful positions within the educational hierarchy. The traditional structure of a teacher's work being shaped by often politically motivated research, and by curricula shaped by "specialists" further up the educational hierarchy, has been perpetuated by a number of factors, chief among them being the asymmetric distribution and valuation of the knowledge of individuals according to their location within the educational hierarchy.

Regarding education as a relational and collective endeavor, encompassing "new kinds of understanding, interaction, and politics" (Licona and Chávez 2015, 97), she calls for relationships to be established so that teachers can truly get to know their students' families and learn from them. She positions personal relationships as foundational to teaching and learning, and proposes how home visits allow for relationships to deepen. She explains: "With each home visit, we teachers become more a part of the socially dense contexts within which our students are growing up" (Amanti 2005, 139–140). She explains that the deeper the relationships, the more she learns about home literacies; the more she learns, the better she is able to teach in a way that reaches her students, communicating to them that their literacy practices—in homes, communities, and (pre)schools—do matter.

How Do You Empower Families Typically Seen From Deficit Perspectives?

Marla Hensley (2005) explains, "Parents in the neighborhood where I teach in Tucson, Arizona, are sometimes viewed as lacking. They are viewed as lacking in parenting skills, lacking in education and lacking in knowledge" (Hensley 2005, 143). Regardless of her perception that she knew the community in which she taught and even with efforts to bring family members to the classroom, she did not recognize many of the rich home literacies her students' families had. For example, a student's father, who was a groundskeeper, helped set up her kindergarten's vegetable and plant garden. As she explains, "As far as I was concerned I had already tapped into a fund of knowledge" (Hensley 2005, 144), but then she came to realize that gardening was not the most important family literacy that parent held.

Through home visits, she learned that Jacob, the father of her kindergartner Alicia, played guitar, wrote songs, and authored poems. Then, visiting the home of another one of her kindergartners, she met Wanda, an African American single mother who had dance literacy and experience. With the parents of two of her kindergartners, Hensley was able to coplan a class musical inspired by the Little Red Hen story. Hensley (2005, 146) explains, "The fact that teachers are enthusiastic when they discover these talents is critical in motivating parents and children." Once Jacob realized how valuable his funds of knowledge were, he became more confident and eventually ran for PTA president and became a leader in his daughter's school. This happened because Jacob saw his family literacy practices being validated and honored in his daughter's school, expanding curriculum and teaching.

There were many other instances where Hensley was able to communicate to family members how their home literacies would add to the learning in her kindergarten classroom, including the use of quilts and quilting as part of a math investigation, based on her knowledge that a child's grandmother made quilts. As she learned about home literacies her students had, the funds of knowledge their families possessed, she reflected on her own funds of knowledge, not regarding them as the truth or as universal experiences, but regarding them as situated—and tapping on them. Her approach did not stem from one single visit, but was inspired by the many home visits she did. She now sees the expertise in her extended classroom community, the families and extended families of her students, who "feel pride in themselves and their accomplishments and feel valued" (Hensley 2005, 150).

Hensley (2005) invites teachers to become interested in moving beyond deficit views of families to identify and document funds of knowledge as home literacies by:

- Engaging in at least a couple of home/family visits with the purpose of learning
- Listening to and learning from students—they will share funds of knowledge their family and extended family members have
- Having students interview family members and share information learned
- Talking with family members—even if at dismissal, field trips, etc.
- Incorporating family funds of knowledge in your planning (you are likely to learn about other home literacies in the process)

Early Childhood Teachers and Researchers as Cultural Workers

Paulo Freire (1998) posits that teachers are cultural workers, and states that the traditional roles of teacher and learner must be blurred. He proposes that humility is an essential component of this blurring of roles, stating, "No one knows it all;

no one is ignorant of everything" (Freire 1998, 39). This necessitates learning from and with families in order to educate children.

To be able to identify, access, and document funds of knowledge, teachers with whom we've worked over the years have taken on the roles of learner, researcher, inquirer, and curriculum maker, seeing these as central to teaching. They saw themselves as continuous, lifelong learners. They engaged in learning through intentional and systematic research, emanating from an inquiry stance. Most of all, they recognized that they can't teach children unless they see them and their families as cultural beings—unless they recognize the value of their cultural practices as well as the value of others' cultural practices.

You Can't Teach Those You Don't Know

Lisa Delpit (2012) proposes, "Knowing students is a prerequisite for teaching them well" (87). To know students, we need to get to know the people and places from where they come. After all, children are social, cultural, and historical beings. They have histories, cultural practices, and are members of multiple communities. Getting to know children within the context of their families is essential. Their knowledges, practices, and languages need to be present in classroom materials, informing curriculum and teaching (Souto-Manning et al. 2018). It is also essential to recognize that children are capable and as individual human beings, their voices have to be present.

In a kindergarten inclusive classroom in New York City, Carmen Lugo Llerena engages in a literacy engagement documenting where students are from—the places they go, the foods they eat, the sayings they hear, and the people they

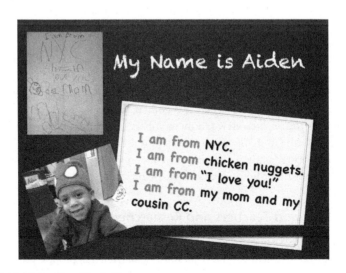

FIGURE 4.3 *I Am From* Book Page

love (based on the idea offered by Souto-Manning and Martell 2016). She read aloud *Momma, Where Are You From?* by Marie Bradby, a book which captures a little African American girl asking her momma where she is from. In the story portrayed in Bradby's picture book, the question is met with the rich details of childhood memories her mother has, such as hanging clothes on the clotheslines tied between trees, the place where the city sidewalk ended, watching her siblings being bussed all across town to a school where all the children were brown. Intentionally and purposefully, she moves away from the *othering* practice that often takes place in classrooms, schools, and society, which asks "different" students where they are from, thus marking them accordingly. Together with her students, Llerena authored a book titled *I Am From*. Instead of asking families to come into the classroom, Llerena asked children to think about where they were from—the places, people, sayings, and foods. The book portrayed their literacies of belonging. She asked them to document what they heard at home, what they ate, and the place and people they felt they belonged to. Figure 4.3 is a page from that book.

In addition to making children's voices and identities visible through curriculum and teaching, as exemplified by Llerena's teaching (above), it is important to help them understand how they are members of families, neighborhoods, and communities, with unique and special practices. This can expand their zones of proximal development (Vygotsky 1978) in potentially powerful ways.

Expanding the Zone of Proximal Development

We posit that to teach to children's potential, it is important to consider the concept of zone of proximal development, proposed by Lev Vygotsky (1978). As touched on earlier, Vygotsky defines zone of proximal development as "the distance between the actual developmental level as determined by independent problem solving and the level of potential development as determined through problem solving under adult guidance or in collaboration with more capable peers" (p. 33). He goes on to explain:

> The zone of proximal development furnishes psychologists and educators with a tool through which the internal course of development can be understood. By using this method we can take account of not only the cycles and maturation processes that have already been completed but also those processes that are currently in a state of formation, that are just beginning to mature and develop.

Moving beyond adults and more capable peers, Gregory, Long, and Volk (2004a) propose that collaboration with peers (regardless of ability or capability) rather than guidance from adults or more knowledgeable others can foster zones of proximal development. After all, there is more expertise distributed than in any one member of a learning community (Ladson-Billings 2012). Thus, Gregory, Long, and Volk (2004b) and Ladson-Billings (2004) lead us to challenge fixed constructs of ability and/or capability and to embrace the distributed expertise in the classroom.

Inviting us to expand the distributed expertise model beyond the walls of the classroom and physical landscape of (pre)schools, Moll and colleagues (1992) propose that *funds of knowledge* extend the more traditional sociocultural understandings of what Vygotsky (1978) called the "zone of proximal development" and thus serve as "extended zones of proximal development" (Moll and Greenberg 1990, 344). That is, they allow for more of the home practices to enter schools and classrooms, calling for a movement inverse to that which blames families' lack of academic work with their children for their children's failing in schooling. They underscore the key importance of drawing on family funds of knowledge when seeking to engage in equitable teaching, learning with and from diverse children.

Countering deficit perceptions of young children as inferior or deprived (Goodwin et al. 2008, Valdés 1996), the concept of funds of knowledge allows teachers to see young children and their families as skillful and resourceful. Inherent in the notion of funds of knowledge is that all families have worthy language and literacy practices (Souto-Manning and Martell 2016). Some of them will enter the classroom; others may remain within the context of homes. Regardless, it is important for teachers to realize that all families have worthy knowledge. They all have rich albeit unique cultural practices, what some call funds of knowledge and others call home literacies.

We acknowledge that we can continue to embrace the practice of excluding children and keeping inequities in place by ignoring the rich funds of knowledge existent in families and communities—but which are often absent from (pre)schools and classrooms. We propose that instead we embrace them, making curriculum and teaching more critically inclusive. Here, we position funds of knowledge as essential for reenvisioning the role and space of family literacy practices as we propose that funds of knowledge are indeed family literacies—even when they don't fit easily under traditional definitions of literacy. After all, (pre)school literacies must be representative and inclusive of diversities.

Looking Back, Moving Ahead

Throughout this chapter, we have invited early childhood educators and researchers to open "curricular closets in regulated times" (Dyson 2010, 307), replacing decontextualized route exercises with sophisticated and rich family literacies. We explored concepts and shared examples of possible pedagogical keys, such as documenting assets (García and García 2012), which can help early childhood teachers identify the strengths of young children and their families. Through the examples presented in this chapter, we situated family literacies (Gregory et al. 2004a; Souto-Manning 2010a) as integral in understanding the resourcefulness of cultural communities, especially those that have been traditionally viewed as deficient or inferior (Goodwin et al. 2008; Valdés, 1996), effectively coming to see family literacies as funds of knowledge, cultural practices with depth and important for household functioning. Here, we re-mediated family literacies, redefining them not as school literacy practices entering families' homes, but as funds of knowledge. In Chapter 5, we situate literacies within larger relational collective contexts: neighborhoods and communities.

Note

1. Deferred Action for Childhood Arrivals, a U.S. immigration policy established in 2012 under President Obama, allowed certain undocumented immigrants in the U.S. who entered the country as minors (and met specific criteria) to receive a renewable two-year period of deferred action from deportation and to be eligible to work in the U.S.

5

LANGUAGES AND LITERACIES IN NEIGHBORHOODS AND COMMUNITIES

Neighborhoods have smells, sounds, colors, and rhythms. They have particular cultural practices within the context of highly textured landscapes. For example, in the neighborhood of East Harlem, New York, bodegas are much more common than Starbucks stores, which punctuate the Wall Street area in New York City's financial district. In Chinatown, bubble tea, dumplings, and egg custard smells saturate the air. In the Bronx's Little Italy, bubbling cheese on top of pizza dough comes out of coal-fired ovens. Each neighborhood has certain characteristics. Within each neighborhood, there are literacies at play.

In her bilingual picture book, *What Can You Do with a Paleta?* (2009), Carmen Tafolla takes the reader through her reading of her *barrio*, explaining how a *paleta* travels throughout the neighborhood. She describes the "sassy and sweet" sound of the accordion, "the smell of crispy tacos or buttery tortillas or juicy *fruta* floating out of every window," bringing readers to the heart of her barrio. Then, she goes on to introduce *paletas* (popsicles) in "every color of the sarape." Not only are both English and Spanish used, but particular cultural referents are visible. For example, the sarape (Figure 5.1), and not the rainbow, captures every color within that specific community. Thus, children grow up being socialized into community- and neighborhood-specific metaphors.

Sharing common meanings and uses of *paletas*, Tafolla then recounts culturally specific actions involving a *paleta*—embracing artifactual literacies, the understanding that every object tells multiple stories as it interacts with individuals within a variety of settings (Pahl and Rowsell 2010). She writes of how some children suck on a *paleta* until their tongues turn green, embodying a monster and scaring younger siblings. She unveils the skills developed as a result of interacting with *paleteros* in her barrio— for example, decision-making skills "Strawberry? Or coconut?" She goes on to account for the relational aspect of *paletas*, which can collectively mediate friendships

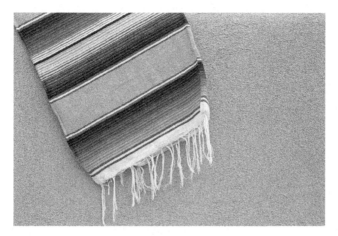

FIGURE 5.1   Sarape
© iStock

and make mamás more comfortable on hot days. In recounting the multiple actions of a *paleta* within the context of her barrio, Tafolla describes the relationships—of siblings, *tíos*, *mamás*—as well as community landmarks, such as "the *señora* at the fruit stand." In Tafolla's barrio, which reminds us of New York City's El Barrio, Spanish overpowers English in many locales; it is likely that if you want a coffee, you are better off asking for a "*café con leche, por favor*" rather than a "soy latte, thanx."

The Ecology of Early Childhood: On Neighborhoods and Communities

Traditional theories of early childhood education—such as Bronfenbrenner's ecological systems theory (1979, 1992, 2005)—position children's growth and development within multiple contexts and systems. While young children are individuals, they grow within the context of families and neighborhoods (what Bronfenbrenner titled microsystems, explored in Chapter 4 and in this chapter) and mesosystems, such as peer groups and communities (explored here and in Chapter 6). Bronfenbrenner defines mesosystems as "a system of microsystems" that "comprises the interrelationships among two or more settings in which the developing person actively participates . . . such as, for a child, the relations among home, school, and neighborhood peer group" (Bronfenbrenner 1979, 25). Bronfenbrenner (1979, 21) underscored that "the progressive, mutual accommodation between an active, growing human being and the changing properties of the immediate setting in which the developing person lives" comprise what he calls development. Yet, while we see Bronfenbrenner's model as a useful organizational device, we employ Cole and Cole's (1996) interpretation of the nested ecological system, which acknowledges the multiple contexts of child learning and development, albeit in nonhierarchical, blurred, and dynamic ways. We reject the assumption that systems are easily definable and delineated as individual and/or communal. Instead, children's participations in different communities are interrelated, impossible to separate in a linear, independent, or hierarchical way.

We see this chapter spanning across and blurring microsystems and mesosystems, rendering them impossibilities as separate spaces and realms, through the exploration of the ways in which young children make sense of and in their neighborhoods and communities—interactionally and physically. As we do so, we position young children as active participants in multiple communities of practice— and not simply as bystanders in a neighborhood. Of course all of these spaces and realms are cultural, and they shape and are shaped by policies and politics in place.

As we explored earlier, notions of appropriateness—albeit foundational to the field of early childhood education as traditionally conceived (Yelland 2005)—are deeply cultural. As New and Mallory (1994) proposed, no word in the English dictionary is more culturally drenched than appropriate. What's appropriate for one cultural group in one neighborhood is not appropriate for another. For instance, in the U.S., many would deem infant caregiving at age six or gardening and selling produce at age four to be inappropriate. Yet, in certain locales, these are not only deemed appropriate, but are expected. For example, Rogoff (2003) documented how a Guatemalan girl was "a skilled caregiver for her baby cousin" and Watson-Gegeo (1990, 87) verified that within the Kwara'ae community of Oceania:

> Three year olds are skilled workers in gardens. . . . In addition to working in the family gardens, young children have their own garden plots . . . [which] may seem like play, but by three or four years of age many children are taking produce they have grown themselves to the market to sell . . . making a significant and valuable contribution to family income.

These are both examples of the cultural nature of children's literacy learning. In the case of three year olds, they are developing important literacies related to gardening, tending to produce, harvesting, and developing literacies related to sales. Such literacies are not present within the context of all neighborhoods and communities. They are culturally situated.

To account for the fact that children are individuals who are members of communities and who live within unique cultural contexts, we recognize that these contexts and communities coexist (at times simultaneously). Young children make sense of multiple contexts, literacies, and cultural practices at once, many times in multiple languages. Neighborhoods and communities are layers of a system. Thus, while they serve as "sociopolitical and economic contexts to households" (Moll et al. 1992, 133) as discussed in Chapter 4, neighborhoods and communities also have languages and literacies. In addition to different sites, rhythms, and smells, neighborhoods also have unique histories. So, before delving into exploring the affordances of the languages and literacies within and across neighborhoods and communities, we briefly review the history of one community, which some would call an urban ethnic enclave, Chinatown. After all, few know that Chinatowns formed to provide protection against threats.

Within the context of San Francisco, as the American economy weakened, White Americans saw the Chinese labor force as a threat to mainstream society.

> Racial discrimination and repressive legislation drove the Chinese from the gold mines to the sanctuary of the neighborhood that became known as Chinatown. The only ethnic group in the history of the United States to have been specifically denied entrance into the country, the Chinese were prohibited by law to testify in court, to own property, to vote, to have family members join them in the U.S., to marry non-Chinese, and to work in institutional agencies. (www.pbs.org/kqed/chinatown/resourceguide/story.html)

Thus, such urban ethnic enclaves emerged not as a concerted effort to stay together out of preference, but for survival. Today, throughout the U.S. and around the world, Chinatowns exist as vibrant communities. Whether in New York City or Washington, D.C., Melbourne or Sydney, they exemplify "how a group of people bound geographically, culturally, linguistically and economically during hostile times has flourished" (www.pbs.org/kqed/chinatown/resourceguide/story.html). Within the context of Chinatowns, children often are bilingual and multilingual. They may speak Mandarin or Cantonese at home while educators expect them to develop English in school—or even before entering school.

Just as neighborhoods have different landmarks, sounds, and smells, they also have distinct literacies. While these are unique and rich, they are often marginalized and racialized (refer to Chapter 2 for a fuller discussion on how families of color, their languages, and literacies have been historically positioned), they are also highly segregated within the context of the dominant U.S. society.

Historicizing Segregated Neighborhoods

> National statistics show that America has been highly segregated racially and economically across the nation. . . . The U.S. Census 2000 shows that growing ethnic diversity in the nation accompanies high residential segregation, especially between black and white. The average racial and economic composition of neighborhoods occupied by whites differs from that of neighborhoods occupied by blacks, Hispanics, Asians, or other ethnic groups. (Li 2008, 7)

The U.S. is becoming ever more diverse while at the same time neighborhoods and communities remain segregated. Some say that segregated neighborhoods allow language and cultural practices to be maintained and spoken outside of the home—as in the cases of El Barrio and Chinatown in New York City. Yet, there are many disadvantages to neighborhood segregation. Lower life expectancy (Saegert and Evans 2003) is one, as "lower socioeconomic and minority status are strongly related to worse health and earlier death" (Saegert and Evans 2003, 569). Political isolation is another prominent issue, and this includes voter suppression and racialized redistricting (Guinier 2001, 2006; Massey and Denton 1989). Without elected officials, ethnically and racially minoritized communities receive fewer resources as compared to racially and ethnically majoritized neighborhoods. Massey (2001, 391) verifies: "Opportunities and resources are unevenly distributed in space; some neighborhoods have safer streets, higher home values, better services, more effective schools, and more supportive peer environments than others." In addition to lack of access to the formal power structures, neighborhood isolation leads to linguistic minoritization. This is how the language practices of many African Americans (African American Language—more fully discussed in Chapters 2, 3, and 4) and Latinxs (Spanish, Spanglish, translanguaging) are relegated and judged in problematic ways. These and many other factors of what Massey and Denton (1993) called "American apartheid" resulted—and continue to result—in "the making of the underclass."

Massey and Denton (1993) explain how during the first half of the twentieth century, there were concerted efforts to isolate neighborhoods ethnically and racially. Such intense neighborhood segregation is referred to as "hypersegregation," and is prominent in urban areas. While we do not fully address the hypersegregation of neighborhoods in this chapter, as it is beyond the scope of this book, we mention it here, as it is a design principle of U.S. society. It is not a result of ethnically and racially minoritized peoples' choices and decisions to self-segregate. It is that the U.S., a society "based on property rights" and endemic racism (Ladson-Billings and Tate 1995, 48), used its foundations to promote segregated neighborhoods. This can be easily understood through the lens of critical race theory, "the intersection of race and property."

Racially and ethnically minoritized neighborhoods—such as El Barrio, Chinatown, and Harlem in New York City—have been cast as problems and dealt with as enemies, as illustrated by the way Ronald Reagan's War on Drugs targeted urban ethnic and racial enclaves, where "THE DRUG WAR IS THE NEW JIM CROW" (Alexander 2012, 3). After all, "enduring racial isolation of the ghetto poor has made them vulnerable in the War on Drugs" (Alexander 2012, 124). These neighborhoods were seen as "poverty-stricken, racially segregated ghettos" (Alexander 2012, 124), until, of course, White people wanted properties in these locales, an easy feat, given the low rates of home ownership in such neighborhoods (Newman and Wyly 2006). But this is another story. For this chapter, it is important to understand that even though there are rich language and literacy practices in ethnically and racially minoritized neighborhoods, they are still grounded on inequities and result from racism. This explains, for example, the lack of fresh produce in some neighborhoods and the availability of organics from distant countries in other neighborhoods.

Languages in Neighborhoods and Communities

Aside from the minoritization of languages spoken in minoritized neighborhoods and communities, children who grow up in urban ethnic and racial neighborhoods develop an impressive communicative repertoire. Many children in Chinatown are learning English alongside Mandarin and/or Cantonese. Many children in East Harlem are learning English alongside Spanish. Even if they do not attend bilingual schooling programs, their communicative repertoires develop within the context of the cultural practices in their neighborhoods. In fact, in such neighborhoods bilingual programs tend to be transitional (home languages are used until children are fluent in English), positioning home languages as crutches to be cast away after the acquisition and development of the language of power—dominant American English in the U.S. Even in bilingual programs, the expectations for English-dominant and Spanish-dominant students differ significantly, with English-dominant students celebrated for every small step they take in Spanish and Spanish-dominant students expected to achieve immediate English fluency (Valdés 1997).

For example, as one enters Tai Pan Bakery on Canal Street in the heart of New York City's Chinatown, interactions in Chinese and English coexist side-by-side. Regardless of whether a customer orders in English or in Chinese, all orders are written on slips of paper in Chinese and placed on top of a tray that moves along the top of the long glass case filled with sweet and savory pastries. It is easy to forget that a few subway stops away, Chinese is not the lingua franca for purchases and for negotiating everyday life.

In East Harlem, as one enters a bodega to order a coffee, utterances in Spanish and English coexist within the syntactic context of the same sentence. Again, a few subway stops down, entering a coffee shop at Trump Tower and placing an order in Spanish or Spanglish, it may not be seen as "normal and unmarked to translanguage in interactions between individuals" (García 2009, 44). Yet, as García (2009, 17) posits, the interactions at the East Harlem bodega illustrate the "linguistic fluidity present in the discourse of the twenty-first century."

While not trying to reduce these entire diverse neighborhoods to these two scenarios, it is important to understand how pervasive the coexistence of languages is. Young children use their entire linguistic repertoires to communicate, at times not yet knowing where one language ends and the other starts, using their linguistic universe to communicate in ways coherent with what García (2009) proposed in terms of bilingualism—not balancing two languages as if riding a bike, but using an all-terrain vehicle and using all available demonstrative resources to communicate across terrains and shifting landscapes. After all, young children's "complex multilingual and multimodal global communicative networks often reflect much more than two separate monolingual codes" (García 2009, 8).

From Languages to Languaging

In urban ethnic enclaves, we see languaging bilingually and/or multilingually as the norm. Yet, in official schooling spaces, even within the context of neighborhoods predominantly populated by a minoritized ethnic or racial group, languaging bilingually and multilingually are often positioned as liabilities—judged from deficit perspectives and constructed as ignorant of dominant American English.

In neighborhoods, young children negotiate not only different languages, but different registers within each language. This happens within relational contexts and families who look very different within and across communities. Extended families figure prominently in ethnic enclaves in New York City.

Lily (莉莉), a four-year-old Chinese American girl, spends many of her days with her grandmother in New York City's Chinatown. Her parents work long hours in neighborhood restaurants. While Lily is exposed to English in (pre)school, her interactions with her grandmother are in Chinese. Lily attends prekindergarten. In the classroom, she is often shy, according to her teacher. Yet, with her grandmother, she is always talking. She knows to stay close to her grandmother as they walk through the busy streets of Chinatown, but experiences freedom as she reaches a public playground. She jumps on the keys of a musical instrument, part of the playground apparatus, giggling with other children. She is emerging as a bilingual meaning maker within the context of her neighborhood.

André, a five-year-old Boricua boy, often goes to his *abuela*'s apartment after school. He attends a monolingual public school kindergarten in East Harlem, New York, and his grandmother lives a few blocks from his school. His parents pick him up from his grandmother's around 5:00 p.m. each day, but he spends at least two hours per day with her on weekdays. Even though his school is monolingual and his parents (second-generation Boricuas) communicate with him primarily in English, his *abuela*'s communication with him is primarily in Spanish. While he responds to her in English, his understanding of Spanish is sophisticated and nuanced. He too is emerging as a bilingual meaning maker, navigating across multiple communicative contexts in his neighborhood.

As we peek at contexts such as a bakery in Chinatown and a bodega in East Harlem and learn from Lily and André, we bear witness to how language varies across neighborhood contexts. In doing so, we underscore the sophistication of language practices within and across neighborhoods and communities. Because we explored oral language development and language minoritization in Part I, here we simply locate the language practices of minoritized individuals across diverse neighborhoods and in ethnic and racial enclaves, often located in urban centers as rich, sophisticated, and worthy—regardless of larger discourses. And, "learning and development cannot be considered apart from the individual's social environment, the ecocultural niche" (Neuman and Celano 2001, 8).

Literacies in Neighborhoods and Communities

The language practices of children in neighborhoods and communities are rich. So are their literacies. They may not be comprised of books or of print materials, and, to be understood, must be conceptualized beyond print (Yelland et al. 2008). Literacies go much beyond print, as explored earlier in this book. Despite the richness of language and literacy practices in neighborhoods and communities, there is a persistent difference between the achievement and learning of children in low- and middle-income families. We further explore this in Chapter 8, when we discuss concepts such as *language debt*.

To date, "much of the literature on differences between middle- and low-income families" with regard to literacy achievement and development

> [H]as given . . . limited attention to the settings in which literacy begins for young children. The environment has classically served as a backdrop for looking at patterns of interaction, but never as a potential explanatory factor. (Neuman and Celano 2001, 11)

While Neuman and Celano (2001) pay attention to the environment, they focus on the availability of print materials, purporting a view of literacy that is attached to school-defined literacies. We posit that the availability of print materials does little to capture the linguistic competence of children like Lily and André. School literacy, specifically attention to print only, defines success in narrow ways, related to practices of power. After all, "the ecocultural structure of a community is more than a matter of material resources . . . it is the social construction of families and the impact of daily experiences on children's lives" (Neuman and Celano 2001, 12). And because the social construction of literacies is complex and harder to document, quantitative studies have often oversimplified the concept of ecocultural communities, thus restricting it to resources and stripping it of its meaning.

Here, as we move to unveil some neighborhood literacies and how teachers can leverage those to benefit students' learning, we embrace the situated nature of relationships, acknowledging that neighborhood literacies are built on relationships and grounded in everyday community cultural events. We propose that we must not only get beyond school-sanctioned literacy definitions (as explained in Part I), but move beyond access to print, unveiling the many literacies present in communities—minoritized and majoritized. We thus offer that neighborhood and community literacies are premised on three principles:

- Every neighborhood and community has particular, rich, and worthy ways to make meaning that are no better and no worse than other community's ways with words.
- Neighborhood and community literacies may or may not be related to print and printed words.
- Community literacies are relational and situated with cultural practices particular to a neighborhood.

Neighborhood Literacies as Changing Participation in Communities of Practice

Young children are active members of multiple communities (see Part I). They not only belong to people, but to places, to neighborhoods, and to communities. Literacy learning is "a process of changing participation in dynamic cultural communities" (Rogoff 2003, 63). Different cultures place value on specific communicative practices, dependent on the context and site of learning, albeit on a farm, at home, in school, and around community centers. Through repeated observation and participation, children are apprenticed into language practices that are vital to engaging in community life (Rogoff 2003).

In the picture book *Something Beautiful* by Sharon Dennis Wyeth (1998), a little girl reads symbols in her neighborhood—for example, she reads the word *die* painted on her front door. While some may think of the reading of words and other printed symbols as neighborhood literacies, we posit that it is the human and nonhuman relationships that comprise the literacies of her neighborhood— the ways of making meaning and making sense of the community in which one lives. As the girl navigates across different sites in her neighborhood, she engages in unique communicative practices. She observes the practice of jumping rope, enacted by her friends on the sidewalk. Then, she reaches Mr. Lee's store with fruit stacked up as high as she can see. Old Mr. Sims invites her to touch a smooth stone he's carried in his pocket, sharing the stories behind an object. Finally, the little girl enters a laundromat, which requires different literacies, such as folding clothes, operating the washer and dryer, calculating time and change. She sees her aunt. She can participate in that community of practice too.

The girl in Wyeth's book was reading her neighborhood and the multiple cultural practices present in them. Here, we focus on the laundromat as these are often positioned as neighborhood hubs, commonly present in low-income and urban settings. Laundromat neighborhood literacy practices can comprise what Ghiso (2016, 1) entitled "literacies of interdependence" that "linked individual flourishing with community wellbeing through their care work in supporting their families" (Ghiso 2016, 2). Ghiso (2016) invites teachers to value children's literacy practices of interdependence and negotiations of identity "as embodied in concrete spaces within their lived experiences" (p. 2). After all, young children's languages and literacies are situated within multiple communities as they take on plural identities.

What Kind of Community of Practice?

Maisha Fisher has written extensively about the power of community and neighborhood literacies, examining participatory literacies where youth are engaged in coconstructing individualized forms of interaction including spoken word, activism, and writing. She drew on the concept of communities of practice (Wenger

1998), complicating "notions of reciprocity and mentoring in the out-of-school literacy practices" (Fisher 2007, 139) to develop what she termed *participatory literacy communities*. Participatory literacy communities (PLCs) are places where learners "can exchange ideas and lived experiences" (Fisher 2007, 139). These places are marked by the role of intergenerational relationships through the commitment of community elders to less experienced members of the community. Here, we learn from her research with youth as we seek to define neighborhood and community literacies as PLCs.

Fisher (2007) studied PLCs in two Northern California bookstores. As she did so, she made visible the importance of intergenerational mentoring to PLCs and its participants. She "came to focus on better understanding these elders' roles and responsibilities and the sorts of literacy practices they modeled and fostered" (Fisher 2007, 140). These elders were often referred to as soldiers; as underscored by Michael Datcher, who participated in both PLC communities she studied, "every city has soldiers" (Fisher 2007, 140). "Through participating in out-of-school literacy-centered events . . . soldiers pass on wisdom and insight . . . and apprentice new people into their communities" (Fisher 2007, 140). She unveiled how soldiers took on the roles of activists and advocates (inviting, encouraging, and inciting), practitioners (blurring the roles of teacher and learner), and historians (knowing the legacy and passing it on), and affirmed that for PLCs, relationships are central. "Members not only share a love for words and language, but they are also passionate about extending themselves to each other in a format that offers fresh ways of thinking about literacy-learning communities" (Fisher 2007, 143), as in neighborhood barbershops.

In another study, Fisher (2003) looks specifically at open mic settings to make sense of African Diaspora Participatory Literacy Communities (ADPLC), "made up predominantly of people of African descent who participate in literacy or literary-centered events outside of traditional school and work settings" (Fisher 2003, 363). She delves into two communities to learn how ADPLC functions as a literacy event. Realizing that "people of African descent did not focus on categorizing aspects of literacy in practices such as reading, writing, and speaking" (Fisher 2003, 381), Fisher proposed that "black people understand literacy by 'making it one whole thing'" (2003, 381). Thus, as we move to explore participatory literacy communities in neighborhoods—and how they enter schools—we do not disentangle language from literacy, or oral from written language. We seek to offer examples of how "literacy learning and education provided people with 'a sense of one's place in that history' and one's 'purpose'" (Fisher 2003, 387).

Participatory Literacy Communities in Neighborhoods

Below we share examples of how participatory literacy communities (Fisher 2007) within the context of neighborhoods can serve to "validate knowledge, help shape visions, inculcate values, and provide the foundation for community stability"

(Lee 1992, 161). Within each of them, we explore the role of intergenerational mentoring as well as how the elder is an advocate, practitioner, and historian, paying attention to what children are learning in terms of purpose and history. In doing so, we move away from innocent and romanticized ideas of young children as helpless and powerless (introduced and challenged in Part I), toward seeing them as capable and active members of multiple literacy communities. We position young children as active and knowledgeable participants in their own right, within and around their neighborhoods.

As we consider PLCs and their role in rethinking early literacies based on the knowledge situated in neighborhoods and shared through the practices of specific communities, we explore the ways in which early childhood teachers leveraged participatory communities of practice particular to the neighborhoods in which the children they taught lived to promote meaningful learning. This not only positioned young children as agents, but also communicated that their communities are worthy and that their practices belong in schools and schooling.

As we share examples of young children fully and capably engaged in participatory literacy communities within and across neighborhoods, we make visible the ways in which literacies are sponsored in spaces outside of the school. We also see how participatory literacy communities in neighborhoods are not simply traditional school-sanctioned literacy practices. These are examples of literacies that are historical, social, and political—essential for the legacy and survival of communities. We depart from the concept of literacy as a set of combined skills, moving toward literacy as cultural practices located within neighborhoods. In doing so, we position literacy as not only a civil right, but a human right. It is a human right because it is foundational to freedom, justice, and peace not only individually, but collectively as well.

As we acknowledge the historical lack of freedom imposed on communities and individuals of color, we build on the concept of literacies as grounded in the experiences and legacies of people of color (Fisher 2003). After all, as expounded by Carmen Tisdale, an early childhood teacher in South Carolina:

> We can no longer teach just according to the ways of the White, middle class. If you are going to reach every student in your classroom, you have to broaden your comfort zone and learn about the lives and communities of your students firsthand. We've been doing it your way long enough. (Long et al., 2013, 419)

As far as we are concerned, defining literacy in colonialist, exclusive, and restrictive ways has kept people of color and minoritized populations at the margins, relegated and segregated. Yet, instead of ignoring the rich cultural practices developed within sites of historical and contemporary struggle, here we center the very concept of participatory literacy communities in neighborhoods on such practices. Because they took place in early childhood settings where children were regarded as capable agents, at times they emanated from issues generated from children's interests; other times, issues were identified by the teacher.

Each of the examples below is unique. We hope this signals how there is no exact formula for engaging with participatory literacy communities in early childhood settings or for exploring literacies existent in communities and neighborhoods. Like Freire (1998), we invite you to reject the notion of importing formulas, but instead, learn from human relationships and reinvent participatory learning communities in your own setting as you learn from and about the rich and varied literacies in communities and neighborhoods.

On the Architecture of the Freedom Tower and Unequal Labor Conditions

It was a sunny day in November in New York City. The World Trade Center building (erected in place of the Twin Towers) glistened over the Manhattan skyline.

Second grader Nico asked, "You ever wonder what makes the buildings so shiny?"

"The sun," Alejandro answered.

"There are window washers cleaning way up high," Nico completed his thought. "And you know what happened yesterday? They got stuck up there on that reeeaaaally tall building," he said as he showed the cover of the *AM New York* newspaper (a free newspaper handed out at New York City subway stations).

Nico and Alejandro continued to talk, seemingly unaware that a number of their peers had abandoned their morning routine of eating breakfast and reading to gather around them. Their classmates organically joined the conversation. Amanda stretched her neck to look at the cover of the newspaper and asked: "Who's up there?" Yolanda tapped Alejandro on the shoulder and asked: "What they do? They still there?" (Souto-Manning and Martell 2017, 252–53)

Noticing that her students were interested in the World Trade Center building, asking questions related to two window washers, Juan Lizama and Juan Lopez being stuck up high, how the broken window was going to be fixed (as well as a number of other questions), teacher Jessica Martell decided to call on the mother of a child in her class to answer their questions. Martell knew this mother and her professional background because she had mapped the human resources of her extended classroom community and had developed relationships with family members (as explained in Chapter 4).

Isaura, a Boricua Spanish-speaking architect and the mother of one of the children in Martell's class, was positioned as an elder who could provide information, advocate for the safety of window washers, and explain the legacy of construction in that region. She was a *soldier*, an elder in the extended classroom community who shared her love for architecture and extended herself, helping children think in new ways as they engaged in the discourse of architecture (Fisher 2007).

When Isaura came to the classroom, she showed the children the gear used by the window washers. She showed the children how to put it on and had them feel the harness. She also brought sample windowpanes constructed in a way similar to the windows of the World Trade Center building. She invited the children to hypothesize about how the broken window would be replaced and then engaged them in considering costs, timelines, and visual consequences of each choice. Then, she got them to design possible solutions for the building, based on the information at hand.

Isaura took on the role of activist, inviting children to join in the community and participate, encouraging children to ask questions, and inciting a participatory literacy community. She shared her role as an architect and compared the questions the children were asking to the questions being asked earlier that day in her office. She also knew the legacy of the field of architecture—and how there are shinier buildings in lower Manhattan (signaling the financial discrepancies of neighborhoods) and the racialized roles in construction and architecture (whereas architecture is punctuated by White men, window washing is overwhelmingly staffed by men of color). She discussed inequities in the profession of architecture.

She mentored the children beyond that specific visit, extending herself and taking them on neighborhood historic walks, pointing out to them features in various buildings (making links to history, legacy, and equity issues) and teaching them about the history of their neighborhood. She pointed out how the southern boundary of Harlem shifted over time, as White families moved in and renamed sections of the larger neighborhood, displacing Black families in an area that had historically been known as the Black mecca. She also shared with them that in New York City, brown street signs "show you the history." The children learned that brown signs identified historic streets and districts and were established by the Landmarks Preservation Commission around the twenty-fifth anniversary of the Landmarks Law. The children learned that only streets within official historic districts could have the brown signs. They learned how to design buildings so that they honor the history and legacy of a neighborhood, and they learned about the architectural and historical characteristics of their own neighborhood in the process. While the children respected Isaura enormously, they also saw her as a member of their extended community, as she learned with them even as they learned from her.

In addition to establishing a participatory learning community, which continued throughout the academic year, Isaura's identity as Boricua made it easier for the children to see themselves in her. Most of the time she spent with them, she spoke Spanish, embodying a counternarrative to the discourse that English is better. Because Martell's class was bilingual (dual language, Spanish-English), Martell expected all students to communicate in both languages, yet the unequal expectations typically persisted within the context of the school and of society writ large.

That is, while Martell communicated the value of both languages, standardized test scores and markers of academic progress accounted by the school and district were only in English, thus a double standard was perceptible. Bringing Isaura to her classroom as a soldier, a mentor, and an elder fostered respect for and admiration of the Spanish language and of Spanish speakers.

Remedies and Healing

Maria's grandmother is a *curandera*, a healer. She had been certified in Arizona before moving to New York. Maria's teacher, Yadira Hernandez, learned this after observing Maria play during class work time (known as centers or choice time in other settings). Maria would gather pretend plants, set them to "boil" with water on the stove, and have peers drink the pretend mix, as healing medicine. Maria's peers were not startled by such a practice, as it was part of their cultural repertoires in the neighborhood and within the context of their extended families. When they got sick, partly because of a cultural tradition emanating from indigenous Mexico and partly due to the lack of affordable and available health care in the U.S. (and, specifically, in East Harlem), they often took natural remedies. Many of them had family members who had been customers of the nearby *botanica*, a place where a variety of medicinal herbs and plants, perfumed waters and oils, candles, incense, and other items of health and religious significance were available for purchase. It is, for example, where one can purchase *siete jarabes*, a common remedy for asthma.

Hernandez did not know the science behind the medicinal herbs and healers, but she was familiar with their prevalence; it was a commonplace cultural practice located in the neighborhood. "Across the park or down Madison, I'm not sure people would go for it, but here, it's where it is." Recognizing this common cultural practice, a neighborhood literacy, Hernandez created space for the children to learn from and with Maria's grandmother, intergenerationally. It is not that the children were unfamiliar with the practice, but that Hernandez wanted to create an official space that valued their out-of-school community literacies. After all, they were already in the unofficial cracks of the classroom—in child-led spaces.

To introduce the idea within the official sphere of the classroom, Hernandez read *My Tata's Remedies* by Roni Rivera-Ashford aloud. As she read the book in the rug area, the children looked at the book and at each other. While the story in the book is set in the southwestern U.S., the children were familiar with natural healing remedies. They knew that plants were remedies and the book reinforced the idea. Interestingly, while Hernandez had experienced difficulties keeping children's attention at the rug area during read-alouds, especially a longer one, the children were very attentive as she read this book, which served as a mirror (Bishop 1990) for many of them.

Just like Tata in the book, Maria's *abuela*, Candelaria, was a family elder who knew a lot about healing. Hernandez knew the power of intergenerational wisdom and learning, especially in a community where extended families are the norm.

Yet, she knew that the school's curriculum did not honor such knowledge and that these cultural practices in which the children participated needed to be repositioned. So, she created space in her classroom for *curanderia*, not only during work time, but throughout the curriculum.

Hernandez had Candelaria come in once a week to exchange her ideas and lived experiences with the children, fostering a participatory learning community within the context of the classroom, but not bound by the school's walls. The PLC extended beyond the school into what she called "the open classroom." As a class, they interviewed Candelaria and also visited the neighborhood *boticario*, learning from its owner. They purchased a few products, such as chamomile and mint, which had distinct smells and well-known uses, and brought them back to the classroom.

Natural remedies had been part of the East Harlem community for years. But the school curriculum and literacies had ignored them. By erasing the classroom and school walls, Hernandez could capitalize on the intergenerational relationships existent in the neighborhood as essential for learning. Candelaria taught the class about remedies, but also about the survival of cultural practices within the context of the neighborhood. Candelaria advocated natural healing, encouraging the children to develop knowledge about the natural world around them and the healing properties of nature. She was committed to socializing less-experienced healers (even if young children) into *curanderia*. She was what Fisher (2007) called "a soldier," who not only engaged in healing, but also knew the history of healing within the community. As she took on a class full of new mentees, she extended herself in relational ways. She validated community literacies, present within the context of their neighborhood, inculcated important values, and laid the foundation for healing literacies to continue to exist for generations to come.

Reading the Subway System: Power Differentials and the Dis/Advantages of Access

In rethinking the role of the elder and disrupting the power balance in the classroom, teacher Jessica Martell positioned the boys of color in her classroom in the role of elders. They had learned from elders in their families how to navigate the New York City subway system, and often at ages seven and eight, did so on their own. Recognizing this as a valuable literacy practice, Martell positioned reading the subway system at the center of her teaching. She thought that positioning boys, who often did not have a lot of chances to display their competence and knowledge, as elders would boost their confidence and allow them to reposition themselves within the context of the classroom. That is, they would see themselves competently and others (peers, teachers) would see them in terms of assets. Thus, just as Gregory et al. (2004a, 2004b) proposed that peers can scaffold each other, building on Fisher's (2007, 139) realization that "every city has soldiers," Martell saw the soldiers (often a role taken up by elders [Fisher 2007]) in her classroom as a group of boys of color who were enthusiastic knowers of the subway system.

It all started with a topic within the second-grade curriculum: New York City. The school where Martell taught is in Manhattan and there are four other boroughs in the city. So that children would be able to visualize the boroughs of New York City, she had a map of the city prominently displayed in her classroom. So that they would become familiar with the names of the boroughs, she had labeled the tables in her classroom according to the boroughs—Manhattan, the Bronx, Brooklyn, Queens, and Staten Island. Yet, knowing where the boroughs were located according to a map and being familiar with names did not make learning real for the children. Martell wanted to build on their experiential knowledge. Then, she realized how the subway (and the overall public transportation system) linked all of the boroughs and could be leveraged for and in learning.

She asked the children to go to their local subway stations and ask for a subway map. They are free. The next day, a group of boys of color (who rarely brought in homework or signed permission slips) showed up with subway maps. Some of the other children who had established their identities as "good students" in her classroom did not bring subway maps. They had to rely on the children who had maps.

As they poured over subway maps (Figure 5.2), identifying familiar sites, it became clear how the map owners were knowledgeable about the subway and public transportation system. For example, when Amanda affirmed, "You can't get to every borough through public transportation; not to Staten Island." Mateo responded, "Yea, you can. There is a free ferry at South Station."

FIGURE 5.2   Reading the Subway and the New York City Public Transportation System

The boys took on the role of soldiers. Although the intergenerational learning was invisible, the boys had learned about the public transportation system from older family members who took them around the city by subway, bus, and ferry. They had experienced the system firsthand. They spoke up for the advantages of public transportation ("there is no traffic underground, well, not as much") and outlined some of its inequities ("some stations in nice neighborhoods are clean, but in not so nice neighborhoods, where rich people don't live, they're all dirty and broken down").

Together, they established a participatory literacy community, where they exchanged experiences and shared ideas. The boys of color, who had been established as the soldiers of this PLC within the context of their classroom, advocated for the class to visit all of New York City's boroughs by public transportation. They took the lead in plotting possible paths, calculating travel time, and discussing possible locations to visit. While the children did not visit all the locations via public transportation (they visited the Bronx via a school bus), the class visited all the boroughs and became familiar with the New York City public transportation system.

La Casa Azul

Bookstores in East Harlem? None! This was the case until Aurora Anaya-Cerda opened La Casa Azul in 2012, East Harlem's independent bookstore. La Casa Azul was a small bookstore, committed to titles written by and about people of color, in Spanish and English. It also hosted art shows and other cultural events. Anaya-Cerda saw La Casa Azul being "more than the average retail store, it is the literature hub in the neighborhood serving as the third place, a meeting space in the community." Although the bookstore is no longer in operation in East Harlem, while it was, it served as a powerful neighborhood hub. Aurora was a soldier who navigated within and across multiple literacy communities.

La Casa Azul was named after Frida Kahlo's house in Mexico, the original Casa Azul. Anaya-Cerda knew a lot about Kahlo and the children in Jessica Martell's second grade had fallen in love with Diego Rivera's work after reading the book *Diego Rivera: His World and Ours* (2011) by Duncan Tonatiuh. Diego Rivera and Frida Kahlo were artists and spouses. So Martell determined that learning about the history of Kahlo and Rivera while becoming familiar with the only bookstore of El Barrio would provide a powerful learning experience, and she arranged with Anaya-Cerda for a visit. Not only did she see La Casa Azul as a powerful space, but as a participatory literacy community in the neighborhood of East Harlem.

On the appointed day, the children were excited. As they arrived at La Casa Azul (Figure 5.3), they settled in the meeting area and listened to Anaya-Cerda engage in a read-aloud of a book in Spanish featuring Kahlo, *Frida* by Jonah Winter, and another one in English and Spanish, *Viva Frida* by Yuyi Morales. She also shared pages from her personal copy of a book featuring Kahlo's paintings, explaining some of the social and political context shaping Kahlo's art. She shared her passion for Kahlo's work with them, explaining how she named the bookstore after Kahlo's La Casa Azul in

FIGURE 5.3 La Casa Azul

Mexico City, Mexico. She also offered a biography of Kahlo, including some of the trauma Kahlo had endured and the pain she withstood throughout her life.

As a member of the community knowledgeable about Kahlo, Anaya-Cerda became a resource for the children, many of whom returned to the space after this initial visit with their families. Anaya-Cerda had taken on the role of activist, establishing La Casa Azul through crowdsourcing. She invited people of color to learn more about texts by and about people of color. She hosted book signings, readings, and special events. She herself was an avid reader, and she knew the power of reading and writing in history. She knew the legacy—not only of Kahlo—but also of many other authors of color. She shared her knowledge with the children, who also became enthusiastic about Kahlo.

Anaya-Cerda offered the time, space, and materials for the children to start pieces inspired by the work of Kahlo, whose paintings dealt centrally with issues of identity and pain. The children found spaces in the basement of the bookstore, on the main floor, or on the long, gray plastic tables to start their own pieces. Because Anaya-Cerda had shown them a painting in which Kahlo had addressed her own mixed German-Mexican heritage openly in *The Two Fridas (Las dos Fridas)* (1939), the children reflected on their own identities as they drafted their sketches. They also referred to another Kahlo piece, housed at New York City's Museum of Modern Art (MoMA), *My Grandparents, My Parents, and I* (1936), which prominently depicts a family tree featuring the artist's interracial heritage. After the visit, the children continued to work on their sketches, reflecting on Kahlo's style as well as who she was. A gender-nonconforming child in Martell's class found Kahlo's *Self-Portrait with Cropped Hair* (1940) reassuring and was encouraged by Kahlo's criticism and refusal to employ traditional images of women—even in 1940.

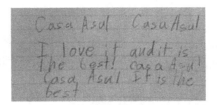

FIGURE 5.4   Song About La Casa Azul Bookstore

The children in Martell's class came to see themselves as members of a partic-ipatory literacy community grounded in the lives and work of people of color. Upon returning to the classroom, during *nuestro tiempo* (a time when students decided what to engage in), two students, Jax and Hanifah, worked on a song about the visit. As Jax came up with the lyrics, Hanifah wrote them down (Figure 5.4). The songwriting was significant to them because it allowed them to share their enthusiasm publically and to display their creativity. But it also served as an opening for an important conversation. Both of them were particularly taken by Kahlo's displays of gender and heritage, and they felt validated, Jax as a gender noncon-forming student and Hanifah as a Palestinian-American child, who sought every opportunity to talk about her heritage. As they sang the song, peers in and outside of the classroom asked them about La Casa Azul, and after a brief description, each time, they went on to describe Kahlo. Jax authored a narrative about how out-of-date traditional images of women are and how Kahlo was already rejecting them "almost like seventy years ago." Hanifah talked about having divided and intersec-tional identities, explaining, "Frida was German and Mexican. I am American and Palestinian. You don't have to be one or the other. It's who we are. We get both."

The children were clearly enthusiastic about La Casa Azul and the participa-tory literacy community it signified—in the heart of East Harlem.

Graffiti

Graffiti is a neighborhood literacy. It exists on its walls, communicating meanings and critiquing social situations. It is a powerful and often subversive participatory literacy community, albeit one often seen negatively by many in society. Despite judgments and personal opinions, the fact is that graffiti is part of the landscape of many communities. In East Harlem, there is a well-known wall called the *Graffiti Wall of Fame* (Figure 5.5).

In a New York City classroom, after reading *Maybe Something Beautiful: How Art Transformed a Neighborhood* (2016) by F. Isabel Campoy and Theresa Howell, second-grade public school teacher Alison Lanza invited her students to docu-ment art (mostly graffiti and murals) in their neighborhood of East Harlem. Lanza then invited the children to share their New York—what they heard, saw, smelled, and felt in their city. They created a graffiti board in their classroom, depicting their city, creating symbolic representations for who they are. They signed their names or added other representations of themselves within a public space (their boards). Through this action, they understood "tagging as a literacy act" (MacGillivray and Curwen 2007, 354), signing their names and embodying authorship. This is significant as they recognized that graffiti "is not simply an act of vandalism or violence; it is social practice with its own rules and codes" (MacGillivray and Curwen 2007, 354). They appropriated the *Graffiti Wall of Fame*, located a few blocks from their school in East Harlem, a longtime site where many well-known street artists displayed their skills on schoolyard walls, capturing, portraying, and re-presenting their own worlds. A social literacy practice, such as graffiti, is comprised of the "general cultural ways of utilizing literacy which people draw upon in particular situations" (Barton 2001, 96), thus departing from what would be considered typical classroom practices, yet honoring the literacy practices present in the school's community of East Harlem.

As the children learned about the rules and codes of tagging from a "graffiti elder," they came to realize how tagging is "a literacy practice imbued with intent and meaning" (Barton 2001, 354). They learned about tagging as a historical literacy practice. They explored alphabetic styles, colors, and lettering script, closely studying tagging as an "evolving symbol system" (Barton 2001, 354). They learned about symbolism and explored the ways that symbols can represent abstract ideas. With Lanza, the children explored artistry through graffiti art. They explored features of tagging. As a crew, they designated a spot in their classroom. They tagged it. They used graffiti to represent their view of New York, much like the *Graffiti Wall of Fame* represented graffiti artists' views and perspectives of their East Harlem.

In learning from their families and community members in the process of planning the graffiti wall, the children explored art and representation, as well as proportion and other mathematical concepts. They became familiar with mash-ups of illustrations and words, understanding the role of each. They engaged in coding what was important to them as a community from their individual sets of images and words portraying their New York, comparing and contrasting. They learned about and communicated through graffiti. They were "placing themselves favorably within a social network of their peers" (MacGillivray and Curwen 2007, 360), making writing more inclusive (validating graffiti in the classroom), and becoming part of a collective.

As a teacher, Lanza knew how essential it was for educators to get to know the children they teach—thinking of their students as individuals from and with whom they can learn. After all, as Gloria Ladson-Billings posits, "You have to study your students." She goes on to explain that culturally competent teachers "don't presume that just because the student is of a particular race or ethnicity, that they already know what that student is like, even if that race or ethnicity is exactly the same as theirs; they literally study the student." This is how teachers start to document and envision children's potential: by getting to know them instead of making assumptions. Lanza got to know her students by listening to and

Figure 5.5 *Graffiti Wall of Fame* in East Harlem, New York

learning from them, documenting their observations and conversations over time. She also established authentic and respectful relationships with families, regarding them as partners in education. She maintained open lines of communication with families and made time for one-on-one conversations. She used the Internet to share photos and stories of what was happening in her classroom. Instead of communicating to families that she had much to teach them, she communicated that she had much to learn from them. Lanza positioned the children she taught and their families at the center of her curriculum and teaching.

From this perspective, the mandated curriculum (or a set of so-called "best practices") should never take precedence over studying the human beings inhabiting our classrooms. As teachers, we have to acknowledge the brilliance in front of us, even if we don't yet recognize the brilliance. Ladson-Billings (2012) reminds us that we must teach as if Martin Luther King Jr., Toni Morrison, and Cesar Chavez are in our classrooms, "because they might be." And where does this brilliance come from? From homes and communities. From students' literacy and language practices. Recognizing the power and possibility of such practices is essential for teaching children as being "at promise," and rejecting the language of risk and its ideology of pathology (Gutiérrez et al. 2009).

Early Literacies as Relational Endeavors

In this chapter, we have positioned cultural practices within the context of communities as important participatory literacies to be repositioned in schooling. Through a number of examples, we investigated the relational and situational nature of early literacy through literacies present in communities. We unveiled the role of community elders in carrying on a legacy, keeping a sense of history alive, and defending their communities. Employing Rogoff's (2003) concept that learning is changing participation in communities of practice and Fisher's (2007) concept of participatory literacy communities, we went beyond neighborhood sites and signs. Finally, knowing that research on literacies "in out-of-school settings does not always translate neatly into implications for schools" (Fisher 2007, 157), we shared ways in which early childhood teachers positioned neighborhood and community literacies centrally in their teaching, learning a great deal in the process.

In the following chapter, we turn to peer literacies and explore childhood cultures as spaces for children to negotiate literacies. We extend the concept of literacy as relational, put forth in Chapter 4, and in this chapter to include literacies in communities, peer groups, popular culture, and digital platforms.

6

LANGUAGES AND LITERACIES IN PEER CULTURE

"The best fashion show is definitely on the street. Always has been, always will be."

Bill Cunningham

The late Bill Cunningham (famed fashion photographer for the *New York Times*) believed that fashion was relevant when it became trends and practices taken up in everyday life by everyday people. In other words, what becomes "popular" and considered "everyday culture" is determined in part by the ways in which people appropriate style and make it their own. Roaming the streets of New York City with a 35mm camera, Cunningham documented fashion across neighborhoods; he appreciated the originality and perspective individuals used to create personal style. He believed that runways provide ideas, materials, and inspiration, but individuals try on styles (literally and figuratively) to create personal fashion.

Whether it is fashion, music, art, electronic media, or print, culture is emergent, "through the process of everyday life, in the form of daily activities, as a frame of reference" (González 2005, 41). Therefore, our frames of reference change as new ideas widely circulate, as new movements gain traction, as available cultural tools evolve, and as practices are created anew. As Cunningham understood, culture is constructed and sustained by everyday people who make an idea popular and fashionable—it is highly dependent on people producing, reproducing, and mass-producing a cultural practice, artifact, and/or idea.

Cunningham's ethnographic documentation of fashion culture aligns with how John Fiske (2016, 16) theorizes the circulation of popular culture, "Culture is the struggle to control and contribute to the social circulation and uses of meanings, knowledges, pleasures, and values." Thus culture, and specifically popular culture, is participatory and collective. Fiske explains that individuals appropriate culture through *popular creativity*; that is, people creatively make meaning, express values, and take pleasure in cultivating resources around them (e.g., street style). When actively producing what is popular, individuals engage in *popular discrimination*—they make choices on which products to use in their immediate social situations. Simultaneously, *popular critical analysis* deepens the meanings associated with what individuals take up. Individuals make active decisions on group affiliations, cultural trends, and counter-cultural movements. Within popular culture spaces are underground cultures and sub-cultures, crucial to social life; therefore, materials cannot be distanced from uses and users. Social life as it unfolds is critical to understanding popular culture—"culture is ordinary and the ordinary is highly significant" (Fiske 1995, 335). Cunningham, then, was right in understanding that the best fashion is not on runways belonging to a select few, but on the street where the people decide what is significant.

Carnival: Playing with Popular Culture in Unofficial Spaces

Bakhtin's notion of "carnival" (1986) adds significance to the importance of popular culture or what is often referred to as common culture—the prac-tices of everyday people. Bakhtin referred to carnival as a playful, festive space where those who are not part of the ruling class would gather together, away from the confines of social order and hierarchy. Carnival, according to Bakhtin (1986), was one such "popular" space, especially relevant in medieval societies where rank, hierarchies, and social classes were pervasive. During those times, the ruling class held significant amounts of power and authority. With status came significant economic benefits: land, servants, and currency. Given the clear inequalities of medieval culture (e.g., kings vs. serfs), these gatherings allowed for the expression of alternate possibilities, underground art forms, freedom from boundaries, and the practice of excess. These carnival practices were undergirded by the notion of play—the joyous, improvised, and sponta-neous engagement of people interacting together without structure nor any particular goal/outcome (Chudacoff 2007; Garvey 1990). Instead, the non-dominant classes came together to amplify the plurality of voices—all within unofficial spaces where boundaries were overturned, and subversive and satir-ical actions were encouraged.

According to Bakhtin (1981), centripetal forces kept in place monological truths often dominated by those in power. However, centrifugal forces disrupted hegemonic spaces as people pushed against singular notions of truth. In carni-vals, individuals challenged the status quo and resisted the cultural script within unofficial spaces. In unofficial spaces (or medieval carnivals), nondominant prac-tices of revelry and play were not just accepted, they were valued as contributive in the new social order. Thus, discourse and ideas were created anew through interactions, offering new possibilities or "ideological refractions" (Bakhtin 1981; Dyson 2013). As individuals engage in creating and playing with popular culture, they transform current ideologies and create new identities that do not have to follow what is considered "normal" or "standard." For young children, play is a cultural space where ideologies are both reproduced and refracted (Dyson 2013)—they follow the status quo but also work to remake ideologies into different versions of accepted beliefs. Children's multiple voices and ideas enter into play spaces, and the ideas that are refracted back are created anew with literacy, in its various forms, as a tool. In the section that follows, we show how these ideological refractions occur.

Baby Dolls Pee, Poop, and Fart: Ideological Refractions at Table 1

The capacity to play calls for creativity and pleasure that does not always have to be rational or "make sense." In the chapter "Going Bonkers," Jenkins (2007) articulates how children watched *Pee-wee's Playhouse* for their own pleasure and enjoyment, often paying attention haphazardly to different parts of the program, be it the color schemes, the catchy sayings, or the strange characters. Rather than paying attention to the content (much of which parents did not approve), children were unstructured and exploratory in their enjoyment of the program. Furthermore, children's enjoyment of *Pee-wee's Playhouse* stemmed from a sense of autonomy and freedom as they could watch something that pushed the boundaries of adult control. Pee-wee, who was seen as a "big kid" by most of the children in the study, was a nontraditional adult who screamed loudly, wore tight-fitting suits with a red bowtie, dressed up in outlandish costumes, tricked his adult friends with glee, and promoted conversations not appropriate for the dinner table.

In the following excerpt, we bring you back to Table 1 in the midwestern U.S., where the children were talking about pooping, peeing, and farting babies. In this segment, Julie was a new member of the table (a White girl), moved from another table. While Jenkins watched children going bonkers over Pee-wee, we share children going bonkers over baby dolls. Regardless of the shifts in material culture, which like fashion may be fleeting, children use subversive humor to participate in their social worlds. Much like the children in Jenkins' work found satisfaction in watching something that adults normally prohibited, we found the children in Table 1 sharing similar sentiments—talking about inappropriate topics within their private, shared space (i.e., their table) away from the ears of adult authority.

> Jolene: I'm taking care of my babies.
> Jaquan: I got a blue shirt.
> Jolene: I'm taking care of my babies.
> Jaquan: I need me some black.
> Lou: My sister made that. [points to his writing]

Jolene: I take care of my babies.

Haeny: You what?

Jolene: I take care of my babies.

Haeny: You have babies?

Jolene: Uh-huh.

Haeny: Where?

Jolene: At home!

Haeny: How many?

Jolene: I pick them up or tell them, we have to watch a movie, and we have to pick something for the babies.

Haeny: Like baby dolls?

Jolene: No, she like to <inaudible>

Jaquan: My cat in space.

Jolene: But, my <inaudible> put her in the way.

Julie: Are they real babies? Is it? Does she poop?

Lou: Her poop?! That's nasty.

Jon: That's disgusting.

Julie: [nods her head vigorously] Now, they're making baby dolls that poop and pee when you put it, I have one at home. . . .

Lou: When you put water up in the baby doll's mouth, it pees?!

Jon: And poops!

Julie: And there's this special food, in this different one . . .

Lou: It farts! And it farts too!

Julie: Yeeaah, it's a gross baby doll [laughs]. And there's special diapers for it to go potty, and I have to put a diaper on it.

Jon: *YOU* have to put a diaper on it!?

Julie: Yeah, it's a baby doll, a baby doll, a baby doll. <inaudible>

Jon: Is it a pretend doll?

Julie: It's a real baby. I have to take care of her baby diaper. That's why I have to be a big sister.

Jon: Pee-ew! I don't get it!

When children play, they are actively constructing a shared space, free from adult-imposed limitations; instead, they engage together in activities that are "characterized by freedom from all but personally imposed rules (which are changed at will), by free-wheeling fantasy involvement, and by the absence of any goals outside of the activity itself" (Jenkins 2007, 163). Upon reading the above transcript as an adult, it can appear disorienting to understand the conversational turns in the sequence. Throughout the conversation, we see multiple topics converging in one place: being a mom who takes care of her babies (e.g., Jolene), baby dolls who poop and pee, and Jaquan's outfit as he took his cat into space. In this scenario, the children are offering up multiple topics into the conversation, some having to do with appropriating adult rules (e.g., Jolene) and others bordering on the fantastical (e.g., Jaquan), but the bodily functions of baby dolls gained the most traction.

The discussion was fluid. No one was required to stay on topic; much like carnival culture, every idea was voiced and acceptable, although not every idea was taken up. However, it is also clear that ideas were connected, borrowed, and reconstructed within the communal space. Jolene told the table about her imaginary babies—babies she took care of by picking them up, facilitating their activities, and choosing stuff for them. Her intention (from what we could tell) was not to steer the conversation in a different direction, but Julie was concerned about whether or not the babies poo, defining this action as whether or not her story could be "real." Picking up on this thread, Jon, Lou, and Julie continued to discuss the evolution of baby dolls— what we would call a philosophical rendering of how realistic some toys have become. Similarly, within the context of her (pre)school classroom, Vivian Paley, a teacher–researcher and master teacher for many decades, noticed that "the children sounded like groups of actors, rehearsing spontaneous skits on a moving stage, blending into one another's plots, carrying on philosophical debates while borrowing freely from the fragments of dialogue that floated by" (Paley 1986, 124). Clearly, from the small yet significant exchange described earlier, we see how children arrive at these unscripted moments: through flexible spaces and open exchanges.

Children's social goals are often more concerned about creating and defining their own kind of carnival experience than meeting adult-sanctioned goals and activities. In teacher Debbie White's classroom, writing workshop (an official curricular activity) often intersected with children's playful conversations (an unofficial child-initiated activity). Thus, the children at Table 1 and the rest of their peers in the classroom engaged in conversations that shifted easily from real to imaginary, jumped from topic to topic, and centered around different individuals. Within the same space and time, children were potentially talking to themselves, talking in pairs, talking as a group. The center of the conversation moved from one person to another. In our example, Julie and her two peers took over the conversation and diverted the attention from caring for babies to mocking them. Thus, in carnival culture and, in this case, in children's playful interactions, the ambiguity and unpredictability of the moment belongs to the children themselves. They are creating the experience, away from authority figures (e.g., teachers, parents, caregivers) who may facilitate and limit their activity. In this particular space, children were able to freely discuss pooping, peeing, and farting—otherwise forbidden or deemed inappropriate in the official classroom space.

Cultivating Peer Cultures: (Be)longing in Carnival Spaces

> Carnival is a way of breaking down barriers, of overcoming power
> inequalities and hierarchies. Festive life is achieved through the playful
> mockery of hierarchical order by individuals oppressed by it. Through free
> and familiar interactions, carnival offers a temporary way of experiencing
> the fullness of life. (Cohen 2011, 178)

Young children's play has often been defined in much the same way: child-initiated,
imaginary, creative, active, and symbolic (Pellegrini 1989; Sutton-Smith 2009;
Wood 2013). As the children who were members of the Table 1 learning community demonstrate for us, play (in the broadest sense) is frivolous and fun
(Sutton-Smith 2009), unbound by goals or even any kind of point—it is often a
"spontaneous, joyous activity" (Chudacoff 2007, 1). The point of playing, arguably,
is the freedom to interact with one another. Children's play spaces are a dialogic
exchange of ideas to make sense of the social and cultural world. Furthermore,
this sensemaking is validated and extended in flexible spaces where social order,
authoritative barriers, and hierarchy are broken down.

Cohen (2011) investigated the similarities between children's social pretend
play and Bakhtin's ideas of the carnival amongst preschoolers in Long Island,
New York. The school used a play-based curriculum where children were given
the freedom to construct their own play scenarios, play with whomever they
chose, and access all materials in the classroom. The teachers observed and guided
the play in unobtrusive ways (e.g., providing more materials, offering suggestions
when asked). Cohen observed children in the "family center area," which housed
typical kitchen items such as appliances, as well as a dress-up corner with costumes, fabric, and accessories. She reminds us that play is often messy, chaotic, and
disorganized, yet complex in how children use "official and unofficial discourse
to develop a sense of identity" (Cohen 2011, 189). As children prepared dinner
in the kitchen, dressed up to go to a party, or satirically reprimanded each other
for misbehavior, they were mediating available words and discourses as ways to
interpret and remake their realities. Furthermore, they were repurposing materials
to progress their own playful interactions—"underwear being worn as outerwear,
clothes worn inside out, nose picking, displaying backsides . . . on occasion they
reversed gender roles" (Cohen 2011, 184). Evident in her work is that play was
embodied by children through materials and space in order to appropriate possible roles and discourses—it was identity work (as discussed in Chapter 1).

Cultural Appropriation on Center Stage: Popular Culture, Play, and the Making of Pop Stars

Children are social beings who are competent meaning makers, interpreting their social worlds by "connecting, communicating, and declaring their

own presence, their own importance, in the social scene" (Genishi and Dyson 2009, 32). School, amongst other competent peers, is an important site for cultural production. As explained in previous chapters, when young children enter their first classroom, they come full of communicative and social practices, specific to their cultural communities (González, Moll, and Amanti, 2005; Heath 1983; Miller and Goodnow 1995; Souto-Manning 2013a)—what Moll, Amanti, Neff, and González (1992) explain as funds of knowledge. As discussed in Chapter 4, when teachers use funds of knowledge as a sociocultural tool, they situate themselves as learners who grasp knowledge from the social, historical, and cultural practices of families. Important to this perspective is a resource-oriented, assets-based view of families from nondominant communities, who speak a variety of languages, maintaining their heritage through various rituals and routines passed-down through generational knowledge, and sustaining their versions of historical knowledge. This is centered on the recognition that every child possesses "culture," and every child and family has resources (or valuable knowledge) that allows them to survive and thrive within their communities.

Thus, children's social practices begin at home and continue to widen as they walk into school (Cook 2002). In classrooms, then, children come into contact with other children who also bring with them unique sociocultural knowledge and practices. Within this space, children develop a shared culture, replete with new ways of knowing and becoming that are distinct to that particular community. While children display communicative competence within their communities, as the previous chapters revealed, children build their own peer culture through their engagement with popular culture. Over time, children accumulate knowledge, language, and practices with each other through play. Children's engagement with popular culture is just as relevant to play scenes as it is to language competence.

In the following scene, three kindergartners use common popular-culture knowledge to carry out their singing show. While the scene takes place in an unofficial moment of play, the three girls appropriate the discourse necessary for a singing show to take place. Their play relied on their language competence—the ability to recall lyrics, take on various roles, and speak to a larger audience. Haeny Yoon met Mona and her friends Tina and Jasmine while studying the intersection of writing and play in a kindergarten in the midwestern U.S. (see Yoon 2014). These three girls were a distinct social group, made clear in their group affiliations and their personal writing. They played with each other often and named each other as major characters in many of the stories they wrote. On one particular day, they set up a Fisher-Price barn with all the Fisher-Price toy people and made a stage where they were singing a song made popular that year (2007) by Rihanna (a pop and R&B artist) and T.I. (a rap artist), both popular and internationally renowned popstars.

All three girls: Mya-hee, mya-ho, mya-ha, mya-haha. Live your life, eyyy, eyyy, eyyy.

Mona: [She switches to an announcer/emcee voice and grabs a fake mic in the air.] Now . . . it's time forthe sisters . . . Tina and Jasmine. Tina and Jasmine are coming up next on the stage. They are going to sing [dramatic pause] . . . what they want to singgggg! [She looks over at them with her eyes shifting and lowers her voice.] Tell me what you want to sing. What do you want to sing? [They whisper in her ear.]

Mona: Ok, I'm goin' down on the stage and we sinnnnng!

Tina: We ready to rock with it. [Starts singing.]

Jasmine and Tina: [They start swaying from side to side in synchrony.] We ready rock with it. We ready rock with it.

Within their play, the three girls demonstrated that language practices are made relevant within a meaningful context where communicative competence is essential to participation with others. The above excerpt shows language is embedded in usage— knowing how to use language to appropriate roles and knowing when to play with the style and rhythm of words (Hymes 1972). Mona used the language of an announcer to bring the other two girls onto the stage. She made a fist with her hand, held it up to her mouth as a microphone, and looked at the audience (the Fisher-Price people); it was evident that she was familiar with the communicative style of emcees. Mona used hand gestures to supplement her talk while holding on to her pretend microphone. She also varied her cadence and volume followed by elongated stretches of words (i.e., "sinnnnng"). Furthermore, she whispered, "Tell me what you want to sing," to Tina and Jasmine, knowing that the audience should not be privy to the unscripted moments where uncertainty and mistakes are evident. Like an experienced emcee, she tried her best to move the show forward despite mishaps and seamlessly carried the "show must go on" attitude, improvising her words to move the show along.

When Tina and Jasmine took their turns, they showed similar sophistication in language as a performative practice. The intonation and variation used to sing the song—varying their voice, using gestures (i.e., swaying from side to side), and identifying themselves as singers—revealed an understanding of singing as performance. In order to participate, Tina and Jasmine needed to know the words to the song they were to sing. Additionally, they needed to synchronize their efforts; they needed to sing the words together, arrange their vocals with a similar melody, and coordinate their movements in rhythm. Thus, the girls anticipated one another's communicative moves, adjusting to each other until they were in sync.

While materials were not central to the narrative, they served as cultural tools for the scene. Materials (like ideas) are not static, but their use is flexible and dependent on the intentions of the play. Typically, the Fisher-Price barn and the Fisher-Price figures came with an intended storyline (as some toys do), but children appropriate and take over these materials in ways that make sense to them. Formanek-Brunell (1998) wrote about how boys and girls engaged in doll play that included the roles of caretaker as well as violent offenders. Girls played with dolls to uphold societal norms for womanhood in the formal space, but they also "killed them off" and created elaborate funerals for their dolls in informal spaces, away from the gaze of the adults. Thus, in the unofficial carnival space is where we witness contradiction, complexities, and resistance using material culture. As the photographer Bill Cunningham said, "the street" or unofficial space is where real meaning is explored and authenticated.

Children are constantly involved in the reappropriation of popular culture. They borrow from multiple resources in order to meet their social goals. For instance, Mona, Tina, and Jasmine used songs that were part of mainstream pop music. They constructed a stage using what was available to them: a Fisher-Price barn as a stage and Fisher-Price figures as the audience members. They took bits of dialogue from singing/talent shows that were popularized on television networks. In play, children figure out possible roles, try out new identities, enact their intentions and goals, and improvise from cultural scripts. While children live within a specific cultural frame, they can deviate from it, violate it, and resist it, creating their own social realities. They play with their own performance in the social scene where they have agency and power. Children do not passively accept the goals set out for them by the media, corporations, parents, and authorities. The resources of popular culture offer a way for children to participate in their peer culture. Knowledge of popular culture are "funds of knowledge" to enter the communities of their peers.

The social worlds of children grow to include a robust peer culture defined by media, toys, and other available materials as "textual toys" (Dyson 2003a) for participation. The content and context of textual toys may change, but children (and youth) perennially borrow from popular culture in their play and literacy. Since peer culture is "public, collective, and performative" (Corsaro 2003, 120), children depend on each other as they interact with ideas from their cultural repertoire, physical environment, and the materials at hand. In peer culture, children form distinct peer groups (e.g., Mona, Tina, and Jasmine) where materials and words signify their belonging in friendship groups.

For example, Kirkland and Jackson (2009) discussed the idea of "coolness," which the 11- to 14-year-old Black males in their study adopted to establish their manhood. They used language and pop culture to resist authority, as well as to navigate their world, exhibit resiliency, and assert strength and power. The boys used literacies to create group identity; for instance, they adopted specific styles, appropriated discourse patterns—of hip-hop lyrics (e.g., bragging), and established "cool talk" borrowed from African American Language (AAL). In addition, they drew pictures on paper, wrote on their shoes, and adopted styles associated with music moguls and sports figures. Appropriating popular culture, then, through fashion, music, and language, were "identity texts" (Kirkland and Jackson 2009, 293) that allowed them to express and construct their own style while solidifying membership within the group. The Black youth in their study used symbolic materials to script coolness, shaping and defining their identities against the current landscape of Black masculinity. The group created and enacted coolness through popular culture literacies in a "public, collective, and performative" way (Corsaro 2003, 120).

From children to young adults, we emphasize that individual *and* collective interests are ultimately the key to participation in literacies, both in and out of school (Dyson 1993; Hull and Schultz 2002; Marsh 2005a, 2005b; Millard 2004). The unofficial work of children provides opportunities to develop literacies that carry cultural capital into the official practices defining literacy (Compton-Lilly 2006; Vasquez 2004a). Therefore, educators must keep cultural forms (i.e., dialects, interests, communication, etc.) flexible, allowing for permeability between children's cultural worlds and the academic world of school (Dyson 1993). In the next section, we discuss the literacy possibilities when unofficial and official worlds meet.

Blurring the Boundaries in (Un)Official Worlds

For researchers and educators, play offers us a window into what the world looks like from the point of view of children—a point of view that is necessary in merging official and unofficial expectations (Dyson 2013). Dyson (2003a) illustrates this in the example of a first grader named Marcel, who was interested in sports. An avid sports fan in an urban school in Oakland, California, in the U.S., Marcel created multimodal texts that included a football field with all the yard lines marked (as if it was an actual football field) on a sheet of paper; he had a scoreboard written at the top of the page, and the talk surrounding this text was undergirded with sports discourse like that of an announcer. This hybrid construction was Marcel's organization of overlapping texts that included the popular media as well as his own appropriations of a football game. Similar to Mona and her friends, Marcel skillfully appropriated the practices of one cultural space (sporting event) to another cultural space (literacy event).

Ranker (2007) discovered a similar phenomenon when an eight-year-old boy, John, started to reappropriate video game texts and TV shows as an entrance into writing. Ranker's qualitative study took place at a midwestern U.S. alternative school which served children who struggled in traditional classrooms. Within an informal writing group, John drew on popular culture (as did many of the students previously mentioned) to engage in written productions. However, upon closer examination, he found that John was not simply replicating the text, but redesigning it. John borrowed video-gaming language, used characters from television/comic book series, and played with comic book forms to produce texts. John's hybrid texts (similar to Marcel's) were remixed and created anew.

Re-referencing Bakhtin's (1981) idea of dialogic, the production of any text is the "remixing" (Dyson 2003b) of several texts in one. Words and texts are always revoiced into a new version—a hybrid of multiple texts, a bricolage

(Dyson 2003b; Merchant 2007; Ranker 2007; Vasquez 2004a). In other words, a single text represents multiple texts and ideas from an available range of discourses (Bakhtin 1981). Children assemble the stories they tell, dramatize, read, and write from varied sources (e.g., popular culture artifacts, storybooks, video games). For example, Paley (1987) typifies the idea of different texts linking together to form a new one—through an example of intertexuality from a kindergartner named Charlotte. The text dictated was as follows:

> One day Princess Leia and Cinderella had a tea party. After that they went for a walk and met Scooby Doo. They said, "Hi, Scooby. Are you looking for a clue?" He said, "Yes, I'm after a mystery. A ghost is somewhere. That's why I'm walking this way." Do you want to come to a party?" said Cinderella. "Who's having a party?" "It's all yours, Scooby. It's your birthday." So they all went to the party. (Paley 1987, 92)

In the text above, Charlotte drew from multiple popular culture figures—Scooby Doo, Princess Leia, Cinderella. These characters exist apart in popular media, but find themselves together in Charlotte's story. Charlotte borrowed discourse patterns from the Scooby Doo show (e.g., "Are you looking for a clue?"), as well as that of Cinderella whose storyline in any version involves attending a party or ball. She also incorporates words relevant to the genre of Scooby Doo (e.g., mystery). Within a single text, Charlotte remixes multiple texts to create her unique version. Texts are remixed by children, whether they are obvious like Charlotte's, subtle like Marcel's, or redesigned like John's.

Remixing Star Wars: Traveling into Intergalactic Worlds

In a time of high-stakes testing and the push for young children to be print literate earlier and earlier, there is increased pressure on kindergarten classrooms to be more of an academic place than a place of play and enactment of popular culture. However, contrary to beliefs that position pop culture and academic rigor in opposition, popular culture can often be used as a mediational tool for children entering into literacy practices, as described in the previous section. Researchers who have studied children's responses to popular culture texts have shown that children actively construct meaning, and interpret and reinterpret their ideologies by interacting with popular culture (Dyson 1997; Gainer 2007; Marsh 2005a; Wohlwend 2009). Children build from each other's utterances, add on the narrative story, and continue others' trains of thought, putting their voices into the conversation as well—remixing storylines and ideas (Bakhtin 1986). Popular culture is a common backdrop for these "textual remixes" (Dyson 2003a) to occur, offering a shared context in which children negotiate and fashion interactions. The following illustrates textual remixing in the present day as children draw from various resources, including popular culture, literacy, and play to participate in their social world.

Trevor, Lucas, and Isaiah were three children with ASD (autism spectrum disorder) in an inclusive kindergarten classroom in a public school in New York City. All three were high functioning and aside from pullout services related to occupational therapy and social development, they were full members of the classroom community. In the year 2016, *Star Wars* had again made a resurgence onto the cultural scene—a movie franchise spanning generations since the original movie's release in 1977. All the children in the classroom were familiar with *Star Wars*, including Isaiah, whose exposure to television and media materials was purposefully limited. However, spending a year in this classroom meant that "the force" of *Star Wars* in classroom play was inescapable (Yoon, Llerena, and Brooks 2016).

Given Haeny's admittedly limited knowledge of *Star Wars*, Lucas educated her and one of his tablemates, Evan, about the nuances of light sabers, the Death Star, and the sordid lineage of family affiliations. Through listening to children discuss intergalactic battles and watching endless clips of *Star Wars* productions, she learned that the line between good and evil is thin and that Darth Vader was not the only figure threatening the empire. In understanding *Star Wars*, it is important to note that "TIE fighters" are not "Thai fighters" or "Tai fighters" (as Haeny originally thought) but an acronym for "twin ion engines." TIE fighters were also different from TIE bombers, a variant enabled to carry warheads and missiles. Evan and Lucas illustrated the differences. TIE bombers represented with Play-Doh by Evan (Figure 6.1) and a TIE fighter represented by Lucas on the whiteboard (Figure 6.2) add clarity to the variations in the TIE fighter line (Figures 6.1 and 6.2). The figures typify the multimodal ways that symbols are represented—in drawings and with Play-Doh (New London Group 1996; Yelland, Lee, O'Rourke, and Harrison 2008).

FIGURE 6.1   TIE Bomber

FIGURE 6.2 TIE Fighter

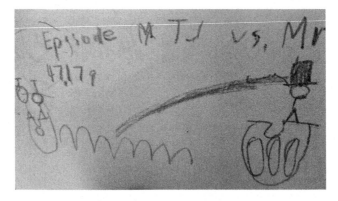

FIGURE 6.3 Trevor's Remix

Star Wars became a cultural mainstay in this classroom of kindergartners. Children used *Star Wars* materials/ideas to create elaborate *Star Wars* scenes on paper and to dramatize familiar scenes during their play. Furthermore, they used their shared knowledge of *Star Wars* to make and sustain friendships. To participate in this classroom, it was necessary for the children and adults in the classroom to have working knowledge of *Star Wars*. Throughout the year, Trevor (who was a history and geography buff) and Isaiah (who was quite the expert in the New York City subway/transit system) became knowledgeable of the *Star Wars* phenomenon to connect socially with Lucas (a bona fide *Star Wars* fan). Soon enough, *Star Wars* was remixed to create new storylines, to mix genres, and to introduce new characters. In the following scene, Trevor shared one of those remixes (see Figure 6.3).

Trevor: I'm gonna show you a really funny one in falcon.

Lucas: What?

Trevor: It is three cannons. [Lucas laughs.]

Lucas: But do you want to see something really funny?

Trevor: What?

Lucas: My Death Star's gonna be very funny. It's very funny, you know why? Because, you wanna see what it looks like? [Lucas laughs.]

Trevor: And look at, look at, um—Lucas, um, Lucas? People go on this one in falcon, they wore hats that have an arrow that they shoot out of.

Haeny: Whoa. [Lucas laughs.]

Trevor: Like this [points at the fire coming out of his figure's hat]. And they shoot fire out of it. Like this. Woooo!

Isaiah: I used the 26 for the one train. It can bend the Millennium Falcon.

Lucas: It's just so many that it just goes like this. Boing, boing, boing, boing, boing. Boing, boing, boing, boing, boing. [Lucas is referring to Trevor's picture and tracing the refracting lines with his finger.]

Isaiah: This is one thing with a Death Star and a TIE fighter.

Trevor: Um, um, um, um-Lucas? Lucas? In this episode, new characters come in *Star Wars*. Like this one. Lucas, look. Look at the episode.

Haeny: Episode 47199? 47 thousand—

Isaiah: One. Look which episode. 0–6. Episode 6. [Isaiah refers Haeny to his paper.]

Much like the idea of carnival presented at the beginning of this chapter, Trevor created a story that tried out different possibilities for an adapted *Star Wars* storyline—he added new characters, altered the genre, and remixed materials so that people stood on cannons, hats shot out lasers; and instead of typical shooting sounds, they went "boing." His satirical account resembled a recognizable version of *Star Wars*, mixed with his own creativity and imagination (Bakhtin 1981). In this version of *Star Wars*, he offered his classmates an alternate way to play out this familiar tale—an offering that Lucas accepted with his subsequent "boings." Throughout, we see the "chaos" that was typical of carnival culture—improvisation and multiple voices. Isaiah attempted to insert his story into the mix, Lucas participated in claiming a similar genre (e.g., "My Death Star's gonna be funny"), and Trevor continued to insist on bringing them both into his world. Their play was more about exploring and enacting creativity and traversing boundaries rather than reenacting the storyline offered by George Lucas, the writer and director of the *Star Wars* series. Popular culture, therefore, is not defined by artifacts and objects. Children negotiate meaning when they transact with these materials for a purpose and use it in their everyday lives (Dolby 2003). They borrow ideas from close-at-hand people (peers), and also from the popular media, producing a remixed version of these multiple voices.

While some of the children informed me that *Star Wars* could be scary, violent, and even bloody, Trevor flipped the genre to make his "episode" funny. Trevor eventually named the character in his remix "Mr. Jabes" and adopted the language of the *Star Wars* genre (e.g., versus, episode, and falcon) to create his scene. Isaiah, in his effort to join in, showed his drawing (which clearly was a picture of a train in the subway stop), pointing at the Death Star and TIE fighters in his remix of *Star Wars*—"episode 6." In his story, the train could bend the Millennium Falcon, Han Solo's famous spaceship from the original *Star Wars* movie (the Millennium Falcon also appeared in four additional *Star Wars* movies through 2015). These three texts were remixed, meaning that traces of their conversations were visible on each of their texts.

All three of the children had little firsthand experience with the movie franchise. In fact, Lucas told me that he could only see the preview because the whole movie was scary and violent, according to his mother. However, the popularity of *Star Wars* made materials, storylines, and ideas accessible to young children. For instance, *Star Wars Rebels* was a cartoon version of *Star Wars* featuring younger versions of the characters. Action figures, Lego sets, clothing, and other consumer goods allowed children to participate without ever viewing the feature films. For someone like Isaiah (whose exposure was minimal), ideas, symbols, and characters were cultural knowledge—funds of knowledge taken up and accumulated through interactions with his peers.

Lucas's drawings of some of the major characters in *Star Wars* served as a "cheat sheet" for those unfamiliar with the *Star Wars* franchise (see Figure 6.4). Lucas was a guide to the galaxy; whether he knew it or not, his willingness to sit down with Haeny, create a reference sheet, and talk her through the intricacies of *Star Wars* was both an act of literacy and an act of social connection. He brought her into a world that was clearly outside of her own experiences.

FIGURE 6.4 Lucas's Reference Sheet

Popular Culture in the Social Life of Children: Children's Cultural Communities

Popular culture, then, is not something that is done *to* children, but it is the result of what is done by children who have "minds and social agendas of their own" (Dyson 2003b, 102). Furthermore, the multiple worlds of children converge rather than occur in separate spaces. For children, these cultural worlds are interwoven, flexible, and permeable (Dyson 1993). We (like many popular culture scholars) are not promoting an "anything goes" attitude toward popular culture, but we are promoting an acceptance of these popular cultural forms as a springboard for entrance into critical literacy (Dyson 1997; Evans 2004; Vasquez 2004a, 2014). Involvement in popular culture is more than just greed or indulgence, but a desire for a community with other like-minded people (Seiter 1995). As children create peer cultures based on these cultural icons, they desire to participate in other children's social worlds and move further away from adult "authority, seriousness, and goal-directness" (Seiter 1995, 50).

As we reenter Debbie White's kindergarten in the midwestern U.S., we can see how in the beginning of the school year, the children at Table 1 simultaneously discussed canivalesque and seemingly inappropriate conversations around bodily functions as they participated in official literacy periods (e.g., writing workshop). Throughout the year, the diverse group of students at this table debated important topics during their writing times, ranging from marriage, sibling relationships, out-of-school activities, and even God (as shown in Chapter 1). Children built community when talking with each other about baby dolls and other resources of popular culture, creating commonalities and connections that might otherwise be absent. The children at this table came to each writing time with the intention to socialize and contribute to the Table 1 learning community. Talking during writing was an important part of participating and belonging with their peers.

Similarly, Mona, Tina, and Jasmine (kindergartners in a different classroom across town) cultivated their friendship group throughout the school year. They built their friendship around shared interests of fashion and pop music. They used literacy to embody their favorite popular culture icons (e.g., the singing show), but they also used formal literacy in many ways to strengthen their affinity group. They included each other in both oral and written stories—they gave each other invitations to birthday parties, drew each other into storylines, and intentionally excluded from the stories those who were not part of the group.

Finally, within the context of an inclusive kindergarten classroom in New York City, Lucas, Trevor, and Isaiah revealed the cultural capital of *Star Wars*. To find one's voice in this classroom and to be included as a member of this particular social group meant that children engaged in what was popular in the classroom. *Star Wars* was an artifact that represented the social complexities in the classroom. Their popular culture texts were far from trivial, but traces of the social affiliations created in the classroom.

Children are involved in ongoing interactions, using available resources to navigate relationships, form social affiliations, understand their worlds, and find their place. As children author cultural communities, they actively choose and decide what they will take up, how they will go about using cultural tools, and whom they will use these tools with. They remix popular cultures in their social lives and in the fabric of their peer literacies.

Such remixing has been documented elsewhere. For example, in *Writing Superheroes* (1997), the second-grade children in Oakland, California, in the U.S. composed writing pieces to "adopt, resist, or stretch available words" (Dyson 1997, 4). In this classroom, participating in the world of X-Men and ninjas was a "ticket" to enter into social life. Children's stories largely consisted of X-Men adventures revolving around X-Men characters that many of the children became familiar with over time. Composing X-Men stories held cultural capital in the classroom; telling or writing an X-Men story gave children power and attention in the classroom. During Author's Theater, a time set aside to act out written stories, children clamored for parts in others' X-Men stories. They often used these stories to initiate new friendships, please one another, and contribute to the social landscape—a "ticket" that signified belonging in the classroom community. When the same boys continued to include each other in their stories, Tina and Holly (two African American girls) wrote their own X-Men stories that allowed their participation in an event that usually excluded them. They creatively wrote in parts for themselves, actively constructed strong female roles, and rewrote the story arc for the hero. Their remixed pieces came to the forefront of the classroom community as their classmates were vying for spots in their piece. Not only did this give Tina and Holly status in the classroom, it also gave them new responsibilities of managing the roles, negotiating relationships, and asserting authority with their own written attempts. X-Men texts became a powerful literacy tool of belonging and participation. Similarly, baby dolls, pop stars, and *Star Wars* were tickets for participation and belonging within the classroom settings featured in this chapter. In all of these examples, individuals were creating for themselves a space to try out different identities and scenarios in the company of others who shared similar social circumstances.

Literacy is useful to young children when it is about "mobilizing agency and available resources in familiar, intention-driven, communicative situations" (Dyson 2003a, 106). Therefore, while the material and scripts are written by producers and marketers of these popular culture icons, children actively seek to author their own identities within their play and literacy. Belonging in peer culture is exemplified in children's engagement with material objects as they play around with images, ideas, and roles (Seiter 1995). Returning to the idea of literacy as a tool for "reading the world" (Freire 1970), we attest that the world is ever expanding for children because of social media, digital tools, and other materials within the cultural milieu of childhood. With these "new literacies" (New London Group 1996) readily available to children, the child is both exploited and empowered (Buckingham 2011), both a consumer and producer. Gainer (2007, 112) adds: "Children are active interpreters of texts who engage in a complex transaction where they are influenced by the messages while at the same time resisting them." While problematic messages are undoubtedly communicated in various media platforms, we have shown in this chapter that children engage and disengage with cultural material in agentive ways.

In free spaces of writing, talk, and play, children are bringing together the unofficial material of popular culture with the official material of school literacy (drawing, writing, reading, and oral language). "Young children are growing up in a time when literacy practices and textual productions are in flux, and they bring to school a range of textual experiences and symbolic tools" (Dyson 2008, 119). Children's literacies infused with cultural resources—an enactment of the media, peers, and materials surrounding their everyday lives. Children clearly build from a cadre of multiple available resources, and play allows them the space to organize those resources, reappropriate their use, and remix their content. They bring their play practices from out-of-school spaces to the stage of the classroom where formal literacy practices immerse with the stuff of everyday (Marsh 2005a, 2005b). Most importantly, the "stuff" characterizes the social worlds of young children. Like the photographer Cunningham, we document and present how children use literacy to "try on" these cultural materials to belong, participate, and contribute to their peer cultures. We look at how children locally produce their own set of practices, "fashioning" their own cultural scene.

In this chapter, we explored childhood cultures as spaces for children's construction of language and literacy repertoires, unveiling how children accumulate practices as they participate within and across varied cultural spaces and multiple communities. As in Chapter 4 and Chapter 5, Chapter 6 reaffirms children as active and capable members of multiple communities. As we turn to Part III, we engage in rethinking school literacies in ways that challenge reductionist literacy practices. In doing so, we examine the potential of curriculum, classroom interactions, and research in bringing theories and practices together to create productive and authentic spaces for children to practice multiple literacies.

PART III

Rethinking Early Literacies: Children's Literate Identities in Contemporary Times

In Part III, we rethink school literacies and challenge reductionist practices shaping children's identities. We consider the complexity of children's literate identities and challenge socially constructed literacies related to gender, race, socioeconomic status, and linguistic varieties. Drawing on examples presented throughout the book, coming from infants, preschool, and kindergarten through second-grade classrooms, we seek to unveil the ways in which young children capably orchestrate complex literacies. In doing so, we theorize from the examples we present and make visible the ways in which children critically negotiate multiple spaces and construct multiple sets of participatory rules (Bhabha 1994; Gutiérrez 2008; Gutiérrez, Morales, and Martínez 2009), even within current social and political discourses and policies which seek to standardize and constrain possibilities. We examine the potential of curriculum, classroom interactions, and research in bringing theories and practice together in ways that create productive and authentic spaces for children to practice multiple literacies.

In *Chapter 7: Rethinking (Pre)School Literacies*, we interrogate narrow ideas of literacy (as conceived by curricula and assessments) and consider literacy as a complex set of *changing* practices used to participate in the sociopolitical context (Apple 2004; Souto-Manning 2007; Yelland et al. 2008; Yoon 2013). We re-examine the disconnect between school literacy and contemporary times. We consider curricula as ideologically positioned to reduce literacy to the "basics" (Dyson 2013). Thus, we explore possibilities for making curricula "permeable" (Dyson 1993) as well as negotiating literacy through dialogic interactions (Souto-Manning 2010b, 2010c; Vasquez 2014).

In *Chapter 8: Reproducing and Challenging Societal Literacies*, we critically examine dominant ideologies, which pervade societal perceptions and dominant definitions of early literacy. We discuss the complexity of children's literate identities, moving beyond standardized, fixed measures of linguistic competence towards a more nuanced, fluid understanding of languaging competence. We refute the problematic idea of a word gap, and build on Ladson-Billings' (2006) concept of "education debt," to establish the understanding that there is no word gap, but a language debt owed to minoritized individuals and communities in society.

We conclude with *Chapter 9: Orchestrating Complex Literacies: Considering the Power of Young Children's Repertoires and Identities*, where we rethink the world that children in contemporary society encounter to understand shifting notions of literate practices and their use. We adopt "third spaces" as a negotiable space where children and teachers orchestrate and construct multiple sets of participatory rules (Bhabha 1994; Gutiérrez, Baquedano-López, and Tejeda 1999; Gutiérrez 2008). In doing so, we consider political policies related to young children's literacies. We address questions such as: What are teachers to do in the midst of conflicting ideologies about literacy? How do teachers negotiate standardized literacy curricula with diverse sociocultural language practices?

7

RETHINKING (PRE)SCHOOL LITERACIES

As we reenter Debbie White's kindergarten in the midwestern U.S., we hear her signaling to her kindergartners that writing workshop is over. She usually refers to them as "writers" and reminds them that they need to put their stories away and join her to debrief.

> Tonea: Darn! I was going to finish my story! I was gonna finish my story. I was writing words.
> Jolene: But I was already finished.
> Tonea: I am not finished! 'Cause I need to write my words. I need to write my words.
> Jaquan: I'm done Jolene. You like my story?
> Jolene: I wrote all my words.

As mentioned in Chapter 1, Tonea had been constructed as underperforming in reading and writing, based on the school district's literacy assessments. But over time, Tonea began to show confidence in her language abilities and raised her social status. Only a month earlier, Tonea had struggled to engage during writing workshop, whereas now she maneuvered her textual representations to enact stories and connect with social others. As Debbie White announced the end of writing workshop, Tonea was disappointed because she was just about to write words. She knew her stories needed to have pictures and words, and thus she needed time to complete the literacy task at hand. However, time was up, and while Jaquan and Jolene proudly announced that they were finished, Tonea's story remained a work in progress. There just was not enough time for her to bring her story to life.

While Debbie White provided space for children to move at their own academic rhythms, she was also constricted by time. Subjects, like writing, were separated into time periods. Debbie White often delivered assessments to children within specific time constraints. Children deemed unready for kindergarten were given interventions to account for their perceived deficits. In fact, educators organize schools in contemporary societies in a way that rushes and hurries children toward meeting benchmarks and predetermined standards (Genishi 1992). Thus, Tonea and other children who demand more time are labeled and categorized as underperforming because they do not have *time* to finish. Genishi and Dyson (2009) conclude that there are four goals for early childhood curricula, two of them having to do with time. They advocate for "unhurried times so that children in contemporary classrooms have possibilities to form vivid memories of childtimes" as well as encourage "practices that are worth taking time with . . ." (Genishi and Dyson 2009, 145). By allowing children the space and time to enact their literacies, we place value and worth on children's activities.

Tonea's declaration of "I am not finished" is significant in the discourse around readiness. In most discussions around kindergarten readiness, children are often asked to complete tasks quickly within a predetermined time frame. Furthermore, these readiness skills are identified along a developmental trajectory that label some children as "normal" and others as "deficient." While many standards, including the Common Core State Standards in the U.S., affirm that children move at their own pace, assessments, boxed curriculum sets with pacing guides, and the idea of "developmentally appropriate" tend to delineate those who are moving at the "right" pace from those who are moving too slowly. As Graue (2006, 53) reminds us, "[c]hildren are not like buses or trains—their timetables are gloriously quirky and often proceed at rates that veer away from the norm." Established benchmarks should thus be considered goals to work toward or "just [signal] a central tendency—something imaginary" (Graue 2006, 53)—acknowledged as social constructions. Some children will meet these goals within the determined time frame, but others will come to those goals later while simultaneously meeting and surpassing other developmental milestones.

For example, in the Illinois School Readiness Initiative report (Illinois State Board of Education 2016, 1)—Illinois is where Tonea and her friends reside—a school-ready child "arrives with strong early language and literacy skills, such as the ability to rhyme, to engage in back-and-forth communication, or to respond to simple requests." The goals outlined here for readiness typify the practices of most communities where interaction, responsive language, and expressivity are valued. However, communicative competence across communities "have their own rhythm, tempo, and volume level, their own amount of communication and interchange" (Genishi and Dyson 2009, 4). Children are developing these competencies within their homes, families, cultural groups, and communities in which language is modeled and used. Strong early language and literacy skills and conversational exchanges are strong components of communication in all familial contexts before children come to school (see Heath 1983). Within the above readiness definition, children's active participation in their own cultural contexts deems them prepared and ready for the new context of schools. However, these same children are evaluated using assessments that test their letter recognition and phonemic awareness within a short window of time; these skills become markers of language competence. Educators do not measure children's competencies against their ability to communicate in social settings (as, arguably, the report articulates); instead they measure children's competencies by timed tests that label their (in)abilities to tackle discrete language tasks.

Language Learning: Nonlinear Paths to Language Competence

It is our view that every child develops language(s) through unique pathways and progresses through literacy learning differently, at varying rates (Clay 1998; Lindfors 2008; Szwed 1981). If we see children's language development as stories, it becomes clear that their "stories are, inevitably, individual, for although every child proceeds as an apprentice, observing and performing as she moves through predictable stages, she does so in her own unique way. Each child creates language anew" (Lindfors 2008, 96).

The motivation to learn language comes from social, intellectual, and emotional pursuits as children explore the world, connect with others, and express themselves. Language develops and builds from this intentionality and from understanding how to participate in communicative events by constructing utterances to convey meaning (learning language); interpreting and organizing their culture with its physical, relational, and social realities (learning through language); and understanding the functional, pragmatic, and syntactic forms of language (learning about language) to communicate (Halliday 1980). Language, from a child's perspective, is "meaningful, contextualized, and in the broadest sense, social" (Halliday 2004, 280). Therefore, learning culture and learning language are interdependent as using language is purposeful and socially significant for participation across settings.

Children's everyday experiences involve "language-in-use"—anything that people "produce and react to, what they say and write, and read and listen to, in the course of daily life" (Halliday 2004, 284). Within each language exchange, we constantly make decisions on symbolic tools to use, modes for conveying meaning, and in which contexts we participate. Language-in-use is different from school definitions of language readiness, which may represent language as "grammar, dictionaries, random words and sentences, and monologues" (Halliday 2004, 280). In other words, language is functional as individuals use the technicalities of language for the broader participation goal of belonging.

Consider the following conversation between Mona and Corey, two kindergarten children in Illinois in the U.S. (Yoon 2014, 115):

> Mona: Oooooh! I gotta draw Ronnie [a boy in the classroom]! I gotta draw me too.
> Corey: Mona! Draw me! Did you draw me in there?
> Mona: No.
> Corey: Awww, you mean!
> Mona: I don't have to draw you if I don't want to. Don't I Tina [turning to her friend for support]? Do I have to draw him if I don't want to?
> Corey: You're mean.
> Mona: I don't want to draw you. I don't have to.
> Corey: But I want to be in there too!
> Mona: You can't just be in there. You can't just boss me around and say you want to be in there and you just be in there.

For Mona and Corey, literacy held greater consequence than just written work done at school; it was a tool to include and exclude people. Language (in this case, writing stories) represented an artifact of friendship and a risky proposition that can either be accepted or denied. As Mona so aptly said, you can't just ask to be in a story and "just be in there."

Throughout this book, many of these young children demonstrated that language in the form of texts are (re)presentations of ideas, values, intentions, and expressions. In this particular classroom, Mona held a great deal of cultural capital, but from previous chapters, we know that her peer group of Tina and Jasmine was tight-knit. To be included in Mona's story was an offering of friendship that many children like Corey desired. Corey, on the other hand, was an African American boy who educators pulled from the classroom frequently for support services related to speech and language, reading support, and social services. For Corey, asking to be in Mona's story was a plea for acceptance, inclusion in a classroom where he may already have felt excluded. Rejection from Mona's story was also a rejection of friendship that Corey took personally (e.g., "You're mean."). Similarly, Mona grew defensive by the attack on her personal character voiced by Corey. And yet, we are reminded that the rejection and personal assaults revolved around drawing figures on a piece of paper. On the surface, what we consider just a drawing held symbolic significance—"allegiance, authority, and representation, or otherwise put, question of identity, power, and text" (Collins and Blot 2003, 14) were entangled in literacy acts. Thus, literacy was much more than a technical, mechanical exercise; it was a personal, social, political, and cultural practice.

Symbolic Meanings: Experimenting with the Relational Implications of Literacy

In the next example, we return to Table 1 in Debbie White's kindergarten. For days (as introduced in Chapter 1), Lou and Jaquan were arguing about the existence of Michael Myers (a masked character from the horror film, *Halloween*). Lou turned to his tablemates, Tonea and Jolene, for support; they did not seem to be interested or helpful in his quest to win the argument. Instead, Lou and Jolene turned to official literacy skills (letters, symbols, and copying) in order to pursue a new argument (Figure 7.2). They quickly moved from Michael Myers to relational conflict.

> Lou: Ain't Michael Myers real? Tonea, ain't Michael Myers real? [Tonea doesn't answer him.] Jolene, ain't Michael Myers real?
> Jolene: [Jolene paused, looked at him.] Just work.
> Lou: Yea, you just work on your face. Okay? Go ahead! Here, make an x. [Lou makes an x in the air over her face.]
> Tonea: [To herself as she refers to her drawing] Look at mommy.
> Jolene: Check! [Jolene puts imaginary checks on peoples' faces in the air. She starts with Lou, then goes to Jaquan, then turns around and puts "checks" on everyone at the table.] Check, check. X. Check, check, check, check, check, check . . .
> Lou: I'm checking over your name [Lou pretends like he's going to write on Jolene's paper and hovers his pencil over her name, written at the top.]
>
> [At this point, Lou turns over his paper and looks at Jolene's paper, copying down some of the letters on her paper.]
> Jolene: [To Lou] What?! Are you copying me? This says I'm going downstairs with mom. I'm going downstairs with my mom. [Jolene points to her writing.] Why are you copying me? That's not your story. [Lou writes the first two letters on Jolene's page into his own: I-N-.] You have to copy your story. Don't copy mines! You have to copy your story. [Lou laughs.]
> Lou: What? [Lou laughs again.] What else? [Lou looks at her paper.] D? [Lou moves her hand and tries to copy more.]

In the above conversation, Lou and Jolene displayed a fair amount of "readiness" according to the definition shared earlier. They specifically engaged in back-and-forth conversation, infused with humor, wit, and sarcasm. They displayed both responsive and expressive language goals, indicators of early literacy benchmarks (see National Institute for Literacy 2008). When Jolene attempted to control his actions and stop the conversation by saying, "just work," Lou did not miss a beat but replied, "You just work on your face." Coupled with his sophisticated conversational move, he used an "x" to signify an insult to Jolene and drew an imaginary "x" over Jolene's face. Jolene took her turn and made imaginary checks (as opposed to x's) on others' faces, beginning with Lou. Both Jolene and Lou assigned particular meanings to symbols and letters in the above scenario.

They both revealed that print carried meaning. For Jolene, a "check" was a significant marker of one's competence. At another point during the school year, she mentioned the desire to get a "+" from the teacher by doing a *great* job. She remarked, "If you do an 'S' [meaning satisfactory], you get a check, then you get a plus for great job!" She made a "✔+"on her paper and said to herself, "You did it. You did it!" From Jolene's own words and perspective, an ordinary check was the equivalent of an "S," so she willingly gave her classmates a mark that she knew was shy of actually doing a "great job." Similarly, Lou attributed an "x" as a symbolic representation for talking back to Jolene, marking out a figurative "x" on Jolene, who needed to "work on her face." But Lou also took on and adopted Jolene's symbolic tool of a check and threatened to use it back on her.

As the scene moves on, we see literacy being used to assert power over each other. Lou, to annoy Jolene, started copying her text, as if lifting her words from her paper and taking them for himself. Jolene insisted that the story was about her going downstairs with her mom (and eventually sneaking downstairs)—a story that she herself "copied" from Angela Johnson's *Joshua's Night Whispers* (1994) (Figure 7.1). She claimed ownership of her story, asking that Lou get his own story because this one belonged to her. Lou copied and took her letters because he knew that the string of letters on the page meant more to Jolene than alphabetic script on a page (Figure 7.2). The story was evidence that she paid attention

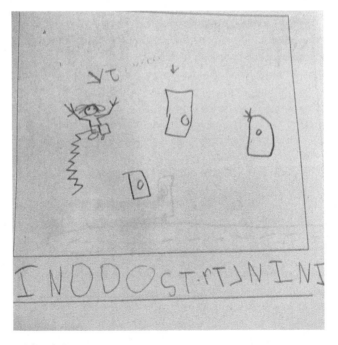

FIGURE 7.1 Jolene's Story

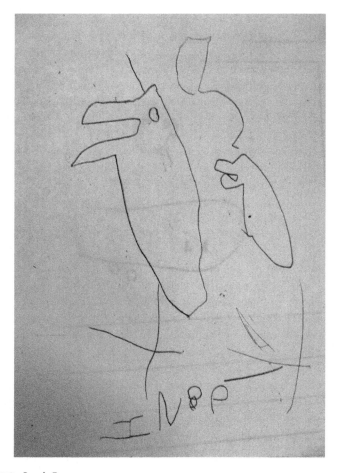

FIGURE 7.2 Lou's Story

during the lesson, that she attempted to write a complete story, that she deserved credit for her ideas, and that she just did her work as she suggested Lou should have done earlier. But—where do children get these ideas of correctness and ownership? How do they come to understand what kinds of stories are valued or what makes a story finished? In the next section, we explain the ideological underpinnings that situate Jolene, Lou, Teona, Mona, and Corey—the curriculum.

Curriculum as Enacted: Constructing and Maintaining Official Knowledge

[E]ven the most scientific matter, arranged in the most logical fashion, loses its quality, when presented in external, ready-made fashion, by the time it gets to the child. (Dewey 1902, 119)

Delivering curriculum in a logical, sequenced, standardized order is even more complicated when applied to language and literacy. Tonea, Jaquan, and Jolene implicitly viewed finished writing as evidence of success, and unfortunately, completing school-related tasks are accompanied by time limits. When children were given the space to interpret literacy tasks, Jolene and Lou showed us convincingly that literacy was a tool to yield symbolic power over one another. The relational potential of literacy was also realized by Mona and Corey, who understood literacy, particularly writing, to forge friendships and to deliberately exclude membership.

We do not deny that official curriculum or the documents, texts, resources, and materials related to what children are expected to know and be able to do are part of the "daily grind" in school (Jackson 1986). Therefore, what is classified as curricular knowledge is never neutral, but ordered by those in power. When referring to curriculum in schools, we often think of curriculum as "the knowledge, skills, abilities, and understandings children are to acquire and the plans for the learning experiences through which those gains will occur" (NAEYC 2009). This normative selection of curriculum is the official curriculum—the materials and resources that are endorsed (and at times, mandated) by schools.

In the earlier examples, there was official curriculum in place for teachers to use in many of the kindergarten subject areas including reading, writing, math, and social studies. The official curriculum is often dictated by state/national standards or claims of scientifically-based research to be enacted with "fidelity" (O'Donnell 2008). Specifically in early childhood, curriculum cannot be separated from the political discourse around readiness that was discussed earlier. Therefore, undergirding official curriculum is a hidden curriculum of values and beliefs around what is important for young children. The hidden curriculum or the dispositions, ideologies, behaviors, values, and norms necessary to be successful in school are always at play in the official classification of knowledge. Both the explicit and implicit conditions construct curriculum as a whole. When examining curriculum, "[n]ot only do we have to include content knowledge, we also have to recognize that what we teach directly implicates how we teach (pedagogy), as well as the form or structure we give to that knowledge as it is communicated" (Au 2012, 32).

Curriculum development and implementation are inherently cultural and sociopolitical productions, as schools and societies sanction what is considered valuable and appropriate for students to know and learn. In this current political climate, curriculum is becoming increasingly standardized and scripted, narrowly defining curriculum as objectives, materials/resources, and texts/manuals to accomplish various political and cultural goals: college and career readiness, global competitiveness, national citizenry, etc. Hence, "curricula are not static, neutral documents of fact, but rather dynamic, ideological, cultural artifacts that do something" (Ladson-Billings and Brown 2008, 153).

Ann Ferguson, in her ethnography of elementary-school-aged Black boys, brings into question the curricular practices that institute a "hidden curriculum" (Ferguson 2001, 2) of power structures. Rewards and punishments are handed out to rank, file, and organize children into distinct, almost impenetrable groups—leading to the success and failure of historically and socially marginalized groups (Foucault 1977). The perception at school that Black males should be feared and consequently isolated was further perpetuated by structures such as the "punishing room" (a disciplinary space) where "troublemakers" (those who misbehaved according to teacher subjectivities) were usually sent. The boys' insistence on maintaining their racial identities, using their vernacular dialect, asserting their physical prowess as males, and maintaining their reputation of being "bad boys" were the only ways that they could retain a sense of self in a system that labeled them as finished before they even started. In this sense, Ferguson (2001, 215) is right in claiming that "troublemakers are not born, they are made" by a curriculum that leads individuals toward failure.

Ferguson reiterates the troubling notion that the standardization of children and the homogenization of language and literacy practices erase diversity in the name of "sociocultural cohesion" (Graff 1987, 341). Thus, educators often use curriculum as a tool to regulate children's knowledge, behaviors, languages, and, in this case, bodies. When examining curriculum, we are also "critically concerned with what is taken to be knowledge in certain times and places rather than what is ultimately true and valid" (Kliebard 1992, 158). We add that certain groups are afforded and given different curriculum, characterized by "intellectual passivity, and ideological quietude" (Anyon 1981). In other words, curriculum for many children of color from low-income communities who speak minoritized language varieties are more regulated, more controlled, and less flexible. Just as Anyon reiterated in the 1980s while studying communities in the northeastern U.S., we see curricular issues at force when we examine dominant hegemony at work in the political and cultural spheres today.

> Class conflict [we would add race, ethnicity, language, gender, ability] in education is thus not dormant, nor a relic of an earlier era; nor is it the outcome yet determined. No class is certain of victory, and ideological hegemony is not secure. Those who would struggle against ideological hegemony must not confuse working-class powerlessness with apathy, middle class ideology with its inevitability, or ruling-class power and cultural capital with superior strength and intelligence. (Anyon 1981, 38)

Nonetheless, if given the space, teachers and children have the capacity and agency to transform curriculum by questioning whose knowledge becomes official (Apple 2004; Sleeter 2005). While structures, institutions, and those in power propagate hegemonic ideas that attempt to sustain dominance, power structures are not stable and those without institutional power are not *powerless*, as Anyon iterates. Official curriculum acts as a regulatory tool, but the creative ways that individuals engage with and interpret curriculum can help educators refocus and rethink early literacies for young children. Through interactions and improvisations among their peers, we see children making sense of official meanings, creating and recreating their own unique literacy enactments (see Souto-Manning 2010a; Yoon 2013).

Curriculum as Enacted: (Dis)ordering the Language Script

Curriculum in its enacted form is a dialogic exchange as participants (both teachers and students) give meaning to curricular documents when they interpret the "linguistic features, functions, and communicative intents" (Yoon 2013, 150). In essence, teachers are acting as curricular translators who make decisions on the words to choose, the materials to incorporate, and the ideas to take up. Despite the best-laid efforts to script teaching practices, teachers are exercising a certain amount of curricular flexibility through the process of translation.

The *Oxford Living Dictionary* defines translation as the process of translating texts from one language to another (2016). To translate is to express the sense of words or texts in another language, "rendering the meaning of a word or text." We linger on this idea of expressing the sense of words or texts, which becomes a highly complex task requiring translators to not only understand the words being written or spoken, but to extract the intent, meaning, and sense attributed to those words. Since words have emotional and ideological connotations, a literal translation would not do justice to the words represented. Furthermore, translation is complicated because those who receive those words are also making sense of them based on their experiences, perspectives, and framing (Benjamin 1968). Therefore, translations are far from perfect, much like curricular scripts are hardly foolproof. Curricula

> [P]rovide teachers with ready-made ways of dealing with the complexities of strange student populations, alien socio-cultural contexts, and peculiar learning styles. In the positivist tradition, methods are considered value-free instruments that avoid the clumsy mediation of human subjects and thus, accomplish one's objectives efficiently. Especially if these methods are formulated through systemic research, they are believed to offer final solutions to the complicated pedagogical problems. (Canagarajah 1999, 103)

We thus consider the ways in which language is ordered and supposedly delivered to children in ready-made ways via the curriculum. In the following excerpt from Arizona in the U.S., we enter a kindergarten classroom with a majority of children labeled "English language learners." This classroom was located within a context framed and influenced by regulatory measures used to create "English-only" classrooms, place bans on ethnic studies, and punish bilingual and multilingual children for their supposed English language deficiencies (Combs and Nicholas 2012). Implicit in these policies was a move toward lifting up the so-called "Standard English," placing value on the history of Whites (e.g., favoring U.S. history over Mexican American history), and diminishing the linguistic flexibility of children who communicate using multiple languages.

Unsurprisingly, within this context, language curriculum was often didactic and mechanical. Many classrooms followed similar structures to the one that follows. Literacy instruction emphasized the formation of letters, punctuation and capitalization, spacing, and other mechanical skills. This overattention to mechanics, then, was the basis of instruction, feedback, and evaluation. In this kindergarten classroom, young children made an art project representative of the holidays and seasons (e.g., an egg for Easter, a baby chick for spring, a pumpkin for Halloween). The following day the children knew to write a story about their art project using familiar guidelines: four sentences, starting with "I see" or "I like," spaces between their words, capitalization, and punctuation. These were the guidelines that teachers used to guide and evaluate children's work (see Yoon 2016). The stories consisted of a formula that the children knew very well.

This type of writing practice became an exercise that many of the children appropriated and learned over time. And while the official curriculum (as taken up by teachers) called for an attention to language mechanics, children interpreted these ideas in varied ways. For instance, Yema (a Somalian immigrant) counted up the lines (not sentences) in his story and was confused by the teacher's remark telling him he needed to have at least four sentences. When he counted his story, he had seven lines, which he thought meant seven sentences. Other children dutifully used their spacemen (a clothespin that children placed on their paper to delineate enough space between words); using the spacemen took painstakingly long, infringing on their recess time when they couldn't complete their pieces on time. Mohandus (a Somalian immigrant) and Shiksha (Indian American) used their aptness at writing letters to get through the writing task as quickly as they could—they often used the same sentence patterns and words, they attended to the mechanics without their tools (e.g., spaceman), and they placed their punctuation marks with emphasis to indicate four sentences (just in case the teacher needed clarity).

> Other children used a combination of different strategies. Some children, like Marvin, used color words because they were prominently portrayed and easy to identify. Some children used the common clauses "I like . . ." and "My egg is . . ." because it was suggested and written by the teacher. Others used sight words that were accessible as a way to complete their writing exercise. Others, like Mohandus (a Somalian student) sounded out every word, figuring that this was the most efficient way to expedite the writing process. Eventually, the stories with the supplemental art project was a rotating showcase in the hallway of the school, a marker to document the passing of time and events in the life of Williams Elementary School. It also became the kind of writing that was valued in the classroom and seen as "presentable." On any given day, a visitor could walk down the hallway and see 20 stories, written in similar fashion and accompanied by a teacher-directed art project. (Yoon 2016, 9)

Scenarios like this are commonplace in many schools and hardly limited to the Arizona context. The displayed writing sample speaks very little to children's writing process. As Yoon (2016) illustrated, most of the children created a process for writing the texts that displayed pieces hardly revealed. While looking seemingly homogenous on the surface, children's literacy acts were far from uniform when approaching the task at hand. Thus, while the teacher devised a plan (typical of writing instruction in regulated schools), children interpreted and enacted these plans with a wide range of goals, intentions, and outcomes. Therefore, children and teachers co-constructed curricular translations.

Using Official Curriculum in Authentic Spaces

After finishing the writing assignment described in the previous section, within the context of the Arizona kindergarten classroom where Marvin, Mohandus, Shiksha, and Yema were students, another student, Mark, got a notebook and a blue marker and headed over to the pocket chart where children's lunch cards and pictures were housed. He copied down some names on his notebook, children he intended to invite to his birthday party. On the list were Roland, Yema, Marvin, Dahlia, and Urie. However, instead of writing the children's first names, he proceeded to copy down each child's last name, as presented on the chart. In the pocket chart was a picture of each child with only their last name listed, not their first. B—* was Roland's last name. A—* was Yema's. S—* was Marvin's. C—* was Dahlia's. W—* was Urie's. He wrote these names with precision (as a list) and was very careful to write down the correct names because surely he was only including his friends. He said he was writing down a list of people he was going to invite to his birthday party (Figure 7.3). Mark was interested in reaching out, in taking a chance and building a social network, much like adults build similiar networks through social media and group affiliations. Upon writing down the names, he embarked on a social excursion.

He walked over to Yema and asked, "What's your real name? How do you spell it?" He knew that the names on the chart were not the first names. So, in a moment of recognition, he understood that "A—" was not Yema's "real name" or the name that he called himself on a daily basis. Yema explained to him that his last name was part of his name, but Mark kept on moving around the classroom to find out everyone's "real name." He went around confirming with the children that the last name listed represented the right person—his list was important to him and so he spent some time looking back and forth from the pocket chart, traveling from table to table, and ensuring that the children he invited recognized and confirmed their own names on the paper. Unsurprisingly, the children (including those excluded from the list) were very interested in Mark's writing. Whereas reading each other's written stories resulting from the official kindergarten curriculum often bore little significance for the children (many of them seemed to be intent on finishing quickly rather than reading each other's work), landing on Mark's birthday list held social significance.

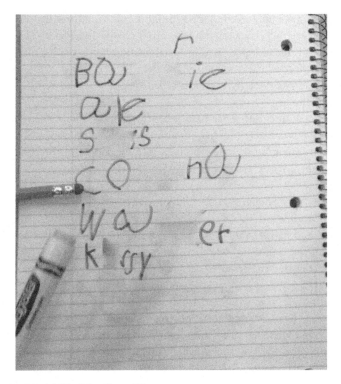

FIGURE 7.3   Mark's Birthday Party List

Johnny's name was not on the original list, so when Mark declared that he was going to invite the people on the list to his party, Johnny said he wanted to be invited. Mark resisted at first, but finally agreed to invite him after Johnny's multiple pleas. Johnny took Mark's notebook and wrote his name, but in the spirit of the author's list, Johnny added his last name, "K—," on Mark's notebook for consistency's sake. Mark read his list out loud to all that were listening, which included Dahlia, the only girl on the list. Johnny emphatically stated, "Don't invite Dahlia." Dahlia, upon hearing this, said nothing and kept working on her story. Mark looked over at her, seemed contemplative for a bit, but kept her on the list. He said that he wanted to invite her. Later on in the day, during lunch, Mark and Johnny got into an argument, leading Mark to retract Johnny's invitation. Seeing this as an opportunity, Melody asked, "Can I come to your party, then?" Mark replied, "Yes, but don't tell Johnny."

In this unofficial literacy practice, Mark's text was an artifact of social accord and discord. It was a piece of writing not to be displayed in the hallway, corrected by the teacher, or worthy of an art project. But it was a social text that accomplished several different aspects of writing as a social act: words on paper were associated with identity. The act of writing someone's name on a list was a social marker, an offering of friendship—an act of inclusion, and in some cases, exclusion. The written words also held significance as a text that moved across contexts—from the classroom to recess and to the lunchroom. The text also moved across time and space within social relationships—the list marked friendships that withstood the test of a whole day, revealed that it can be revised (by adding people like Melody), and showed that it can be reduced through social tensions and fights.

There is a distinct difference between writing as an assignment versus writing as social and cultural activities used to connect with others and to build relationships. At the same time, literacy skills related to mechanics, or the basics, as Dyson (2013) outlined in her work, were apparent and clearly recognizable:

- *Symbolic value of print*: As the children in the Arizona kindergarten described in the earlier part of this section revealed, literacy in the form of letters, words, and names were symbolically significant. That is, Mark and the children in the classroom (whether or not they were part of his birthday party list) recognized the symbolic value of print.
- *Words and letters as representative of meaning*: Names and words were meant to represent people. The words associated with Mark's friends were their last names, and while he understood that the string of letters came to stand for one's identity, he asked for their first names (another representation connoting self). It was clear that print was meaningful and stood for something or someone.
- *Patterns and repetition*: Johnny followed the pattern that Mark started when he wrote the list; instead of writing his first name, he also listed his last name. Johnny's markings were consistent with the pattern that Mark began.
- *Genre with purpose*: Mark wrote his birthday party invitees in a list form, as is consistent with the purpose of making lists. Every line had a new person's name; furthermore, Mark made an accurate and unscripted decision on his genre choice. Clearly, he chose the right format or mode for the task at hand.
- *Capitalization*: Many of the last names started with a capital letter followed by lowercase letters. Therefore, we can assume that he understood that names were capitalized.
- *Use of print resources*: While word walls, alphabet charts, color words, and other materials around the room were used to act as literacy tools, Mark attended to resources around the room, including the pocket chart intended for attendance and lunch counts. He creatively saw this chart as a useful way to meet his social intentions and goals.
- *Copying*: Copying down words from one text to another is a skill that we often ask children to do (Dyson 1985)—from copying down letters, to writing sight words. In this classroom (as in many others), words were also written down on sentence strips or on the board so that children can copy down key words (e.g., earth). Mark took up this strategy within a different context, away from a prescribed school task.

As we made visible, the kinds of authentic literacy practices in which the children engaged allowed them to move toward the use of conventions and mechanics and to negotiate their membership within and across cultural communities. They engaged with literacy practices that allowed them to participate in the social life of the classroom while also developing traditional literacy skills. For Mark and the rest of the children, writing meant inclusion in the group, an opportunity to connect socially with others, and a chance to understand the purpose of writing as a useful social activity rather than just a decodable skill to accomplish.

Similar to the context of the Arizona kindergarten we visited and the literacy practices in which kindergarten students engaged, Hull and Rose (1989) found parallel habits when working with college students in a remedial writing course— overattention to mistakes, continued structural/conventional issues, an emphasis on the form/function of language mechanics rather than content, and the fear of looking like a copier. Thus the labeling of "struggling" or failure and those of a "literate" person are attributed to these skills not just in the larger discourse, but in individual perceptions of literacy abilities in kindergarten through college. Within and across contexts, the technical aspects of language are reinforced by language instruction (e.g., teacher expectations of good writing), the language arts curriculum (e.g., four-sentence writing projects), and reductive forms of feedback and evaluation (e.g., assessment measures). We argue that these mechanical habits are often formed early, beginning with our youngest learners, who are taught that literacy is a set of skills that need to be mastered rather than an expression of meaning.

Connecting the Past, Present, and Future: Reimagining the Literacy Curriculum

Language and its use have always been about participation in social worlds. Scribner and Cole's (1981) study of the Vai people in northwestern Liberia further highlights this very notion. The Vai invented a phonetic writing system, but most of this script was transmitted to members outside of institutional settings. The Vai script was learned and passed down from one generation to the next through social practice rather than formal schooling. In this region, English was the political and economic language of power, Arabic was the religious script, and the Vai script served personal and public needs. The actual uses of Vai literacy (practical, everyday language) were learned through interactions with others in the community, making language personal and inherently social. Therefore, while the script possessed a functional, linguistic quality, the purpose of learning the script was communicative, used in daily life. Furthermore, different languages (English, Arabic, Vai) served different functions and were used in purposefully chosen instances that reflected different social practices.

Communicative competence and linguistic flexibility represent an individual's ability to use multiple modes, which are context appropriate. Most children learn to be communicatively flexible as they move between existing structures and multiple linguistic codes and dialects. Dialects, as defined by Adger, Wolfram, and Christian (2007), refer to the languages associated within a regionally or socially defined group of people. Dialects vary among speech communities (Hymes 1974) in terms of pronunciation, vocabulary, grammar, structure, and accents that participants acquire and learn as members of these communities. This problematizes the notion of a "standard" form of English since language varieties exist around the world. The idea that some dialects are perceived as better or more intellectual than others is the result of "broader social attitudes that surround language" (Hymes 1974, 11). Like the Vai, we use forms of language appropriate for social situations. Similarly, young children show competence as they move across different communicative situations, especially those who speak multiple languages, revealing abilities to switch among codes, modalities, and styles.

However, placing value on specific forms ignores the situated nature of languaging. For example, African American Language is often met with racial prejudice and stereotyping in mainstream ideologies (Adger et al. 2007; Delpit and Dowdy 2008). These stereotypes lead to assumptions about intelligence, class, and social status, making it especially troubling for young children of marginalized and minoritized speech communities. Making judgments on appropriate forms of language and their usage are not simply corrections of linguistic formalities or syntax, but a correction of an individual's sense of self and culture. Language is a social and interactive process of participation. On one hand, children learn the language of their communities, and participate in the registers and dialects of these communities to become competent language users and active participants. On the other hand, those who possess power control, distribute, and regulate literacy, inflating and deflating certain types of literacy. Thus, language is deeply connected to identity, culture, belonging, and power (Canagarajah 1999; Collins and Blot 2003). Ferguson (2001) draws upon this when she illustrates the ways in which children used language to represent and assert themselves against the authorities in school. Many of the boys used African American Language to form group identity and show solidarity in their experience. The boys were intentional with their talk, using language as an expression of self and a mechanism for excluding outsiders—as a marker of belonging. Their language and literacy choices were intentional.

Whereas once literacy was seen as a way to participate in religion, then to participate in government, and then to establish community, it is now also a way to produce practices relevant in the digital age. "Cultural and social organizations of a particular economy create reservoirs of opportunity and constraint from which individuals take their literacy" (Brandt 2001, 207). Becoming literate is not simply a description and knowledge of surface-level features, but knowing how people use languages and present them as texts. Literacy is multiple—literacies—as the discourse changes from moral literacy to digital literacy to school literacy, essentially defining literacy as "any body of systemic useful knowledge" (Collins and Blot 2003, 3). For instance, learning the discourse patterns, the participation norms, textual scripts, and the digital publishing required to participate in social media is a relevant and contemporary literacy practice.

Consequently, literacy changes across time, space, and community. It does not remain the static set of skills that school curriculum promotes. Social participation requires individuals to move beyond a fixed skillset toward maneuvering literacy flexibly and creatively across various social contexts. To reimagine literacy for young children requires paying attention to the language-in-use rather than narrowly focusing on "proper" language usage. Lou and Jolene showed us in the beginning of this chapter that letters and words are symbolically useful and powerful. Tonea's attempt at writing words in order to finish texts leads us to question our ideas about language-in-use: Is time really the ultimate marker of doing literacy right? Are Jolene and Jaquan better at maneuvering texts because they finished faster than Tonea who really wanted to write words with her picture to communicate a story? In the Arizona kindergarten, are those who picked up quick strategies in order to finish faster, more literate than those who took their time to write creative stories?

> Rather than teaching rules in a normative way, we should teach strate-
> gies—creative ways to negotiate the norms operating in diverse contexts.
> Rather than developing mastery in a "target language", we should strive
> for competence in a repertoire of codes and discourses. Rather than simply
> joining a speech community, we should teach students to shuttle between
> communities. Not satisfied with teaching students to be context-sensitive,
> we should teach them to be context-transforming. (Canagarajah 2003, xiii)

Official Curriculum at Work: Children Enacting Curricular Goals

Basic skills and language mechanics have a place in the literacy learning of young children. Learning the common rules that institutions require for participation are especially important in giving children access to the language of power (Delpit and Dowdy, 2008) and the language of the wider culture (Adger et al. 2007). Within social settings, children have the opportunity to use these skills with purpose and vitality. Mark used literacy skills for a social purpose. He experimented with genre, encoding, and representation for a larger purpose than just getting it right. In the final example, we return to Lou and Jolene as they engaged in official literacy tasks. The conversation between these two children exemplifies the permeability of official and unofficial worlds. Rather than dividing children's cultural worlds between school culture and children's culture, we have argued that children fluidly take up cultural tools within their unofficial social worlds. These two children saw writing as a time to play just as much as they saw writing as a time to work. We interrupt their play to show an example of how official literacy tasks permeated their cultural space (Figure 7.4).

FIGURE 7.4 Lou's Story

Lou: How do you write wuh?

Jolene: Huh?

Lou: How do you write wuh?

Jolene: Wuh?

Haeny: Like walking? Right? What word do you want Lou?

Jolene: Wuh? W.

Lou: I was walking to tree.

Haeny: So, was?

Jolene: W.

Lou: I already wrote the W. [Lou does already have this on his paper.]

Jolene: I.

Jon: Now I'm on my third page. I'm getting busy on it. I'm really getting busy.

Lou: K? K? [Lou thinks he hears a "k."]

Jolene: No, no, wait, wait. W-I-K . . .

Lou: I already wrote I and K and W [In fact, Lou did do this.]

Jolene: Okay, K.

Lou: K?

Jolene: Ah. Wuh-k-ing.

Lou: What else . . . I don't—Oh [Lou looks up at the chart that Debbie White put up on endings.] Ing! I-n-g [Lou points to it.]

Jolene: Ing. Like "ing" on the wall.
Lou: I.
Jolene: I-N-G.
Lou: I:I:I:I. I . . . am . . . walking.

Throughout most of the year, these children deliberated over popular culture icons, towed the line between reality and fantasy, argued over just about anything and everything, and engaged in philosophical wonderings of all sorts (see Chapter 1). Embedded within these socially constructed events were moments like the one above, where they discovered literacy on their own terms. These discoveries were nonlinear, meaning children rarely understood literacy in a predictable, developmental progression. Instead they were spontaneous and largely tied to social motivations (e.g., birthday invitations) or within social circumstances like this (Figure 7.4). Just like in Bakhtin's carnival, children moved from joking around and laughing to writing down letters. They weaved back and forth from completing and engaging in literacy tasks to play and social interactions. Kindergarten teacher Debbie White, instead of worrying about children staying on task, allowed for permeable boundaries where children could freely move back and forth. Lou, in the above example, showed language proficiency across several mechanical skills valued by the curriculum: beginning sounds, middle sounds, word endings, capital letters, use of print resources, transferal (copying down letters). Regardless of his sophisticated communication skills and social capacity, he could often be mistaken as having deficits in literacy. He often sidelined his writing productions in favor of talking and playing with his friends at the table. He rarely finished a piece of writing and was not "getting busy on it," as Jon mentioned. However, it was clear that he was knowledgeable about the basic skills that educators expected children to know.

Permeable Textual Boundaries: Opening Up Spaces for Literate Identities

Vasudevan, Schultz, and Bateman (2010) studied fifth graders' multimodal compositions as sedimented identities on texts, arguing for opening up possibilities for children to share, write, and author their lives. Like Lou in the previous example, children displayed a myriad of literacy skills when flexible spaces allowed for authentic practice. While many scholars articulate the scripted, standardized practices that often define language arts, Vasudevan et al. (2010, 446) show possibilities for children's composing. They argue for the "productive disruption of these normative definitions of what it means to be literate within classroom boundaries" as a way to reconceptualize literacy for children in diverse times. Literacy, according to their work, is embedded in the lives that students create between multiple spaces that are "increasingly permeable and overlapping" (Vasudevan et al. 2010, 462).

As iterated multiple times throughout this book, a "funds of knowledge" (González, Moll, and Amanti 2005) approach to identity presumes that children come to school with resources, practices, linguistic capabilities, and cultural experiences that contribute to their literacy development. A teacher's role is to foster "complex scenes that are spacious enough for children's diverse ways of being" (Genishi and Dyson 2009, 10), giving them opportunities to carry out personal literacy intentions. Underlying this notion is that children's range of literacy enactments in diverse forms should influence our understanding of what counts as literacy, interrogating our own preconceived notions of what practices we deem worthwhile.

Permeable textual boundaries are vital to the lived experiences of children's identities, but in many cases, these boundaries are narrowed by perceptions of children as innocent and incapable, uncritical of their world (Jenkins 1998). Arguably, children's literacies upon entering school are often highly regulated, as adults feel obligated to apprentice children into school-approved literacy practices, oriented toward basic skills (Dyson 2013). Attached to the "back-to-basics" orientation are discourses on achievement in the U.S., related but not limited to "readiness" discourse (Graue 2006), perceptions of achievement gaps (Delpit 2012), and threats of international competition (for the U.S., with Finland and Singapore). However, as we have learned throughout this book, children draw on a combination of materials/resources, tools (including school literacy), time, and space to "expand their identities as writers and enact multiple ways of communicating" (Kuby, Gusthall-Rucker, and Kirchhofer 2015, 415).

As we continue to learn from diverse children's rich literacies and sophisticated language practices, in Chapter 8 we problematize dominant ideologies, which pervade societal perceptions and definitions of early literacy.

NOTE

* Full last names are hidden to protect student's anonymity.

8

REPRODUCING AND CHALLENGING SOCIETAL LITERACIES

> In order to transform schools into democratic sites, we must analyze and
> understand the structural and causal realities that produced undemocratic and
> unequal schools in the first place. Thus, on the one hand, it is imperative to
> analyze and describe the social and historical conditions of the United States
> so as to explain the ideology that produced undemocratic schools and is
> presently reproducing educational inequalities through systemic mechanisms.
> On the other hand, educators need to also understand the students' cultural
> production, including their resistance, and develop pedagogies that speak to
> the reality of the culture produced by students. (Macedo 1994, 171)

Literacies produce and reproduce identities, ideologies, and epistemologies.
They can liberate some while oppressing others. Individuals and communities
define literacies within the context of structures in societies (Archer 2000, 2003).
Literacies influence the "production of ideas, of conceptions, of consciousness"
(Marx 1998, 42) and inform what we say, imagine, and envision.

Literacies inform and are informed by systems of ideas and beliefs and in
turn inform our ideas and beliefs about how the world works. "Literacy—of
whatever type—only has consequences as it acts together with a large number of
other social factors, including political and economic conditions, social structure
and local ideologies" (Gee 2015b, 65). That is, experiences and theories play an
important role in the claims we make to justify our beliefs, and are all located
with an organized structure or system of integrated sociocultural and political
claims, concepts, ideas, and purposes. Literacies are thus highly historicized and
racialized.

While we have dedicated much of this book to unveiling the ways in which
young children, families, and communities—especially those from minoritized

backgrounds—produce powerful literacies and are agents, in this chapter we focus on the ways in which literacies (re)produce who we are as individuals and cultural groups and how we are positioned in the world. This is framed by an ideology of neoliberalism (Yelland and Kilderry 2005). Neoliberalism is "the most dangerous ideology of the current historical moment" (Giroux 2002, 425), as it ideologically revisions the very meaning and purpose of education while also cultivating neoliberal attitudes and pedagogies. Instead of seeing education as inherent to a democracy, it seeks to prepare workers who are "ready" for the workplace. Neoliberalism replaces civic engagement and participation discourses with discourses of commercialization, privatization, and deregulation (Giroux 2002), which are central to corporate cultures. Students are positioned as objects, meeting the needs of corporations. Teachers are positioned as technicians. For teachers and students, curriculum has been narrowed because of neoliberal pedagogies and attitudes (Apple 2006, Yelland and Kilderry 2005).

Neoliberalism takes root through a variety of actions grounded in the commercialization of education (Giroux 2002) and is instantiated through concepts such as the "language gap" or "word gap," which blame families and children for the supposed word gap they possess instead of positioning historical injustices as obstacles to learning (discussed later in this chapter). A neoliberal ideology fails to acknowledge the segregationist nature of (pre)schools, neighborhoods, and societies (discussed throughout this book). Instead, it sponsors a grand narrative, which weaves together "'back to the basics,' 'grading kindergarten,' and 'no child left behind' to defend testing and stringent accountability measures" (Yelland and Kilderry 2005, 2). As a result, neoliberalism narrows and dehumanizes teaching and teachers.

At its roots, neoliberalism excludes cultural values inherent in populations of color—such as interdependence, collaboration, and familism (which mark Latinx and African American communities, for example). Instead, it assumes competition "as a defining characteristic of human relations" (Monbiot 2016) without acknowledging the cultural nature of such a statement and operating ethnocentrically. It frames citizens primarily "as consumers, whose democratic choices are best exercised by buying and selling" (Monbiot 2016). It propagates racist myths, such as meritocracy—that is, dominant populations and individuals convince themselves that their accomplishments and social locations are unswervingly linked to merit, without any acknowledgment of racial privilege and intersectional notions of superiority and inferiority; such discourses colonize minoritized populations and individuals, who even come to blame themselves for failing instead of recognizing how the system was stacked against them.

Neoliberal ideologies exist in discourses which re-produce inequities. Young children, families, and communities are discursively constructed in particular ways and attributed identities. These discursive constructions are foundationally informed by epistemologies, which are "concerned with providing a philosophical grounding for deciding what kinds of knowledge are possible and how we can ensure that they are both adequate and legitimate" (Maynard 1994, 10).

At times, these discursive constructions are dismissed as "just words," without the recognition that uttering words often leads to acts and actions (Austin 1962). As Fennimore (2008, 190) reminds us, "language is a form of cultural power that serves to retain and reinforce structures of stratification and privilege."

Ideologies informing discourses are drenched in cultural assumptions—whose knowledge is legitimate, who is capable, etc. From a neoliberal ideological perspective, discourses of inequity are justified under the guise of "choice" and other code words and firmly grounded in a system of meritocracy. Minoritized individuals are positioned as choosing not to work hard enough, choosing to live in government-assisted housing, choosing not to go to college without any regard for racist legacies (such as slavery). These very neoliberal ideologies are omnipresent in discourses framing early literacy and early schooling in the U.S. and throughout the world. They continue to position children whose families and communities have been historically minoritized as lesser than, without acknowledging the "power relations and processes by which certain groups are socially, economically, and politically marginalized within the larger society" (McCarty 2002, xv).

In this chapter, we reflect on the sophistication of early literacy practices portrayed in Part I of this book and on the (r)evolution of the concept and definition of early literacies, which we defined as inherently relational (Part II). Now we focus on challenging societal literacies and ideas, which justify and reify problems affecting education and society writ large. That is, we explain how discourses such as the achievement gap and notions such as remediation, both of which pathologize minoritized individuals and populations and blame them, are problematic and colonialist; they serve to excuse societies and their structures from any answerability or responsibility. After all, from a neoliberal ideological standpoint, inequities in society are recast as righteous. They are justified by the myth that individuals and communities receive what they merit, without any acknowledgment to the systems of oppression we discussed in Part I and Part II of this book. We reaffirm our belief that this myth is highly exclusionist and racialized, and it is meant to keep the status quo in place and to strip democracy of its very purpose. Through examples, we discuss the complexity of children's literate identities, moving beyond standardized, fixed measures of linguistic competence toward a more nuanced, fluid understanding of language competence. We also challenge reproductive practices that perpetuate gender, race, and class stereotypes (Blaise 2012; Delpit 1995, 2006, 2012; Dyson and Smitherman 2009).

Literacies of Power—Or Literacies of Those Who Have Power

Who gets to define which literacies are worthy? Which literacies are more sophisticated? Which have more power? These are key questions in redefining literacy more broadly. Throughout this book, we have shown many examples that elucidate how literacies of power are the literacies of those who have power.

We make this visible here, as too often the literacies of those who have power are unproblematically upheld as the rule against which all other literacies are rated—without a clear understanding of how power in society influences concepts and definitions of best, appropriate, and right.

Although many of today's educational inequities are blamed on a supposed gap, we posit that there is no gap. Rather, there is a debt to minoritized children, their families, and communities. There is a lack of understanding and valuing of multiple literacies (note that there is more than one literacy, as affirmed throughout the book). Over time, as more investments have been made in the practices of the dominant class, more value has been attributed to their practices.

The reason why so many children of color and other minoritized groups are deemed to be failing in schools, not developing as readers and writers (per the school-sanctioned definition of literacy), is that there is a misalignment between the sophisticated and rich literacies young children from nondominant and minoritized backgrounds enter early educational settings with, and what is valued by their teachers and administrators (see Chapter 7). A norm for literacy practices is thus defined based on the literacy practices of those in power. This norm defines what is best and what comprises developmental appropriateness—albeit in highly cultural ways. Delpit (1988, 283) explains:

> Children from middle-class homes tend to do better in school than those from non-middle-class homes because the culture of the school is based on the culture of the upper and middle classes—of those in power. The upper and middle classes send their children to school with all the accouterments of the culture of power; children from other kinds of families operate within perfectly wonderful and viable cultures but not cultures that carry the codes or rules of power.

When linguistic diversities are not understood and valued, young children may be excluded from schooling and schools (Souto-Manning 2009a). This is the case of an African American kindergartner, George, who had not previously been exposed to institutionalized, dominant American English. During his kindergarten year, he spent most of his school days in detention due to the fact that his language practices were misaligned with those of his teacher, the dominant language practice in place (see Chapter 3).

George was a public school student in Georgia in the U.S. He had grown up not far from the school he attended, but in a distinct communicative universe. This caused him to be constructed by his teacher as a behavior problem, not because of how he intentionally behaved, but because he was unaware of the conventions inherent to dominant American English. Again and again, when his teacher asked him if he would like to sit, for example, he understood this polite middle-class request (marked by indirectness) as a real question, which prompted him to respond with his honest and preferred answer, "No, ma'am." This happened again and again—more than half of his kindergarten days. Whenever he answered a question used as a polite request with the teacher's least preferred answer, defying the expected adjacency pair, he was seen as defiant by the teacher, for "talking back." He was then sent to time out. On his way to time out, he tried to explain that he was only answering a question, but his fight to communicate was seen as his behavior "escalating to the next level," and he was sent to the Opportunity Room (also known as detention). While some may be tempted to say that he was resisting through defiance, in talking with George, it was clear that no one had taken the time to teach him the rules of the language of power (Delpit 1988). Here is an interaction, which took place between George and Jordan, a White classmate who was facilitating calendar time (a common fixture in U.S. primary grades— also known as morning meeting—facilitated by teachers and/or students) in first grade. George elucidates his learning of the language of power:

> Jordan: Would you like to sit down?
> George: You know, you aks me if I want to sit down, right?
> Jordan: Yes, please.
> George: So then, this a question or you tellin' me to sit down?
> Jordan: I am asking you to sit so that I can get on with calendar.
> George: Then just tell me to sit down.
> Jordan: Then I'd be rude.
> George: Not in my momma home. You want me to sit. I will. You don't care if I wanna sit. It just a different way of aksin', you know. I get it. In kindergarten I didn't know. But I ain't dissin' you or you momma.
> (Souto-Manning 2009a, 1090)

Prior to schooling, George had been socialized into direct communicative practices that were not aligned with the school discourse (Gee 1996). In kindergarten, he was initially unaware that his teacher's questions were in fact requests guided by the tyranny of politeness and indirectness, defined by dominant American English language structures. This resulted in many misunderstandings and to his assigned labels of unsuccessful and defiant. Pragmatically, George and his teacher operated within different literacies. Furthermore, because of his teacher's power within the context of schooling, her limited understanding of George's language practices put him in jeopardy; she positioned her own communicative referents as literacy norms against which George's communicative practices were measured, imposing dominant ways of communicating on George and excluding him from learning.

Such misunderstandings also influence children's views of each other's communicative repertoires and very identities. Building on Delpit's (1988) understanding that the culture of power is the culture of those who have power, we reaffirm that the language of power is the language of those who have power. The following assertions ground this affirmation:

- The language of power is sanctioned in classrooms and other learning contexts by teachers and students alike—as well as by teaching materials and mandated curricula.
- There are specific ways (and unstated rules) used by those who have power to communicate in the language of power.
- The rules of the language of power reflect the communicative practices of those who have power.
- Those for whom the language of power is not the language of the home or of the heart must be explicitly taught its rules in order to develop access; not teaching these rules effectively denies access and further perpetuates inequities (as was the case with the kindergartner George). This does not mean that home languages should be erased; they must be cultivated and sustained alongside the language of power.
- Those who speak the language of power rarely recognize the existence of a language of power while those who do not are keenly aware of its existence as a barrier to success.

Children enact such concepts in unofficial settings as well. For example, Souto-Manning (2013a) found that in a dual-language after-school program setting in New York City, first graders imposed their own rules on group membership. They perceived academic success to be closely linked to communicative practices in dominant American English, which excluded those who spoke other languages, such as Spanish and African American Language. Thus, they used this epistemological standpoint to justify the social exclusion of their peers from play based on linguistic competence and performance, with alignment to the dominant language. In that setting, they not only needed to command a repertoire related to the affinity group and play in place, but also had to prove their fluency in dominant American English to gain entry during play.

The following interaction took place when five boys who were in first and second grades (ages 6–8) and were doing homework (away from adults). It illustrates how linguistic misalignment influenced not only academic success, but also social belonging (transcription notation: colons show degrees of elongation of the prior sound; the more colons, the more elongated the sound):

> Malik: You smart, you know!
> Juan: ¡*Muy listo*! [Very smart!]
> Luis: Sometimes—when I wanna be. Sometimes people think I'm not smart. But I know Spanish and English.
> Malik: ¡*Y yo también*! [And me too!]
> Juan: And me too!
> Luis: And I gotta do my homework all by myself.
> Juan: ¡*La tarea*! [Homework!]

Elvis: Sometimes I don't cuz I don' like them books. *No porque no pueda, pero no quiero hacer.* [Not because I can't, but because I don't want to do (it).]

Xavier: Yea.

Elvis: The books in Spanish are not as good. But I am better in Spanish. So, if I wanna read what I want, I gotta read English and if I wanna read in Spanish I gotta read something I don't like. And then some boys in Ms. [Teacher's] class think I'm stupid. I'm not.

Xavier: And they don't want to play with you. It don't matter if you like Bakugan or even if you got them. You know, you only gotta play with people who talk like you.

Juan: *¿Por qué?* [Why?] Why you sayin' that?

Xavier: Cuz, man, you know, they don't want to play with me.

Luis: Do you wait for them to ask?

Xavier: Yea.

Luis: I don't. I just say, "Hey, my Zoompha can beat your Hurrix!" And then, "Let's bra::awl!" That means let's battle in Bakugan. You gotta know that=

Malik: =Yea=

Luis: =You gotta show them what you know. In English. If I wanna play with them, I talk like them.

Malik: A::and you gotta know the rules.

Luis: And put your cards down like this. [Luis shows with his hands how the cards need to be put together.]

Xavier: I get it.

Malik: You gotta show them what you kno::ow.

Luis: And really re:::eally know it.

Juan: *En inglés.* [In English.]

(Souto-Manning 2013a, 310–311)

The interaction above illustrates how young children took up ideologies framing English as a superior language and enacted them in their everyday discourses. For example, to participate in Bakugan play, it was not enough to know about Bakugan. In addition, one needed to abide by the rules of the dominant language in place: English. Privileging singular practices is exclusionary and problematic, failing to honor diverse children's multiple ways with words in multiple languages.

In this excerpt, the boys interrogate and critique the structures of power—the dominance of English. They also flip the script about who is deemed smart by recognizing their bilingual repertoires, while also admitting that they are, in fact, othered. They are sophisticated in how they "play the linguistic game"—they know when to speak English for play, for school, for social reasons, for inclusion.

They also connote that language must be performed ("you gotta show them"). Power determines not only which literacy practices are sanctioned, but also whose literate identities are included and excluded. Thus, literacies produce not only competence, but competent beings. As seen in the children's talk about the Bakugan play, the situation, context, and participants determine competence.

On the Cultural Nature of Best Practice and the 30-Million Word Gap

Early literacy (in its singular) assumes one "best practice" for all and thus embodies a legacy of debt. It is grounded in the practices enacted by those who have power in society—historically as well as contemporarily. Such restrictive definitions of early literacy exclude and devalue family literacies (Chapter 4), participatory literacy communities in neighborhoods (Chapter 5), and peer literacies (Chapter 6). Children, families, and communities whose literacies are not aligned with the literacy of power are immediately positioned as having a gap. This view privileges White, middle class families as communicatively competent, rendering the language competencies of nondominant communities as invisible and less valuable.

It is easy (and all too common) to point out the word gap children from minoritized backgrounds exhibit (Hart and Risley 1995, 2003). Hart and Risley (2003) pinpoint a thirty-million-word gap, which minoritized children *supposedly* have by age three, labeling it a "catastrophe." Such misinformed and deficit-ridden findings (explained later in this chapter) have informed many programs, including the White House's *Bridging the Word Gap* campaign under President Barack Obama and *Too Small to Fail*, an initiative of the Clinton Foundation. It is important to understand that such an approach places the blame on the individual and/or family and seeks to remediate the child; a problematic approach, which ignores systemic racism and historical inequities (Gutiérrez, Morales, and Martínez 2009). We see such claims as similar to the way in which Ladson-Billings conceptualized the education gap—as a fabrication that continues to blame the child, his/her family, and the child's community. Instead, we seek to work against historical policies and practices that have been built on deficit understandings of young children's practices—especially those of color, those from low-income households, and those who have been colonized, minoritized, and disadvantaged by dominant interests (Goodwin, Cheruvu, and Genishi 2008).

Goodwin et al. (2008) explain how early childhood education itself was established based on the idea that nondominant families were unfit to raise their own children. Unstated in such a paradigm framing early childhood education is the conflation of *dominant* and *appropriate* (as explained in Chapter 2). For example, in the U.S., the Common Core State Standards for kindergarten mandate mastery of "academic language," which is code for dominant American English. In Australia, for example, even in the Northern Territory, White teachers sought to educate Aboriginal children in English (read: colonialize and assimilate), at first through "the Australian Federal Government's earlier policy of Assimilation of Aboriginal people" (Nicholls 2005, 161) and then through bilingual education programs, which were closed due to "poor standards in English literacy" (Nicholls 2005, 161), resulting in indigenous languages' "death by a thousand cuts" (Nicholls 2005, 160). Such actions continue to privilege English, which is deemed more important than indigenous languages.

Throughout the world, many children are not educated in their home languages, and in many countries their formal education is conducted in languages they themselves do not understand—"as much as 40% of the global population does not have access to education in a language they speak or understand" (UNESCO 2016, 1). This is dehumanizing and disempowering. It communicates to young children that they are not knowledgeable, and that who they are (one's identity) does not matter. We thus call for a reorganization of the learning environment, tools, and the definition of what counts as literacy and how literacy success is assessed—especially in the early years—based on understandings of literacies explored in Part II of this book, which recognize early literacies as relational (Anzaldúa 1987; Licona and Chávez 2015; Martin 2013).

In the early years, concepts of basics and readiness permeate what counts as literacy and educational success. They further reify dominant models of literacy and learning as the norm by which all young children are to be rated. Thus, educators reward young children for having their home language and literacy practices aligned with schooling practices (Souto-Manning 2013a). Such an approach continues to position minoritized children as unsuccessful, effectively blaming them for society's drive to sustain continued inequity.

From Word Gap to Language Debt

Instead of measuring early language and literacy against dominant practices, as with studies such as the one conducted by Hart and Risley (2003)—blaming individual children, their families, and their communities for a perceived word gap—it is important for us to understand the language debt that dominant groups have to minoritized communities. As Ladson-Billings (2006) explains, this is not a one-time deficit, but a debt that has been accumulated over time, resulting from policies and practices that have, throughout history, disempowered diverse language and literacy practices. Simply deeming the results of such actions a gap continues to reinscribe the fallacious "pull yourself up by the bootstraps" mentality. Such a mentality continues to privilege the privileged and disempower those who have been colonized and stripped from their humanity. Thus, we propose that educators and researchers must move from seeing minoritized children as having a word gap to understanding that dominant populations have a language debt to pay to minoritized children, families, and communities.

Building on the work of Ladson-Billings (2006), we recognize that the concept of a word gap is one of the key contemporary concerns related to early literacy—whether in scholarship or in the popular media. Foundations, politicians, and policymakers evoke this "word gap" often, despite its deficit framework and multiple critiques that highlight the ways in which the "word gap" pathologizes linguistic and cultural differences and diversities (Dudley-Marling and Lucas 2009; Michaels 2013; Quintero 2013). Some researchers highlight that there is an opportunity gap (Neuman and Celano 2012) while others pinpoint the fact that the researchers who conceived the 30 million word gap never entered children's homes (Orellana 2016).

In their study, Hart and Risley (2003) proposed that low- and no-income children are language deficient. The authors blame the children's families for playing "a significant role in perpetuating the cycle of poverty" (Dudley-Marling and Lucas 2009, 363). That is, without acknowledging societal injustices, which keep the socioeconomic status quo in place, they blame families for keeping their children within the same socioeconomic bracket they grew up in. Interestingly, they reached these conclusions based on a study comprised of one hour of observation per week of 13 upper-socioeconomic status (SES) (1 Black, 12 White), 10 middle-SES (3 Black, 7 White), 13 lower-SES (7 Black, 6 White), and 6 welfare (all Black) families—all from Kansas City, Missouri (Hart and Risley 1995). They make strong claims and issue evaluations based on limited data, which do not warrant such claims about the quality of the language and communication between parents and children. That is, Hart and Risley's analysis of a small subset of families in one city made harmful, evaluative assertions about the language competencies of all minoritized families. Their study fails to recognize the cultural and linguistic repertoires minoritized families do have, as documented in Chapters 4 and 5, where teacher-researchers go into the homes of families and communities and gain in-depth understandings of families' cultural and linguistic repertoires. That is, the teachers portrayed in Chapter 4 and in Chapter 5 learned from their students' families, acknowledging that "learning does not take place just 'between the ears,' but is eminently a social process." They believe that "people are competent, they have knowledge" (González, Moll, and Amanti 2005, ix).

We believe that the focus on a word gap is misguided at best—or an explicit attempt to maintain language hierarchies and to reinscribe the superiority of dominant language practices at worst. As highlighted by researchers like Orellana (2016), Heath (1983), and Dyson and Smitherman (2009), language is learned and cultivated by the cultural communities in which children are actively involved. School literacy practices do not acknowledge these sophisticated language practices. We thus elucidate the existing language debt, "accumulated over time. This debt comprises historical, economic, sociopolitical, and moral components" (Ladson-Billings 2006, 3).

This language debt is historical—as American schooling used English as the language of assimilation. In fact, American schooling initially sought to assimilate and Americanize immigrants (Goodwin et al. 2008) and those enslaved—e.g., enslaved Africans were separated per language to avoid communication (Smitherman, 2006), with the intent of domination and linguistic genocide. Yet, they creatively developed African American Language, which served "to bind the enslaved together, melding diverse African ethnic groups into one community" (Smitherman, 2006, 3). Historically, language has served a key role in disempowering and dehumanizing—not only regarding enslaved Africans, but for immigrant groups as well.

In Arizona, Proposition 203 required all children not fluent in English to be placed in intensive English-immersion programs regardless of their fluency in their respective home languages. The law cites that English is the "leading world language for science, technology, and international business, thereby the language of economic opportunity," and to be productive members of society, literacy in the English language is deemed the most important skill (Arizona Secretary of State 2000). Embedded in the policies are "English-only" instructional mandates, constant language proficiency tests, and the marginalization of children's first languages—the languages of their communities, homes, and families. In this example, it is clear that policymakers believe that English is the language of power and should be privileged above other languages in order to "fully participate in the American Dream of economic and social advancement" (Arizona Secretary of State, 2000). In addition, other language programs that move away from English-only policies are seen as "wasting financial resources on costly experimental language programs whose failure over the past two decades is demonstrated by the current high dropout rates and low English literacy levels of many immigrant children" (Section 1. Findings and Declarations—Arizona Secretary of State 2000). Rather than pointing at systemic racism toward immigrant children, policies blame children's English-language skills for failure in schools. Noticeably missing from language policies like Proposition 203 is the responsibilities of schools, teachers, and communities to cultivate and value multiple languages. In the same ways, immigrant children are seen as language deficient rather than language resourced.

The language debt—as the education debt (Ladson-Billings 2006)—is also economic, sociopolitical, and moral. The language debt is economic—as policymakers make more investments in dominant language schooling and provide more money for those who speak the dominant language in school. That is, for those fluent in the dominant language, learning an additional language is often framed as an asset. For those fluent in nondominant languages, learning English is seen as a necessity to address a dire deficit. This results in inequitable expectations in dual-language programs, as identified by Valdés (1997). The language debt is also sociopolitical as decisions regarding the civic process in a country are all-too-often made in the dominant language, in writing. The judicial process is overpopulated by members of the dominant population, which benefit from keeping the status quo in place under the excuse of legality. So, historically and contemporarily, sociopolitical contexts have excluded nondominant language practices and those who are speakers of nondominant languages are deemed unworthy and inadequate. Finally, the language debt is moral, explained by Ladson-Billings (2006, 8) as the "disparity between what we know is right and what we actually do." Ladson-Billings's (2006) concept of "education debt" serves as a powerful framework for understanding early language debt, moving beyond the simplistic count of words young children speak. By counting the words a child speaks, the field distorts the bigger issue: how dominant languages continue to privilege dominant groups and individuals, as well as how language has served to discriminate, segregate, disempower, and dehumanize. Unfortunately, this continues to be the case in (pre)schools today as we hear statements from teachers such as, "He has limited language," applied to a child whose linguistic knowledge, practices, and flexibility are much more advanced than those of his teacher(s). Such language debt extends to literacy—and continues to grow as traditional models of literacy reign in classrooms and (pre)schools.

As Genishi and Dyson (2012, 20) eloquently argue, "teachers are accountable not to some narrow "top" but to the rhythms and rhymes of their developing students." That is, instead of judging the language repertoires and literacy practices children acquire at home and in their neighborhoods against dominant ideas of language and literacy, it is important to identify, document, and learn from them. Taking a critical anthropological approach is important as we seek to understand the function of certain practices (as explored in Chapter 4, Chapter 5, and Chapter 6). It is important to recognize that

> The field of literacy has expanded considerably in recent years and new, more anthropological and cross-cultural frameworks have been developed to replace those of a previous era . . . . The rich cultural variation . . . lead us to rethink what we mean . . . and to be weary of assuming a single literacy where we may simply be imposing assumptions derived from our own cultural practice onto other people's literacies. (Street 1993, 1)

The Debt We, As a Society, Owe: Standardized Curriculum and Punitive Measures

A major paradox frames the field of early literacy. While the field of literacy research has expanded to account for the cultural diversity in children's, families,' and communities' cultural practices (Street 1993), official texts and curricula in (pre)schools have been more and more standardized. "There is a very puzzling contrast—really an awesome disconnect—between the breathtaking diversity of schoolchildren and the uniformity, homogenization, and regimentation of classroom practices, from pre-kindergarten onward" (Genishi and Dyson 2009, 4). Such uniformity and regimentation is not value-free, but grounded in dominant cultural assumptions, giving credence to cultures and languages of power, or to those who have power (Delpit 1995/2006).

With an increasingly diverse landscape, tensions occur when curricular mandates clash with diverse cultural communities. This is particularly the case for curricula with pacing guides operating under the premise of "one-size-fits-all." "There is a profusion of human diversity in our schools and an astonishingly narrow offering or curricula . . . [grounded in] the view of children as empty vessels to be filled by behaviorist-oriented, scripted lessons" (Genishi and Dyson 2009, 10). This comes to life in a kindergarten class in New York City, composed primarily of African American children. Teachers Mary Hill and Jessica Garcia (pseudonyms) encountered such tension—all royalty in the Core Knowledge Kings and Queens unit of study were White (this is E. D. Hirsch's curriculum, introduced and discussed in Chapter 1).

The school where Hill and Garcia taught had adopted Core Knowledge as its official curriculum under the promise that a Whiteified curriculum would result in higher test scores for its student population (more than 70 percent of whom were children of color). The school was a K–5 school in New York City, where 70 percent of its students qualified for free and/or reduced lunch, a U.S. program typically associated with low- and no-income levels. *Tell It Again! Read-Aloud Anthology* was the main text of the Core Knowledge read-aloud curriculum. Instead of teachers selecting books to read to their students, Core Knowledge provided picture cards to be shown while teachers read mandated and pre-selected stories, which purport to include high-level vocabulary. Differently from books, the figure cards did not contain any text. The specific anthology associated with the unit (Kindergarten ELA Domain 7: Kings and Queens, Engage NY) did not include any kings or queens of color. The cover of the anthology portrayed the picture of a White king, queen, and child against a background of green grass and hills. In the twenty-nine image cards to be presented during the read aloud, none included a person of color (Hirsch 2013), all while twenty-four of the twenty-five students in their kindergarten were children of color. These mandated, behaviorist, and scripted lessons did not honor the rich cultural practices and experiences brought by the children. In fact, they effectively invisiblized them. Kindergarten ELA Domain 7 specifically focused on White kings and queens (mostly kings) from northern Europe—not a very relevant topic for four- and five-year-olds in New York City. This was part of the schoolwide curriculum, resourced with curricular materials that determined who was made visible and invisible in read-alouds and in curriculum at large. The curriculum set a landscape which overprivileged Whiteness and dominant American English. This landscape brought to life what Myers and Myers (2014, para. 4) had titled "the apartheid of children's literature . . . in which characters of color are limited to the townships of occasional historical books that concern themselves with the legacies of civil rights and slavery but are never given a pass card to transverse the lands of adventure, curiosity, imagination or personal growth." Children of color were made invisible in classroom materials and books. This is representative of the "all-White world of children's books," which is not new. It also highlights how failing to include people of color in children's books routinely offer White children "gentle doses of racism" via the books they read (Edelman 2015).

Noticing that the curriculum did not reflect children's images, identities, languages, or worlds, Mary Hill and Jessica Garcia, both first-year teachers at the school, decided to add children's books featuring African princesses and queens as well as real royalty, such as Queen Rania of Jordan. They read *Mufaro's Beautiful Daughters: An African Tale* (1987) by John Steptoe. They also challenged gender roles put forth by tales such as The Princess and the Pea, Cinderella, and Snow White (part of Core Knowledge) by reading books such as *The Paper Bag Princess* (1980) by Robert Munsch and *The Princess and the Packet of Frozen Peas* (2012) by Tony Wilson. They also read *The Sandwich Swap* (2010) by Her Majesty Queen Rania Al Abdullah (of Jordan) and learned more about her.

When an administrator observed the teachers in the classroom, they were "marked up" for critically adapting and supplementing the curriculum in place. They were admonished by their administrator for disadvantaging the children in their class by "distracting them from the curriculum," and given a rating of "Ineffective" in Domain 1: Planning and Preparation. They were also rated Ineffective in "Demonstrating Knowledge and Content of Pedagogy" according to the Danielson evaluation (Danielson 2014, adapted to New York City Department of Education) because they were making content errors and in "Designing Coherent Instruction," because materials did "not meet instructional outcomes" (Danielson 2014, 7). The administrator also rated them Ineffective in "Domain 4: Professional Responsibilities" on similar grounds. Such a system of surveillance continues to sanction the message that the lives and experiences of children of color do not matter. Schools are sites where a "war on the vulnerable" is waged, rendering the lives of children of color as invisible and disposable, as *nobody* (Hill 2016). This illustrates the language debt we owe children, families, and communities from minoritized backgrounds.

This toxic combination of a standardized curriculum, diverse communities, and punitive measures keeps the status quo in place and distorts the bigger picture—and the real problems emanating from a restrictive definition of early literacy—by blaming teachers (Kumashiro 2012). In briefly reviewing the paradoxical situation experienced by first-year teachers Mary Hill and Jessica Garcia within the context of a New York City public elementary school, we can easily see how the standardized literacy curriculum communicates to children of color that they do not matter, standing in stark contrast to the society in which we live—which is rapidly becoming more and more racially diverse. When teachers like Hill and Garcia try to make the curriculum more inclusive and relevant to the children they teach, they are (or may be) punished via standardized teaching evaluations. Unsurprisingly, both Hill and Garcia left the school after that first year of teaching. They no longer teach in New York City, but continue to hone their teaching practices in urban settings, working with children who are "at promise" in other locales in the U.S., and acknowledging the reparations needed and the debts owed to children, families, and communities from minoritized backgrounds.

On Paying the Debt and Positioning Literacy as a Transformative Tool

In Chapters 1 through 7, we offered examples—glimpses of hope and possibility— of teachers redressing inequities through curricular materials, pedagogies, and social policies. The featured teachers show us diverse ways of teaching that honor children's home languages and community cultural resources. Economically, they invest in materials that allow minoritized children's practices to be present; they allocate time for such culturally situated and important topics to be positioned centrally in the curriculum. They also know that morally, they cannot continue to enact curricula and engage in teaching that invisiblizes young children from minoritized backgrounds and their families. They recognize that not every policy in place is just—and that, in fact, most are designed by those in power to keep the status quo in place.

As we reflect on the literacies accepted, valued, and honored by teachers such as Debbie White in Illinois (Chapter 1), Maria Helena Mendonça Buril (Chapter 2) and Phillip Baumgarner in Georgia (Chapter 3), Carmen Lugo Llerena (Chapter 4), Abigail Salas Maguire (Chapter 4), Jessica Martell (Chapter 4), Yadira Hernandez (Chapter 5), Alison Lanza (Chapter 5) in New York City, we reaffirm our beliefs that we have the responsibility to create spaces for young children to develop as capable and competent literate beings. Through examples from their classrooms and the rich practices of the children they teach, their families and communities, they show us ways in which curriculum can (and should) include social opportunities to use language(s) fluidly and flexibly with other children (through practices such as translanguaging, as illustrated in Chapters 1 and 5).

To do so, we must acknowledge the historic obstacles that have been put in place, as well as the Whiteified and exclusionary way(s) in which early literacy is conceived. As we look at the (r)evolution of early literacies in ways that account for the debts society owes to communities of color and their children, we must acknowledge, as Maya Angelou underscores, that children come to us with rich histories and sophisticated cultural practices, bearing gifts from their ancestors. We educators have to be able to acknowledge, value, and leverage such gifts, instead of ignoring them. It is our responsibility. It is our debt to our students. Not to judge, but to learn from and with them and with the people from whom they come. Even when children's languages and literacies may seem inappropriate to us—and especially then—we must ask ourselves their function and come to recognize that languages and literacies can serve as sites of resistance and of transformation.

Educational philosopher Paulo Freire (1970) proposed that education has the power and potential to transform individuals and collectives, who can in turn transform the world. This transformative stance urges us to critically consider how early literacies can and should be repositioned as transformative tools, and not simply as tools for re-production of the current inequitable and unjust society. Literacies alone do not transform the world; yet, they can and do transform the people who then change the world, alongside their ideologies and epistemologies.

9

ORCHESTRATING COMPLEX LITERACIES

Considering the Power of Young Children's Repertoires and Identities

In his book, *Lives on the Boundary* (1989), Mike Rose gives an autobiographical account of living in the margins as a child of immigrant parents in South Los Angeles. He poignantly highlights his own working-class background, his time "accidently" placed in the vocational education track, his struggles with trying to catch up with the other students in the college preparatory courses and finding himself grossly underprepared as he entered college. His schooling experiences were marked by a familiar labeling and sorting system where placements and tracks left minoritized individuals and communities with few options, narrow curricular standards, and limited opportunities. Schooling for children in lower tracks "isn't designed to liberate . . . but to occupy . . . [and] train" (Rose 1989, 28). Rose's later experience teaching veterans with limited schooling, ex-convicts, remedial students who skated into the university, and low-income students in El Monte, California, U.S., reinforced the idea that minoritized children and families have the odds stacked against them. Fewer resources, static academic labels, limited curricular options, escalating educational costs, and competition for selective schools managed to create "the perfect storm of bad conditions for working-class students" (Rose 1989, 252) in particular and students from historically minoritized backgrounds in general.

While Rose's work was written in the late 80s, the same dilemma is still of great concern in this era of high-stakes testing and standardization. A close examination of classrooms, children, and communities today reveals that "scores are many levels of abstraction away from daily life in the classroom" (Rose 1989, 247). Yet, neoliberal discourse and policies (discussed in Chapter 8) continue to define curriculum, schooling, and teachers' work. The push for charter schools, high-stakes testing, and school choice, ironically, limit the choices and opportunities for students whose "lives are on the boundary."

Throughout this book, we emphasized that as communities grow more diverse, it is important to consider the multiple communities, literacy practices, and child-hoods of which children are members as they enter the community of school. Of even greater importance is interrogating systems, ideologies, and practices that punish children for this diversity. Rose's autobiography shows how predetermined categories (often correlated with race, language, culture, and class) limit educators' insights on children's language depth while simultaneously obstructing their opportunities. These divisions were structurally clear in Rose's narrative, where tracks sorted students into specific life trajectories. Although Rose's work focuses on older age ranges, the phenomenon he describes is persistent and pervasive in early childhood education. That is, young children are also subject to the same sorting methods through curriculum, instruction, and assessments (Souto-Manning 2009b; Yoon 2015). Consequently, the teacher acts as a mediator, facilitating opportunities to develop sophisticated literacy repertoires. While the children who populate this book bring literacies to life, we now turn the attention to teachers who make classrooms, structures, and languages "permeable" (Dyson 1993).

Humanizing Teachers: Moving Beyond Public Discourse

The cover of the March 5, 2010 issue of *Newsweek* magazine showed a picture of a chalkboard with a straightforward message written on it: "The Key to Saving American Education: We Must Fire Bad Teachers" (cover). Clearly, the declining state of the American education system has caught the nation's attention, with "failing" teachers being the focus of interest. Arne Duncan, former U.S. Secretary of Education, continued to call teachers and teacher education programs mediocre, at best, in preparing teachers for diverse schools. The National Council on Teacher Quality (2013) published (and continues to publish) guidelines that prescribe interventions and increased regulations on the preparation and development of teachers. This rhetoric shows no sign of slowing down as we have moved to an administration led by venture capitalists and businesspeople whose commitments to public schools are questionable. In each instance, ill-prepared teachers with little accountability are blamed for children's failure to perform in a global world.

Scholars (Cohen and Barnes 1993; Darling-Hammond 2010; García-Coll and Marks 2009; Kumashiro 2012) agree that high-quality teachers can be crucial agents of change in education reform, and more importantly, student success. Additionally, new models, new curriculum, new policies mean nothing without good teachers. However, by placing the blame for the woes of contemporary schools on teachers alone, we ignore the pervasive problems associated with other social issues such as poverty, hunger, homelessness, violence, racism, and other inequalities. Firing bad teachers, then, becomes a simplistic solution to a complex issue. As Noguera (2009) articulates, this simplistic solution ignores the fact that children come to classrooms with a myriad of social dilemmas as well as a depth of cultural practices from diverse cultural communities (Genishi and Dyson 2009;

González, Moll, and Amanti 2005; Heath 1983; Li 2008). The common space of the classroom, then, becomes the place where identities are practiced, negotiated, constructed, and reimagined for both students and teachers.

Undoubtedly, while there are teachers who are incompetent and harmful for children's social and intellectual growth, we argue that the media and the public obsessively perpetuate extremes: heroes and saviors vs. delinquent and misfit teachers; both images are problematic to understanding a teacher's work. Instead, this section addresses the "unchallenged presumption that there are too many incompetent teachers, protected by unions, and prepared by mediocre teacher-certification programs" (Kumashiro and Meiners 2012, 41). Thus, we discuss the efforts teachers make to resist and push back on capitalist priorities and neoliberal agendas imposed on children in public schools (as discussed in Chapter 8). We share the struggles and the victories that teachers throughout our book face because "any reform enacted on the backs of teachers is doomed to fail; any reform that discounts the experiences and wisdom of teachers and parents will be stillborn" (Ayers et al. 2016, 15). Educational policies, especially those related to core subjects like math and language arts (the focus of this book) are quantified in linear progressions apart from the expertise of teachers who understand that children's development is far from linear (e.g., *Common Core State Standards* written by the National Governor's Association Center for Best Practices). Hence, the work of teachers is mediated by increased competition, privatized educational funding, and regulated curriculum. In response, there are many ways to organize and resist the attacks on public education from protests to marches to teach-ins, all of which are valuable in their own right. Here, we make public the experience and wisdom of teachers as a way to resist the script written about their daily work.

Tightening, Scheduling, and Regulating Schools

We began this book by introducing Lou, Jaquan, Tonea, Jolene, and Jon, and we close this book by returning to that same classroom in the midwestern U.S. Their sophisticated and rich conversations were made possible because teacher Debbie White allowed permeable spaces in her curriculum despite neoliberal efforts to regulate her work. In this chapter, we honor the voices of teachers who strive to create the conditions for all children's participation in languaging experiences. Navigating the political and social landscape of schools and curriculum are not devoid of frustrations as illustrated by Haeny's reflective journal entry below.

> Debbie informed me [Haeny] that it's been a rough few days since I last came. She recently got a terse note from the resources specialists telling her that it was very hard to accommodate for "those things you do." They really wanted her to just stay on schedule and go with the plans that she had, but Debbie felt the need to adjust. However, she was also very conscientious about the schedule as well, so I know she tried really hard to make sure that

she was on time to things. There were just some things that were unpredictable. She's very adamant about students staying in class and making sure that they could participate in the classroom community.

Debbie White was a twenty-three-year veteran teacher. She was a White woman, a native of the small urban community featured, and a "lifelong learner," to use her own words. She enrolled in courses at the university, pursued continuing-education classes, and spoke up in all of the grade-level meetings observed. White spent several summers writing curriculum with other teachers, participating in the National Writing Project, and continued her involvement with coursework far beyond her master's degree. She acknowledged having far more flexibility in her teaching because of her status, her experience, and her popularity among staff and parents. She was well known in the community, and it was clear that the principal (who was fairly new to the school) listened to and trusted Debbie White, even when their opinions differed.

Even a teacher as experienced as Debbie White struggled to meet regulations. At an informal meeting, she described her lesson plans for the week, which teachers were required to turn in, complete with standards attached since they were now as Debbie White put it, "trying to *do* the Common Core." There was writing in every corner of the small boxes of her plan book, handwritten in pencil. The lettering was very small (so as to fit everything), and a cursory glance at the book made it overwhelming and impossible to read. She noted, "I can't even look at this because it's so hard to read. I used to be able to look at it and say, 'Okay, read _____', but now I don't even use it." In the future, they would have to attach assessments onto their lesson plans and write follow-up plans if children did not pass the assessments. She sighed and shook her head, "What's the point of lesson plans if you can't even use them?" Debbie White was a planner—she spent many mornings, nights, and weekends preparing experiences for the children, including bringing tomatoes from her garden, coordinating field trips, organizing storybook "buffets," introducing composting projects, to name a few of the classroom events witnessed. Therefore, being asked to "plan" was far from the issue. Instead, she was being asked to document the standards, mandates, and assessments being addressed in her teaching, regardless of whether or not it was occurring inside her classroom. On many occasions, Debbie White would report that the lesson plans and the actual teaching were two separate and distinct actions. The lesson plans were perfunctory as they had little to do with curriculum as an enacted practice. For her, plans were supplemental, even apart from the input and ideas that children brought to the curricular experience or moment. Her plans came from, in her own words, a "trust the children" mindset making it impossible to carry out prescriptive, detailed lesson plans.

When Debbie White taught thematically, when topics, ideas, skills found authentic connection, she felt the most like herself as a teacher. At the end of November, when the rhythm of the school year took its own side roads and unpredictable turns given the holidays, the school breaks, the school performances, etc., Debbie White (and other teachers) were given a little bit of space to create their curriculum.

Amidst the chaos of holidays and school breaks, Debbie White found a space to teach thematically and creatively—a welcome relief from the tightly monitored district curricular calendar. Even district regulation and curricular mandates took a break for the holidays. She remarked, "I've loved everything that I've done, I've almost completely pulled out of the district materials except that, I'm pulling all of the concepts we are supposed to be covering . . . but everything is tying in together and the kids are just having a ball with it. We just flow from one thing to another. I didn't realize 'til this week how much I missed that."

When Debbie White talked about curriculum, she did not struggle with the intellectual and time-consuming work of bringing ideas together. In fact, she had a firm grasp on curricular goals and aligned her own teaching to match the guidelines presented. Her knowledge of the children in the classroom coupled with the situated time and context made it possible for her to create authentic connections or bridges between content and children. Given the space, time, and freedom, she created curricular opportunities that were not just stuff to get through, but moments to slow down and enjoy.

Creating "New" Literacies: Expanding the Curriculum

> Those who never disrupt may be withholding too much. Until they tell us more of what is on their minds they may not be able to listen to what *we* have to say. There is a tendency to look upon the noisy, repetitive fantasies of children as *non-educational*, but helicopters and kittens and super-hero capes and Barbie dolls are storytelling aids and conversational tools. Without them, the range of what we listen to and talk about is arbitrarily circumscribed by the adult point of view. (Paley 1990, 38)

In Vivian Paley's classroom, listening was curriculum and planning. At times, it is easy to dismiss the musings of children—the obsessions with Barbie dolls, the reenactment of superhero adventures, and the arbitrary conversations that sustain children through play and interaction. Our "adult point of view" often gets in the way of realizing the depth of cultural knowledge and understanding that children need to participate in such play and interaction. Overreliance on scripts and curricular plans limits the contributions children make to the scene.

During the school year in Debbie White's classroom, one child was chosen each week to share something about themselves ("superstar of the week")—a practice that many early childhood teachers might employ to build community (a.k.a., "All About Me" posters or "Show and Tell"). She invited the children to bring toys, objects, and/or pictures from home to share with the class. Opportunities for the rest of the class to interview the superstar and ask questions were included. The other children eventually drew a picture and wrote words for the superstar, which Debbie White compiled into a book for the superstar to keep. During Jaquan's superstar week, he brought in three variations of a Spider-Man toy: the regular Spider-Man, the Black-Suited Spider-Man, and the Venom Spider-Man. He went on to describe the physical differences and special powers of each of the Spider-Men. Debbie White noted that many of the boys expressed continued interest in Spider-Man and believed that some of this was sparked by Jaquan's conversations about the trio of Spider-Men. Jaquan was not the only one who knew about Spider-Man, but he was the first one to bring the toys into the classroom.

Debbie White admitted that although Jaquan was not very adept with academic language, she said that he presented a very sophisticated discussion about the variations of Spider-Man, a distinction of which outsiders were not aware. It was for this reason she relished the superstar time, because it allowed her to recognize children's experiential knowledge. It helped her see their capacity and potential with language-in-use. Jaquan had a way of using language to confront and convince others. Jaquan made sure to portray accurate information about Spider-Man, doing so with confidence and expertise. As we saw earlier, he was willing to engage in arguments with his peers (e.g., Michael Myers vs. Chucky) in order to display knowledge and prove a point. During his superstar week, he monitored his tablemates' drawings of him—he made Jolene draw him with a green shirt, and he asked others to make sure that they drew him with a "football in one hand and a pizza in the other" (two of his favorite things). Their teacher viewed this time as more than just a "cute activity," but as a tool to understand children's popular culture literacies, family literacies, and cultural literacies that were usually invisible in formal assessments.

In sharing this example, we emphasize that Debbie White enacted a practice in her classroom that is typical—a structured sharing time where children talk about their identities. The practice, in and of itself, is not transformative. However, we highlight her engagement in this activity as a way to unearth hidden creativities and to bear witness to children's capacities. While Jaquan could easily be seen as "slow" (a term assigned to him by many students and educators), viewing him in varied situations positioned him as a capable and competent language user. Thus, changing practices is not the sole remedy to unstandardizing curriculum. Transforming dispositions, attitudes, and ideas about children, curriculum, and teaching practices is key to dismantling deficit perspectives about historically marginalized populations (Sleeter and Carmona 2017). In the following section, we follow Debbie White's curricular moves through the official curriculum.

Co-constructing Curriculum: Creating "New" Literacies with Children

One day, Jon, all on his own, decided to turn his paper over and write a story on the back of it about him and Tonea. The photocopied paper for writing was blank on the back side, the top had a line to write the "Superstar's name" (this week it was Tonea), and the rest of the page was blank to accommodate for a drawing. There was nothing official or magical about the paper given to children. Instead, the paper served as a tool, prepared by the teacher to compile the books. Jon, on this particular day, used the back of his paper to "say more" about his relationship with Tonea. Debbie White jumped on this opportunity to show the rest of the children what he had done, and consequently, many of them ended up writing a story on the back of their pages as well. The idea was a spontaneous event that happened in the course of children's experimentation with different ideas.

This idea carried over into writing workshop time. Within a three-page booklet, the children began to use the back, blank sides in order to continue their stories. One of the children commented that the stories looked like "real books" that contained writing on both sides. The idea was not part of the curricular tool-kit, yet it was a useful and productive one. The children strived to create longer stories as a way to use the full range of a page, not to mention the environmental gains of consuming less paper. Debbie White did not have to change or subvert the direction of her instruction. Jon's addition only added to her idea and perhaps this new practice added dimension and momentum to a weekly practice. She simply opened up the space for children to construct ideas, making them official through acknowledgment and recognition. Children's intellectual contributions to the literacy curriculum were common, as the next section illustrates.

Continuing Down Curricular Side Roads: The Reality of Storytelling

Angela Johnson's story, *Joshua's Night Whispers* (1994), is about a young boy who hears the sounds of the night (e.g., the wind, the creaks of the house) and walks down the stairs to his father's room where he feels safe and comforted. When he is finally safe in his daddy's arms, they sit and listen to the wind together. Debbie White read the book to the children, as the curriculum suggested, to introduce them to writing true stories that focused on one moment in time (Calkins 2003). She reiterated the goal of reading this small story, "Here's what I want you to see. A small moment. Something tiny that has *happened* to you. Joshua sat in bed, walked down the stairs, and went to his daddy's room. Was that a small moment?" The children nodded their heads enthusiastically and shared their own small moments one by one.

> Jake: Um, one night when I was little, I actually rolled out of bed 'cause I didn't have any stuffed animals. [Some children laugh.]
>
> Debbie White: Jake, that sounds sooo interesting. Could you turn that into a story? [Jake nods.] You could, and you know exactly what details you need 'cause it really happened to you. Anybody have another small moment? Benji?

Benji: When I was little, I heard the wind, and I went in my daddy's and my mommy's room.

Julie: When I was a little baby, I rolled out of bed because I couldn't walk yet and I went into the hall and I could hear my cat sleeping, and then I went to my mama's room, and I listened to the wind.

Debbie White: And you got all the way to your mama's room, and what happened?

Julie: I, listened—

Debbie White: You got sent—

Julie: I, was, um, I listened to the wind, um, to the wind, um, that was whispering. [Julie cupped her hands by her ears.]

The three stories above were iterations of the story in *Joshua's Night Whispers* (1994). Jake started off by telling what seemed to be a true story about falling off the bed, which elicited laughter from his fellow classmates. And soon enough, children built off of Jake's momentum. As seen many times throughout this book, children used language in order to connect with social others. Stories that were uttered during writing workshop were crafted by young children that went beyond meeting curricular goals; instead, they were opportunities to bring language to life and elicit reactions from those around them.

Benji built off of Jake's seemingly true story, intermixing it with Johnson's character Joshua. Benji claimed that, like Joshua, he heard the wind and went into his parents' room. Julie, however, went one step further in the retelling of her "small moment." She brought several almost impossible elements into the story: she was a baby who could not walk, but eventually made it out of bed to creep around the house and listen to her cat. Somehow, Julie ended up in her parents' room and listened to the wind. It was obvious that while she was focusing on a small moment, there was little truth in the crafting of her story. She paused with "ums" while telling her story, as she carefully constructed what her next action would entail. Like Joshua, she made sure that on route to her parents' room, she noticed one thing in the hallway (i.e., she replaced a cat for the toybox featured in the story). Her story was a replica of Johnson's story with elements of Jake's story (i.e., "being little") and Benji's story (i.e., "going into mom and dad's room") mixed into it. She drew from the work of many "authors" to produce her own unique rendition with familiar elements of others' words. However, Debbie White responded to the story with interest, asking her questions as if the story really did belong to her, "And you got all the way to your mama's room, and what happened?"

Debbie White, of course, had literacy goals related to the structure of a story: a zoomed-in, focused moment of time that was opened up and detailed across several pages. Children, on the other hand, found meaning in connecting ideas with others, including the author of *Joshua's Night Whispers*. As a deliberate curricular move, Debbie White honored the words of the children, allowing their engagement with language to serve as a resource for her teaching and their learning. There were many directions she could have taken in this curricular moment, but instead she followed the momentum of the young storytellers who saw value in building off of each other's ideas rather than learning about focused stories. We presume that as a teacher, Debbie White decided how she addressed the curricular side roads that inevitably children bring us down.

Resisting Scripted Curriculum: Undoing Cookie-Cutter Teaching

When asking Debbie White and her kindergarten colleague why scripted curriculum does not work, they replied,

> Debbie White: For the same reason there is "no child left behind." You know what, we are just not cookie cutter kids or teachers. And, how do you? Where does the script say somebody just threw up on the rug and two other children lost their teeth just now.
>
> Aliyah: Right, none of the programs that they purchase could ever cover every different child you have in the classroom.
>
> Debbie White: Or situation.

Children, teachers, and schools are not cookie-cutter factory lines. Similarly, as long as language is viewed as mechanical—specified inputs yield predictable outputs—we miss the sophisticated language moves that children make, much like the ones discussed earlier. They fluidly mix ideas together; personal stories and small moments intersect with popular culture and classroom culture. They use language for genuine, communicative purposes: to assert their identities, to voice their affiliations, to build ideas in response to each other, and to show that they are naturally literate beings. Debbie White articulated that curriculum could never account for the cultural events present in every classroom—the mishaps like throwing up or the milestones like losing teeth. Instead, she took an approach to teaching that embraced these turns, attributing them to unique differences in personalities, experiences, and situations. The cultural "trends" in her classroom were the stuff of curriculum as intended, the co-construction of shared meaning that allowed Debbie White (after twenty-three years) to be curious about young children's ideas about the world, through the medium of language.

Inclusion and Belonging at Table 1: From Community to Family

We bring the world of this kindergarten classroom to a close by bringing Tonea to the foreground. After several months of being in this kindergarten classroom, listening and documenting the interactions at Table 1, Haeny Yoon finally had the privilege of appearing in Tonea's text (Figure 9.1).

FIGURE 9.1 Tonea's Drawing

Tonea: [To Haeny Yoon] And you're going to have a dress on you.

Haeny: Yay.

Tonea: A skirt on you too.

Jaquan: [To Tonea] Write me in your picture.

Tonea: You be in my picture too. And Jolene and Lou and my and my . . .

Jaquan: Write me. Write me.

Tonea: Okay. I'm writing her first. [She points at Haeny Yoon.]

Jaquan: Tonea! Write me in your picture, Tonea.

Tonea: Okay! I'm writing you in the kitcher, picture.

Jaquan: I'm in the kitchen?

Tonea: Picture.

Jaquan: Oh.

Tonea: Not, kitchen. Oops. [Tonea starts drawing a head but messed up, so she's erasing now.]

Jaquan: That's okay.

Tonea: That could be your pants! [Tonea points to the figure on the far left.] That could be your pants, right? It could be your pants.

Jaquan: No, do my hand. Then, you do my hand first there. [Tonea starts to make it.] Yeah.

Tonea: Like that?

Jaquan: Yeah.

Tonea: Okay.

Jaquan: Tonea, you in this big spaceship. [Jaquan points at his drawing.]

Tonea: Whooooa! I am?!

Jaquan: Yeah.

Tonea: I'm writing you in my picture too. And I'm writing Jolene in my picture and Lou and Jon. [Lou looks up.]

As seen here and earlier in the book, having a part in each other's stories was important to the children. Jaquan wanted a spot in the story. Lou looked up with interest when Tonea declared that he would also be in it. Tonea also made a point to include everyone currently at the table. The finished product included Haeny Yoon (the tall figure in the middle) and the rest of the children with either pants and spiked hair (to connote boys) or skirts and long hair (to connote girls). The story seemed fitting given the fact that together in this space, these children found ways to share their lives, question their ideas, and make social connections. Tonea's offer of inclusion was reciprocated by Jaquan who changed his story to make Tonea the main character. Throughout the year, the texts were rewritten and even retold to fit shifting social purposes—Jaquan's same story was once a cat going into space, or his mom taking him to the park, or Michael Myers coming to get him. Tonea's piece, however, represented the people around her (peers and even an adult bystander) who made literacy valuable. The children in the story are the ones who motivated her literacy life, who helped develop her penchant for stories, who gave her a purpose to participate in literate acts.

Going from whole group lessons to their independent writing time was an opportunity for the children to develop and cultivate their own space. Their teacher was virtually absent in the philosophical debates and social renderings at Tonea's table; partly because in authentic third spaces, no one is the sole arbiter of knowledge. As highlighted throughout this book, Debbie White put together a group of children at each table that brought with them a wealth of experiences—funds of knowledge. Therefore, it was up to the children to build their repertoire of literacy tools, and Debbie White trusted them to do this. In these third spaces, there is an emphasis from "teaching to learning, from individuals to collectives, from classrooms to communities, and from habitual to reflexive practice" (Gutiérrez et al. 1997, 372). Children (and adults) are part of multiple, overlapping communities, and for the kindergartners at Table 1, they found a new community in the relationships fostered within this group. They illustrate for us how literacy practices are invented as individuals participate in shared events. They wrote trademarked stories about rainbows, upheld and attempted to impose classroom laws on copying, and wrote each other into "true stories" that may have never taken place.

Unstandardizing Literacy Curricula

At the time of the study in Debbie White's kindergarten, literacy curriculum was idiosyncratic, drawing from multiple programs with congruent or competing language theories. For example, while using a writing workshop approach to writing instruction (Calkins 1986) where children were encouraged to independently construct ideas and create stories, teachers were also encouraged to use intervention programs for the class that focused on whole-group language exercises. Where the writing curriculum focused on encoding words to form a story, the reading programs focused on decoding words out of context. The teachers were also given two literature programs, one promoting good habits for readers and another focused on comprehension. Due to time constraints, all three of the kindergarten teachers in Debbie's school admitted to taking ideas from one curriculum or the other, integrating ideas in ways they saw fit, and bypassing the time limits that were allotted for language units.

Debbie, and her colleague Jennifer, likened curriculum to a revolving door.

> Jennifer: It's been a while now, things have definitely settled. For a while, and I don't know how many years ago, every time we turned around, there was something old going and something new coming. And, you would barely just get a good mastery of teaching the way you were needing to be teaching the latest curriculum or whatever and off it would go, and then it would come this new curriculum.
>
> Debbie White: Something was always going and something was always coming.

Curriculum was reduced to a set of materials that could be applied and discarded. Our view is that curriculum is a sociopolitical act made up of ideologies and big ideas that teachers apply and discard in spite of the "comings and goings" of curricular materials (Freire 1970; Sleeter and Carmona 2012).

In sociocultural approaches to language and literacy, we view language practices as an "identity kit" (Gee 1991, 3). Thus, young children use language to grow their ideas and literacy in the broadest sense (e.g., interactions, translanguaging, oral/verbal competence, communication, etc.). Furthermore, the multiple worlds of children converge rather than occur in separate spaces. For children, these cultural worlds need to be interwoven, flexible, and permeable (Dyson 1993). Languages and cultures embody values and ideologies that are not "biologically encoded on human brains; they are rituals and rules that have evolved within cultural contexts" (Ramsey 2015, 107).

Returning to the idea of literacies as tools for "reading the world" (Freire 1970), we attest that the world is ever expanding for children because of social media, digital tools, and other materials within the cultural milieu of childhood. With these "new literacies" (Gee 2015b; New London Group 1996) readily available to children, literacy is evolving and changing within this new landscape of communication options. Most importantly, children learn language both individually and collectively—they develop innate language systems through participation in social and cultural communities (Chomsky 1968), and they cultivate innovative language practices within and across communities of practice. For example, Alison Lanza, the second-grade teacher in New York City, celebrated children's keen attention to literacy in social worlds. While engaging in more traditional literacies, such as reading books, her students also unpacked graffiti as a socially significant literacy act with rules, meanings, and intentions. They inquired about ideas related to tagging and to symbolic placement of pictures and words. Graffiti, a contested literacy, was repositioned as a legitimate way to use conventional literacy while intermixing various other multimodal forms (images, art, texture). Within their neighborhood in East Harlem, this enabled children to engage in critical literacy, examining, learning about, and problematizing the "social and political conditions that unfold in communities in which we live" (Vasquez 2004b, 1).

Teaching as Advocacy: The Politics of Languages and Literacies

As we reflect on the cases shared in this book, we are reminded of the teachers we met—like Phillip Baumgarner, Jessica Martell, Alison Lanza, Carmen Lugo Llerena, Abigail Salas Maguire, Maria Helena Mendonça Buril, Yadira Sanchez, and Mary Martin, who allowed children's concerns about their social world to seep into their curricular spaces. Their practices displayed a deep commitment to repositioning literacies as tools for social justice. Literacies were thus foundational to their teaching as they sought to engage young children in transforming inequitable realities, righting the wrongs that plague a continually unjust world. For example, the children in Jessica Martell's classroom used literacies to question racial stereotypes (e.g., service workers as Mexican immigrants). She made space in the dominant curricular structures (e.g., morning meeting, shared writing, read-aloud) for children's concerns to be expressed, addressed, and legitimized. Jessica was willing to shift the curriculum and offer time, space, and resources for genuine engagements with literacies; and she carefully coordinated these experiences with the mandated learning standards in mind. She, like many other teachers, recognized that it is essential to create spaces where

> [C]hildren become critical of aspects of the culture that denigrate or humiliate them or anyone else. . . . Instead of prohibiting things that tempt children, this means allowing them the freedom to explore things while trusting them to make sensible and humane judgments. (Kohl 1995, as cited in Jenkins 1998, 31–32)

This is also the challenge for educators: to hand over power to children and simultaneously provide tools to explore the cultural world around them.

Therefore, it is important to take the work of children seriously, not as trivial pursuits but as windows into their meaning-making process as both participants and contributors of languages, literacies, and cultures. Each teacher whose stories and practices populate the pages of this book created spaces of hope and possibility where children's cultural and linguistic practices were sustained. In these spaces, children's ideas were legitimized and identities affirmed as inequities were questioned and injustices were interrupted.

Yet, instead of sharing formulas and offering solutions, we recognize that teaching is much more complicated than many think it is. "The actions of teachers, like those of everyone else, are constantly responsive to that vast and largely unarticulated network of shared understandings that comprises much of what people mean when they talk of common sense" (Jackson 1986, 11–12). In other words, teaching practice (like common sense) is elusive, largely comprised of individual ideologies and experiences. Moreover, there is no one way to describe good teaching as it is inherently the cumulative sum of peoples' social and cultural experiences—it is differently defined rather than singularly constructed. Teachers use their intuition and beliefs to teach young children, a form of common sense that requires thoughtful analysis of children's social, linguistic, and cultural identities.

Education is about liberation and democracy as articulated at the beginning of this chapter and reiterated throughout this book—ideas that Mike Rose (1995) did not have access to given his marginal status. We see many of the children featured in this book in danger of experiencing those same conditions of learning: reductionist curriculum, mediocre teaching, and narrowly defined language and literacy opportunities. Instead, the children whose stories, experiences, voices, and practices we share are meant to reveal the breadth and depth of languages and literacies as communicative tools; as ways of reading and rewriting the world. As the political environment becomes more hostile to children's linguistic flexibility, while many children of color are denied their right to play, while children from low- and no-income families continue to populate under-resourced schools, we believe that teachers can offer transformative possibilities through rethinking curriculum, languages, and literacies—centering democratic aims. "This is the moment within which we have to choose who we want to be as scholars and intellectuals, as teachers and researchers, as citizens, most of all, as liberatory curriculum activists" (Ayers et al. 2008, 319).

We thus call for a reframing of early languages and literacies—redefining and reconceptualizing them in ways that create pedagogical spaces where students are encouraged to draw from language and literacy practices and repertoires that speak to their being. This stands in stark contrast to simply using "their stuff" to teach the "real stuff" (Kirkland 2008). Such a reframing entails deliberately moving toward upholding students' rights to their own languages and cultural practices as means to interrogate and challenge their world(s). After all, literacies are how we challenge orthodoxy and confront injustice, through signs, materials, and our very voices. By highlighting the various ways that literacies are practiced, we honor the rich linguistic competencies of children and bring to the forefront nondominant communities whose languages and identities are often swept under the proverbial rug. Teachers honoring students' experiences in order to teach them the dominant culture is simply not enough. Instead, we affirm the need for third spaces, open, flexible instructional spaces where teachers bring the "artifacts of student life (e.g., rap, body art, graffiti) into classrooms to not only help advance students' academic literacy development, but to ultimately adjust how literacy is conceived of, practiced, and assessed" (Kirkland 2008, 73).

As we made visible throughout the chapters of this book, literacies are deeply personal and inherently ideological. They are situated and relational. They go much beyond the combination of phonemes or the correspondence of letters and sounds. Literacies are cultural practices negotiated by young children, passed down from generation to generation, and taught in varied cultural contexts. Literacies and languaging are "intricately linked to the construction of social roles, cultural affiliations, beliefs, values, and behavioral practices" (Li 2008, 14); and children enter school occupying multiple spaces— within, across, and in between cultural worlds.

As we reflect on the problematic legacy of early literacy and of unequal (pre) schooling opportunities in the U.S., we offer an inclusive definition of early literacies, which encourages teachers and researchers to advocate for children's linguistic flexibility, honoring their incredible ability to navigate within and across varied cultural spaces while sustaining their own languages, literacies, and identities. In doing so, we reaffirm our call for ongoing systematic studies of young children's family and community cultural practices as the basis for curriculum development and planning. We call for spaces where teachers can learn and grow together as inquirers, curriculum makers, and advocates. We also call for engagement and partnership with families and community members. Only then will we be able to honor who young children are and the diversities they represent.

May we be inspired by the sophisticated cultural practices of diverse children, families, and communities featured in this book; they showed us a number of powerful ways to rethink early literacies. May we learn from teachers whose teaching invites us to unveil worlds of transformative possibilities as we commit to recognize the brilliance of minoritized children and build on their strengths. Most of all, may we—as a field and as individual educators—move away from prescribing curriculum as if it were medicine to remediate perceived ailments children bring with them to classrooms and (pre)schools. After all, young children's multiple literacies, language repertoires, and ways of being in the world must be recognized, valued, and sustained as we rewrite a more just tomorrow. It is a matter of humanity.

AFTERWORD

Luis Moll

This is a terrific book, lively and informative, immersing the reader into multiple and revealing pedagogical scenarios. The authors summarize a sociocultural or "processual" approach to early language and literacy development where the children are the main protagonists, and play and imagination become the leading activities for their learning. The teachers are certainly not absent from this formulation; teachers are always key, creating and mediating the conditions under which teaching and learning become transactional, never directive or scripted, especially given the emphasis on learning about and from their students. At the heart of this book, then, are multiple "case examples" (as I call them), all sources for theorizing, which bring children's learning to life, involving classroom or community-oriented activities where the children actively create themselves, shaping their subjectivities through the use of multiple social, cultural, and linguistic resources. As Vygotsky (2004, 66) put it: "The best stimulus of creativity in children is to organize their life and environment so that it leads to the need and ability to create." Such is the goal of the activities featured in this book. The environment, then, is considered not only as a setting but as a source of learning and development.

In this brief Afterword, I want to add a couple of examples that I think may complement the text, moving beyond the early childhood years. One is an example (gathered by Ruth Sáez) from a bilingual classroom that features two girls' collaborative writing about ethnic conflict and then finding a resolution. I have used the example previously (e.g., Moll, Sáez, and Dworin 2001) because it captures not only the power of biliteracy in elementary schooling (they were third graders), but also the cleverness and creativity of the two girls in conceptualizing the story, and of the teacher in arranging classroom circumstances for such novel and risky writing to occur. It is the sort of story, however, that could lead to classroom-wide discussions of social and political issues that affect all of us, most certainly the children and their families as well. The second example (from Moll 2014) is about how teachers collected household observations and interviews, as part of their documentation of "funds of knowledge," and then participated in study groups with university researchers and other schoolteachers to share what they learned about families and students. This was knowledge that could lead to innovations and improvements in teaching. The claim here is that teacher development, especially as they learn about and from students and families, must always accompany student development. This is a subterraneous yet present aspect of the teacher-student interactions Souto-Manning and Yoon presented throughout this book.

My first example features two girls, who were good friends, collaborating in writing this fictional bilingual story about a new girl in the neighborhood, Raquel, a Spanish speaker, and the resentment she encountered from a White girl, Michelle, in the same neighborhood and school (from Moll, Sáez, and Dworin 2001, 444). The story has a cordial albeit brief and unexpected ending, given the tense exchange of words by the girls. (I have included a typed version of the handwritten original, but one that retains the girls' punctuation and spelling.)

THE NEW GIRL IN THE NEIGHBORHOOD

By L. and R.

One day a new girl moved in my neighborhood. She was poor. I did not like her. She also was a Mexican girl. I went to her house and asked her name. "Mi nombre es Raquel," she replied. "I know a little bit of Spanish," I told her. "I know a little of 'ingles,'" Raquel told me. "Mi nombre es Michelle. I don't like you." I yelled and then I yelled "Your not supposed to be holy today your supposed to be holy Sunday." she started to cry, then ran inside.

The next day my teacher said, "we have a new girl," "her name is Raquel." I screamed "What's the matter the teacher asked. "nothing I thought I saw a spider"

After school I went to Raquel's house and asked "What were you doing in MY classroom"? "Para aprender a escribir y leer en ingles." She answered. "If YOU SHOW UP TOMorrow at my school Ill hurt you. And then she said. "No te entiendo." I got so mad that I screamed and ran away. The next day I went to her house and we talked and I found out that we had lots in common. And we were friends for ever.

The End

There are various themes found in this brief bilingual text: bilingual exchanges, humor, irrational dislikes, literacy learning, hostility to others who are different, threats, and similarities leading to friendship. With the teacher's help, any one of these themes could have been elaborated more fully in writing, or through discussions in class or study groups. As we wrote then, "The text represents an example of bringing life into the writing, and of using writing, and its conventions, to examine issues of life. But it also represents the extent to which languages can interconnect and interact with each other as part of the children's writing" (Moll et al. 2001, 444). What we did not mention at the time was how affect-laden the text is; how emotions permeate (or mediate) the storytelling and how both languages are used, indeed, cleverly manipulated, to capture and display those essential elements of the story and their experiences. By the way, "Your [sic] not supposed to be holy today" is a play on words that the students used to tease classmates when they had a hole in their pants or shirt; it did not have religious connotations. Also notice how quickly third graders resolve a tough and difficult ethnic conflict. In case you missed it, "The next day I went to her house and we talked and I found out that we had lots in common. And we were friends for ever." At least dialogue and diplomacy prevails in the story, if not in life, especially nowadays. As I have written elsewhere (Moll 2014, 102), "Literacy in two languages mediates thinking not only by supporting access to the real worlds of both language communities and the resources of books in both languages, but also by helping these children imagine new worlds that have not existed before. This kind of imagination is a profoundly metacognitive activity, as the children acquire control over their thinking."

The next example also involves achieving control over one's thinking, but in relation to teachers' representations of their students and their families. This was a central goal of our funds-of-knowledge research with families. Our main strategy involved creating a study group with teachers who would be conducting household visits with some of their students, mostly from working-class families (González, Moll, and Amanti 2005; Moll 2014). The purpose of the study group was to reflect on the work and what we were learning, address problems in data collection, and for teachers to take the lead in suggesting pedagogical initiatives based on the information generated by the household observations and interviews.

Within the context of my study (Moll 2014), the study group turned into a key setting, the center of gravity, as I called it, mainly because it served as a place to discuss what we were learning and its relevance to the schooling of the students, and a place to scrutinize classroom lessons based on the household visits. It also was a flexible setting, and it was transportable, as we met in colleagues' homes, in cafeterias or restaurants, in school libraries, and in university classrooms. And these discussions served to curb stereotypes, which were invariably challenged by the information gathered from the home visits. Here is a sample of some of the study group activities (adapted from Moll 2014, 147):

Study Group Artifacts and Activities

Fieldnotes based on household visits	Analysis of project-related concepts
Interviews with family members or students	Discussion of ethical issues
Discussing academic articles on culture and education	Practicing an interview
Reports on household visits or classroom activities	Discussion of case study
Discussion on details of data	Discussion of specific family visit
Challenging stereotypes about family or community	Planning of classroom activity

These study groups, then, served to mediate and clarify the relationship between household visits and classroom teaching and learning (much like the teaching and learning opportunities portrayed in Chapter 4 of this volume). They were also settings where the teachers' agendas were always present and respected, and they took the lead in developing and addressing issues and opportunities. The household visits, thanks to the grounding achieved through the study groups, became a way of engaging teachers strategically with their cultural environments for teaching. I take the study groups, then, as an example of what Edwards (2005) calls "relational agency," the capacity to work with others and recognize and acti-vate them as resources to expand our thinking. This also includes the "capacity for interpreting and approaching problems, for contesting interpretations, for reading the environment, for drawing on the resources there, for being a resource for others, for focusing on the core objects of the professions whether it is children's learning or social inclusion" (Edwards 2005, 179).

In closing, allow me to reiterate my praise of the impressive achievement of my colleagues in preparing this volume. It has been a delight to read their book. I have offered two examples from previous studies that I hope relate critically but also admiringly to the present work, extending it beyond second grade, making visible the promise and possibility of this work beyond the earliest years. The first example resembles the sort of student agency that the authors highlight in this volume, however, featuring writing that, in my view, no English monolingual student could produce. The clever translanguaging displayed in the text, giving this brief story tremendous authenticity, is missed completely in monolingual settings. A consequence is that teachers and students may also ignore completely that such switching of languages, often disparaged, is at the heart of the intellectual power offered by bilingualism, the ability to read in one language, either word or world, and discuss what is read in another. The gift of biliteracy is found in this sort of flexibility, in providing a broad array of cultural resources for thinking. The second example addressed how to produce a social structure, in this instance a study group for teachers and others, that may be the beginning of sustaining an innovation and producing the social and cultural capital necessary for teachers to collaborate, and become important, expansive, and lasting professional resources for each other. This sort of collaboration is at the heart of the present book as well. The many cases they share offer us hope and possibility. But beyond offering examples, Souto-Manning and Yoon offer an urgent call for transformative action. As the authors have proposed,

> We reaffirm our call for ongoing systematic studies of young children's family and community cultural practices as the basis for curriculum development and planning. We call for engagement and partnership with families and community members. Only then will we be able to honor who young children are and the diversities they represent.

I agree. Count me in.

References

Edwards, A. (2005). Relational agency: Learning to be a resourceful practitioner. *International Journal of Educational Research*, 43, 168–182.

González, N., Moll, L. C., and Amanti, C., eds. (2005). *Funds of Knowledge: Theorizing Practices in Households, Communities, and Classrooms*. Mahwah, NJ: Erlbaum.

Moll, L. C. (2014). *L. S. Vygotsky and Education*. New York, NY/London, UK: Routledge.

Moll, L. C., Sáez, R., and Dworin, J. (2001). Exploring biliteracy. *Elementary School Journal*, 101(4), 435–449.

Vygotsky, L. S. (2004). Imagination and creativity in childhood. *Journal of Russian & East European Psychology*, 42(1), 7–97.

ABOUT THE AUTHORS

Mariana Souto-Manning, Ph.D., is Associate Professor of Early Childhood Education and director of the Doctoral Program in Curriculum and Teaching and the Masters Programs in Early Childhood Education and Early Childhood Special Education at Teachers College, Columbia University. From a critical perspective, she examines in/equities and in/justices in early childhood teaching and teacher education, focusing on issues pertaining to language and literacy practices in pluralistic settings. In her research she critically considers theoretical  and methodological issues and dilemmas of doing research *with* communities of color. Souto-Manning has published seven books, including the 2016 winner of the American Educational Studies Association Critics' Choice Award, *Reading, Writing, and Talk: Inclusive Teaching Strategies for Diverse Learners, K–2* (with Jessica Martell). Her work can also be found in journals such as *Linguistics and Education, Journal of Teacher Education, International Journal of Qualitative Studies in Education, Research in the Teaching of English*, and *Teachers College Record*. She is the recipient of a number of research awards, including the 2011 American Educational Research Association (AERA) Division K Innovations in Research on Diversity in Teacher Education Award and the 2017 AERA Division K (Teaching and Teacher Education) Mid-Career Award.

Haeny Yoon, Ph.D., is Assistant Professor of Early Childhood Education at Teachers College, Columbia University. She teaches courses on curriculum, language/literacy, and children's play. Her work focuses on how teachers can create curriculum and orchestrate spaces for children to use language and acquire literacy while engaging in meaningful social relationships. Previous to joining Teachers College, she was an assistant professor of early childhood education at the University of Arizona. She had the privilege of taking part in an early childhood program created with communities and families as integral partners in early childhood education. Their collective work can be found in *Re-Designing Teacher Education for Culturally*
and Linguistically Diverse Children: A Critical-Ecological Approach. Yoon's interest in curriculum, teacher development, and children's play stems from working as a staff developer and primary schoolteacher. She currently studies the intersection of children's cultural practices (e.g., play, language development, social interactions), teacher practice, and curriculum within classroom contexts. Her work can be found in *Research on the Teaching of English, Journal of Early Childhood Literacy, Multicultural Education Review*, and *Contemporary Issues in Early Childhood*. In addition, as department editor of "Language Arts Lessons," a column in *Language Arts*, she works to bridge theory and practice together with the work of scholars in the field of literacy.

REFERENCES

Abdullah, Q.R. (2010). *The Sandwich Swap*. New York, NY: Disney-Hyperion Books.

Adger, C.T., Wolfram, W., and Christian, D. (2007). *Dialects in Schools and Communities* (2nd ed.). Mahwah, NJ: Lawrence Erlbaum Associates.

Adichie, C. (2009). *The Danger of a Single Story*. Retrieved from http://www.ted.com/talks/chimamanda_adichie_the_danger_of_a_single_story.html

Alexander, M. (2012). *The New Jim Crow: Mass Incarceration in the Age of Colorblindness*. New York, NY: New Press.

Alim, S. (2003). "We are the streets": African American Language and the strategic construction of a street conscious identity. In S. Makoni, G. Smitherman, A.F. Ball, and A. Spears, eds., *Black Linguistics: Language, Society and Politics in Africa and the Americas* (pp. 40–59). New York, NY: Routledge.

Alim, S. (2005). Critical language awareness in the United States: Revisiting issues and revising pedagogies in a resegregated society. *Educational Researcher, 34*(7), 24–31.

Alim, S., Rickford, J.R., and Ball, A.F., eds. (2016). *Raciolinguistics: How Language Shapes Our Ideas About Race*. New York, NY: Oxford University Press.

Amanti, C. (2005). Beyond a beads and feathers approach. In N. González, L.C. Moll, and C. Amanti, eds., *Funds of Knowledge: Theorizing Practices in Households, Communities, and Classrooms* (pp. 131–141). Mahwah, NJ: Lawrence Erlbaum Associates.

Anderson, G., and Irvine, J. (1993). Informing critical literacy with ethnography. In C. Lankshear and P. McLaren, eds., *Critical Literacy: Politics, Praxis, and the Postmodern* (pp. 81–104). Albany, NY: SUNY Press.

Anyon, J. (1981). Social class and school knowledge. *Curriculum Inquiry, 11*(1), 3–42.

Anzaldúa, G. (1987). *Borderlands/La frontera: The New Mestiza*. San Francisco, CA: Aunt Lute Books.

Apple, M. (2004). *Ideology and Curriculum*. New York, NY: Routledge.

Apple, M. (2006). *Educating the Right Way: Markets, Standards, and Inequality*. New York, NY: Routledge.

Archer, M. (2000). *Being Human: The Problem of Agency*. Cambridge, UK: Cambridge University Press.

Archer, M. (2003). *Structure, Agency and the Internal Conversation*. Cambridge, UK: Cambridge University Press.

Au, W. (2012). *Critical Curriculum Studies: Education, Consciousness, and the Politics of Knowing*. New York, NY: Routledge.

Austin, J.L. (1962). *How to Do Things with Words*. Oxford, UK: Oxford University Press.

Ayers, W., Kumashiro, K., Meiners, E., Quinn, T., and Stovall, D. (2016). *Teaching Toward Democracy: Educators as Agents of Change*. New York, NY: Routledge.

Bakhtin, M.M. (1981). *The Dialogic Imagination*. M. Holquist, trans. Austin: University of Texas Press.

Bakhtin, M.M. (1986). *Speech Genres and Other Late Essays*. V.W. Mcgee, C. Emerson, and M. Holquist, trans. Austin: University of Texas Press.

Baldwin, J. (1963). A talk to teachers. In T. Morrison, ed., *Baldwin: Collected Essays* (pp. 678–686). New York, NY: Library of America.

Banks-Wallace, J. (2002). Talk that talk: Storytelling and analysis rooted in African American oral tradition. *Qualitative Health Research, 12*(3), 410–426.

Banks, J.A., and Banks, C.A.M. (2009). *Multicultural Education: Issues and Perspectives*, 7th ed. Hoboken, NJ: John Wiley & Sons.

Bartolomé, L.I. (1996). Beyond the methods fetish: Toward a humanizing pedagogy. In P. Leistyna, A. Woodrum, and S.A. Sherblom, eds., *Breaking Free: The Transformative Power of Critical Pedagogy* (pp. 229–252). Cambridge, MA: Harvard Graduate School of Education.

Barton, D. (1996). Family literacy programmes and home literacy practices. In D. Baker, J. Clay, and C. Fox, eds., *Challenging Ways of Knowing in English, Maths, and Science* (pp. 52–61). London, UK: Falmer Press.

Barton, D. (2001). Directions for literacy research: Analysing language and social practices in a textually mediated world. *Language and Education, 15*, 92–104.

Baugh, J. (2007). Plantation English in America: Nonstandard varieties and the quest for educational equity. *Research in the Teaching of English, 41*(4), 465–476.

Bauman, R., and Briggs, C. (2003). *Voices of Modernity: Language Ideologies and the Politics of Inequality*. New York, NY: Cambridge University Press.

Benjamin, W. (1968). The task of the translator. In H. Arendt, ed., *Illuminations* (pp. 69–82). New York, NY: Schocken Books.

Bentley, D.F., and Souto-Manning, M. (2016). Toward inclusive understandings of marriage in an early childhood classroom: Negotiating (un)readiness, community, and vulnerability through a critical reading of "King and King." *Early Years: An International Journal of Research and Development, 36*(2), 195–206. doi: http://dx.doi.org/10.1080/0957514 6.2015.1104899

Bhabha, H.K. (1994). *The Location of Culture*. New York, NY: Routledge.

Bishop, R.S. (1990). Mirrors, windows, and sliding glass doors. *Perspectives, 6*(3), 9–11.

Bishop, R.S. (2015). *Mirrors, Windows and Sliding Doors* [Video file]. Retrieved from https://www.youtube.com/watch?v=_AAu58SNSyc

Blaise, M. (2012). *Playing it Straight: Uncovering Gender Discourse in the Early Childhood Classroom*. Hoboken, NJ: Taylor & Francis.

Bomer, R., and Laman, T.T. (2004). Positioning in a primary writing workshop: Joint action in the discursive production of writing subjects. *Research in the Teaching of English, 38*(4), 420–466.

Boutte, G., and Johnson, G. (2013). Funga alafia: Toward welcoming, understanding and respecting African American speakers' bilingualism and biliteracy. *Equity and Excellence in Education, 46*(3), 300–314.

Boutte, G., and Johnson, G. (2014). Rethinking family and community involvement in urban schools: Learning about and from urban families and communities. In R. Milner and K. Lomotey, eds., *Handbook of Urban Education* (pp. 167–187). New York, NY: Routledge.

Bradby, M. (2000). *Momma, Where Are You From?* New York, NY: Orchard Books.

Brandt, D. (2001). Literacy learning and economic change. In S.W. Beck and L.N. Olah, eds., *Perspectives on Language and Literacy: Beyond the Here and Now* (pp. 201–220). Cambridge, MA: Harvard Educational Review.

Bronfenbrenner, U. (1979). *The Ecology of Human Development: Experiments by Nature and Design*. Cambridge, MA: Harvard University Press.

References **223**

Bronfenbrenner, U. (1992). Ecological systems theory. In R. Vasta, ed., *Six Theories of Child Development: Revised Formulations and Current Issues* (pp. 187–249). London, UK: Jessica Kingsley Publishers.

Bronfenbrenner, U. (2005). The bioecological theory of human development. In U. Bronfenbrenner, ed., *Making Human Beings Human: Bioecological Perspectives on Human Development* (pp. 3–15). Thousand Oaks, CA: Sage.

Buckingham, D. (2011). *The Material Child.* Cambridge, UK: Polity.

Calkins, L. (1986). *The Art of Teaching Writing.* Portsmouth, NH: Heinemann.

Calkins, L. (2003). *Units of Study for Primary Writing.* Portsmouth, NH: Heinemann.

Canagarajah, S. (1999). *Resisting Linguistic Imperialism in English Teaching.* Oxford, UK: Oxford University Press.

Canagarajah, S. (2003). Foreword. In G. Smitherman and V. Villanueva, eds., *Language Diversity in the Classroom: From Intention to Practice.* Carbondale, IL: Southern Illinois University Press.

Carter, R., and Goodwin, A.L. (1994). Racial identity and education. *Review of Research in Education, 20,* 291–336.

Cazden, C. (2001). *Classroom Discourse: The Language of Teaching and Learning,* 2nd ed. Portsmouth, NH: Heinemann.

Chomsky, N. (1957). *Syntactic Structures.* Berlin, Germany: Walter de Gruyter.

Chomsky, N. (1959). Review of Skinner's verbal behavior. *Language, 35,* 26–58.

Chomsky, N. (1968). *Language and Mind.* New York, NY: Harcourt, Brace, & World.

Chouliaraki, L., and Fairclough, N. (1999). *Discourse in Late Modernity.* Edinburgh, UK: Edinburgh University Press.

Chudacoff, H. (2007). Introduction. In *Children at Play: An American History* (pp. 1–18). New York, NY: NYU Press.

Clay, M. (1991). *Becoming Literate: The Construction of Inner Control.* Portsmouth, NH: Heinemann.

Clay, M. (1993). *An Observation Survey of Early Literacy Achievement.* Portsmouth, NH: Heinemann.

Clay, M. (1998). *By Different Paths to Common Outcomes.* Portland, ME: Stenhouse Publishers.

Clay, M. (2000). *Concepts about Print: What Have Children Learned about Printed Language?* Portsmouth, NH: Heinemann.

Cohen, D.K., and Barnes, C.A. (1993). Pedagogy and policy. In D.K. Cohen, M.W. McLaughlin, and J.E. Talbert, eds., *Teaching for Understanding: Challenges for Policy and Practice* (pp. 207–239). San Francisco, CA: Jossey-Bass.

Cohen, L.E. (2011). Bakhtin's carnival and pretend role play: A comparison of social contexts. *American Journal of Play, 4*(2), 176–203.

Cole, M., and Cole, S. (1996). *The Development of Children,* 3rd ed. New York, NY: W.H. Freeman.

Cole, M., and Engeström, Y. (1993). A cultural-historical approach to distributed cognition. In G. Salomon, ed., *Distributed Cognitions: Psychology and Educational Considerations* (pp. 484–507). Cambridge, UK: Cambridge University Press.

Cole, M., and Griffin, P. (1983). A socio-historical approach to re-mediation. *The Quarterly Newsletter of the Laboratory of Comparative Human Cognition, 5*(4), 69–74.

Coleman, E. (1996). *White Socks Only.* Morton Grove, IL: Albert Whitman and Company.

Collins, J., and Blot, R.K. (2003). *Literacy and Literacies: Texts, Power, and Identity.* Cambridge, UK: Cambridge University Press.

Comber, B. (2001a). Critical literacies and local action: Teacher knowledge and a "new" research agenda. In B. Comber and A. Simpson, eds., *Negotiating Critical Literacies in Classrooms* (pp. 271–282). Mahwah, NJ: Lawrence Erlbaum Associates.

Comber, B. (2001b). Negotiating critical literacies. *School Talk, 6*(3), 1–2.

Comber, B. (2003). Critical literacy in the early years: What does it look like? In N. Hall, J. Larson and J. Marsh, eds., *Handbook of Early Childhood Literacy* (pp. 355–368). London, UK: Sage.

Combs, M.C., and Nicholas, S.E. (2012). The effect of Arizona language policies on Arizona indigenous students. *Language Policy, 11*, 101–118.

Compton-Lilly, C. (2006). Identity, childhood culture, and literacy learning: A case study. *Journal of Early Childhood Literacy, 6*(1), 57–76.

Cook, D.T. (Ed.). (2002). *Symbolic Childhood*. New York, NY: Peter Lang.

Copple, C., and Bredekamp, S. (2009). *Developmentally Appropriate Practice in Early Childhood Programs Serving Children from Birth through Age 8*, 3rd ed. Washington, DC: National Association for the Education of Young Children.

Corsaro, W. (2003). *We're Friends, Right? Inside Kids' Culture*. Washington, DC: Joseph Henry Press.

Corsaro, W. (2011). *The Sociology of Childhood*, 3rd ed. Thousand Oaks, CA: Sage Publishing.

Corsaro, W.A., and Eder, D. (1990). Children's peer cultures. *Annual Review of Sociology, 16*, 197–220.

Coutinho, M.J., and Oswald, D.P. (2000). Disproportionate representation in special education: A synthesis and recommendations. *Journal of Child and Family Studies, 9*(2), 135–152.

Cowhey, M. (2006). *Black Ants and Buddhists: Thinking Critically and Teaching Differently in the Primary Grades*. Portland, ME: Stenhouse Publishers.

Crenshaw, K. (1991). Mapping the margins: Intersectionality, identity politics, and violence against women of color. *Stanford Law Review, 43*(6), 1241–1299.

Darling-Hammond, L. (2010). *The Flat World and Education: How America's Commitment to Equity Will Determine Our Future*. New York, NY: Teachers College Press.

Delpit, L. (1988). The silenced dialogue: Power and pedagogy in educating other people's children. *Harvard Educational Review, 58*(3), 280–299.

Delpit, L. (1995/2006). *Other People's Children: Cultural Conflict in the Classroom*. New York, NY: New Press.

Delpit, L. (1998). Ebonics and culturally responsive instruction. In T. Perry and L. Delpit, eds., *The Real Ebonics Debate: Power, Language, and the Education of African-American Children* (pp. 17–26). Boston, MA: Beacon Press.

Delpit, L. (2012). *"Multiplication Is for White People": Raising the Expectations for Other People's Children*. New York, NY: The New Press.

Delpit, L., and Dowdy, J.K., eds. (2008). *The Skin that We Speak: Thoughts on Language and Culture in the Classroom*. New York, NY: The New Press.

Dewey, J. (1902). *The Child and the Curriculum*. Chicago, IL: University of Chicago Press.

Dickinson, D.K., and Sprague, K.E. (2001). The nature and impact of early childhood care environments on the language and early literacy development of children from low-income families. In S.B. Neuman and D.K. Dickinson, eds., *Handbook of Early Literacy Research* (pp. 263–280). New York, NY: Guilford.

Dickinson, D., McCabe, A., Anastasopoulos, L., Peisner-Feinberg, E., and Poe, M. (2003). The comprehensive language approach to early literacy: The interrelationships among vocabulary, phonological sensitivity, and print knowledge among preschool-aged children. *Journal of Educational Psychology, 95*(3), 465–481.

Dickinson, D.K. and Tabors, P.O. (2001). *Beginning Literacy with Language: Young Children Learning at Home and School*. Baltimore, MD: Paul H. Brooks Publishing.

Doake, D. (1981). *Book experience and emergent reading behavior in preschool children*. Unpublished doctoral dissertation, University of Alberta, Canada.

Dolby, N. (2003). Popular culture and democratic practice. *Harvard Educational Review, 73*(3), 258–284.

Du Bois, W.E.B. (1903). *The Souls of Black Folk: Essays and Sketches*. Chicago, IL: A. C. McClurg.

Dudley-Marling, C., and Lucas, K. (2009). Pathologizing the language and culture of poor children. *Language Arts, 86*(5), 362–370.

Durkin, D. (1966). *Children Who Read Early*. New York, NY: Teachers College Press.

Dutro, E. (2010). What "hard times" means: Mandated curricula, class-privileged assumptions, and the lives of poor children. *Research on the Teaching of English, 44*(3), 255–281.

Dyson, A.H. (1982). *The Emergence of Visible Language: Interrelationships between Drawing and Early Writing*. Retrieved from http://files.eric.ed.gov/fulltext/ED230280.pdf

Dyson, A.H. (1985). Three emergent writers and the school curriculum: Copying and other myths. *The Elementary School Journal, 85*(4), 496–512.

Dyson, A.H. (1989). *Multiple Worlds of Child Writers: Friends Learning to Write*. New York, NY: Teachers College Press.

Dyson, A.H. (1990). Symbol makers, symbol weavers: How children link play, pictures and print. *Young Children, 45*(2), 50–57.

Dyson, A.H. (1993). *Social Worlds of Children Learning to Write in an Urban Primary School*. New York, NY: Teachers College Press.

Dyson, A.H. (1995). Writing children: Reinventing the development of childhood literacy. *Written Communication, 12*(1), 4–46.

Dyson, A.H. (1997). *Writing Superheroes: Contemporary Childhood, Popular Culture, and Classroom Literacy*. New York, NY: Teachers College Press.

Dyson, A.H. (1999). Coach Bombay's kids learn to write: Children's appropriation of media materials for school literacy. *Research in the Teaching of English, 33*(4), 367–402.

Dyson, A.H. (2003a). *The Brothers and Sisters Learn to Write: Popular Literacies in Childhood and School Cultures*. New York, NY: Teachers College Press.

Dyson, A.H. (2003b). Popular literacies and the "all" children: Rethinking literacy development in contemporary childhoods. *Language Arts, 81*(2), 100–109.

Dyson, A.H. (2007). School literacy and the development of a child culture: Writing remnants of the "gusto of life." In D. Thiessen and A. Cook-Sather, eds., *International Handbook of Student Experience in Elementary and Secondary School* (pp. 115–142). Dordrecht, the Netherlands: Springer.

Dyson, A.H. (2008). Staying in the (curricular) lines: Practice constraints and possibilities in childhood writing. *Written Communication, 25*(1), 119–159.

Dyson, A.H. (2010). Opening curricular closets in regulated times: Finding pedagogical keys. *English Education, 42*, 301–319.

Dyson, A.H. (2013). *ReWRITING the Basics: Literacy Learning in Children's Cultures*. New York, NY: Teachers College Press.

Dyson, A.H., and Genishi, C. (2005). *On the Case: Approaches to Language and Literacy Research*. New York, NY: Teachers College Press.

Dyson, A.H., and Smitherman, G. (2009). The right (write) start: African American language and the discourse of sounding right. *Teachers College Record, 111*(4), 973–998.

Edelman, M.W. (2015). *It's Hard to be What You Can't See*. Retrieved from http://www.childrensdefense.org/newsroom/child-watch-columns/child-watch-documents/ItsHardtobeWhatYouCantSee.html

Evans, J. (2004). *Literacy Moves On: Using Popular Culture, New Technologies and Critical Literacy in the Primary Classroom*. Portsmouth, NH: Heinemann.

Fairclough, N. (2003). *Analysing Discourse: Textual Analysis for Social Research*. London, UK: Routledge.

Falchi, L., Axelrod, Y., and Genishi, C. (2014). "Miguel es un artista"— and Luisa is an excellent student: Seeking time and space for children's multimodal practices. *Journal of Early Childhood Literacy, 14*(3), 345–366.

Fennimore, B. (2008). Talk about children: Developing a living curriculum of advocacy and social justice. In C. Genishi and A.L. Goodwin, eds., *Diversities in Early Childhood Education: Rethinking and Doing* (pp. 185–199). New York, NY: Routledge.

Ferguson, A.A. (2001). *Bad Boys: Public Schools in the Making of Black Masculinity (Law, Meaning, Violence)*. Ann Arbor: University of Michigan Press.

Ferreiro, E., and Teberosky, A. (1982). *Literacy Before Schooling*. Exeter, NH: Heinemann.

Fisher, M. (2003). Open mics and open minds: Spoken word poetry in African diaspora participatory literacy communities. *Harvard Educational Review, 73*(3), 362–389.

Fisher, M. (2007). "Every city has soldiers": The role of intergenerational relationships in participatory literacy communities. *Research in the Teaching of English, 42*(2), 139–162.

Fiske, J. (1995). Popular culture. In F. Lentricchia and T. McLaughlin, eds., *Critical Terms for Literary Study* (pp. 321–335). Chicago, IL: University of Chicago Press.

Fiske, J. (2016). *Power Plays Power Works*, 2nd ed. New York, NY: Routledge.

Formanek-Brunell, M. (1998). The politics of dollhood in nineteenth-century America. In H. Jenkins, ed., *The Children's Culture Reader* (pp. 363–381). New York, NY: NYU Press.

Foucault, M. (1977). *Discipline and Punish: The Birth of the Prison*. New York, NY: Vintage Books.

Freedman, D. (2007). *Scribble*. New York, NY: Alfred A Knopf.

Freire, P. (1970/1996/2003). *Pedagogy of the Oppressed*. New York, NY: Continuum.

Freire, P. (2000). *Pedagogy of the Oppressed* (30th anniversary ed.). New York, NY: Continuum.

Freire, P. (1985a). Reading the world and reading the word: An interview with Paulo Freire. *Language Arts, 62*(1), 15–21.

Freire, P. (1985b). *The Politics of Education*. Westport, CT: Bergin and Garvin.

Freire, P. (1998). *Teachers as Cultural Workers: Letters to Those Who Dare Teach*. Boulder, CO: Westview.

Freire, P., and Macedo, D. (1987). *Literacy: Reading the Word and the World*. Westport, CT: Bergin & Garvey.

Freire, P., and Macedo, D. (1998). Literacy: Reading the word and the world. *Thinking, 14*(1), 8–10.

Gainer, J. (2007). Social critique and pleasure: Critical media literacy with popular culture texts. *Language Arts, 85*(2), 106–114.

Galdone, P. (1970). *The Three Little Pigs*. New York, NY: Clarion Books.

Ganeshram, R. (2016). *A Birthday Cake for George Washington*. New York, NY: Scholastic.

García-Coll, C., and Marks, A. (2009). *Immigrant Stories*. New York, NY: Oxford University Press.

García, E. (2012, October). *Teaching Young English Language Learners*. QUIERE Seminar Series, New York, NY: Teachers College Press.

García, O. (2009). *Bilingual Education in the 21st Century: A Global Perspective*. Malden, MA/ Oxford, UK: Basil/Blackwell.

García, E., and García, E. (2012). *Understanding the Language Development and Early Education of Hispanic Children*. New York, NY: Teachers College Press.

Garvey, C. (1990). *Play* (Vol. 27). Cambridge, MA: Harvard University Press.

Gee, J.P. (1991). What is literacy? In C. Mitchell and K. Weiler, eds., *Rewriting Literacy: Culture and the Discourse of the Other* (pp. 3–11). New York, NY: Bergin & Garvey.

Gee, J.P. (1996). *Sociolinguistics and Literacies: Ideology in Discourses*, 2nd ed. London, UK: Taylor & Francis.

Gee, J.P. (2001). Identity as an analytic lens for research in education. *Review of Research in Education, 25*, 99–125.

Gee, J.P. (2002). A sociocultural perspective on early literacy development. In S.B. Neuman and D.K. Dickinson, eds., *Handbook of Early Literacy Research* (Vol. 1, pp. 30–42). London, UK: Taylor & Francis.

Gee, J.P. (2004). *Situated Language and Learning: A Critique of Traditional Schooling*. New York, NY: Routledge.

Gee, J.P. (2015a). Discourse, small d, big D. In K. Tracy, C. Ilie, and T. Sandel, eds., *International Encyclopedia of Language and Social Interaction* (pp. 1–5). Hoboken, NJ: Wiley-Blackwell.

Gee, J.P. (2015b). *Social Linguistics and Literacies: Ideologies in Discourses*, 5th ed. Abingdon, UK, and New York, NY: Routledge.

Genishi, C. (1988). Young children's oral language development. *ERIC Digest* ED301361. ERIC Clearinghouse on Elementary and Early Childhood Education. Urbana, IL. Retrieved from http://files.eric.ed.gov/fulltext/ED301361.pdf

Genishi, C. (1992). *Ways of Assessing Children and Curriculum: Stories of Early Childhood Practice.* New York, NY: Teachers College Press.

Genishi, C., and Dyson, A.H. (1984). *Language Assessment in the Early Years.* Norwood, NJ: Ablex Publishing.

Genishi, C., and Dyson, A.H. (2009). *Children, Language, and Literacy: Diverse Learners in Diverse Times.* New York, NY/Washington, DC: Teachers College Press and the National Association for the Education of Young Children.

Genishi, C., and Dyson, A.H. (2012). Racing to the top: Who's accounting for the children? *Bank Street Occasional Papers, 27,* 18–20.

Genishi, C., and Goodwin, A.L., eds. (2008). *Diversities in Early Childhood Education: Rethinking and Doing.* New York, NY: Routledge.

Ghiso, M.P. (2016). The Laundromat as the transnational local: Young children's literacies of interdependence. *Teachers College Record, 118*(1), 1–46.

Giroux, H. (1987). Literacy and the pedagogy of political empowerment. In P. Freire and D. Macedo, *Literacy: Reading the Word and the World* (pp. 1–28). South Hadley, MA: Bergin & Garvey Publishers.

Giroux, H. (2001). *Theory and Resistance in Education: Towards a Pedagogy for the Opposition,* 2nd ed. Westport, CT: Bergin & Garvin.

Giroux, H. (2002). Neoliberalism, corporate culture, and the promise of higher education: The university as a democratic public sphere. *Harvard Educational Review, 72*(4), 425–464.

Gonzalez, M.C. (2017). *When a Bully Is President: Truth and Creativity for Oppressive Times.* San Francisco, CA: Reflection Press.

González, N. (1995). The funds of knowledge for teaching project. *Practicing Anthropology, 17*(3), 3–6. Retrieved from http://www.sfaajournals.net/doi/pdf/10.17730/praa.17.3.a036jlq42223625p?code=apan-site

González, N. (2005). Beyond culture: The hybridity of funds of knowledge. In N. González, L. Moll, and C. Amanti, eds., *Funds of Knowledge: Theorizing Practices in Households, Communities, and Classrooms* (pp. 29–46). Mahwah, NJ: Lawrence Erlbaum Associates.

González, N., Moll, L., and Amanti, C., eds. (2005). *Funds of Knowledge: Theorizing Practices in Households, Communities, and Classrooms.* Mahwah, NJ: Lawrence Erlbaum Associates.

Goodwin, A.L. (2010). Curriculum as colonizer: (Asian) American education in the current context. *Teachers College Record, 112*(12), 3102–3138.

Goodwin, A.L., Cheruvu, R., and Genishi, C. (2008). Responding to multiple diversities in early childhood education. In C. Genishi and A.L. Goodwin, eds., *Diversities in Early Childhood Education: Rethinking and Doing* (pp. 3–10). New York, NY: Routledge.

Graff, H.J. (1987). *The Labyrinths of Literacy: Reflections on Literacy Past and Present.* New York, NY: Psychology Press.

Gramsci, A. (1971). *Selections from the Prison Notebooks.* New York, NY: International Publishers.

Grant, C.A., and Sleeter, C.E. (1996). *After the School Bell Rings,* 2nd ed. Philadelphia, PA: Falmer.

Graue, E. (1992). *Ready for What? Constructing Meanings of Readiness for Kindergarten.* Albany, NY: State University of New York Press.

Graue, E. (2006). The answer is readiness—Now what is the question? *Early Education and Development, 17*(1), 43–56.

Graves, D. (1983). *Writing: Teachers and Children at Work.* Exeter, NH: Heinemann Educational Books.

Greenwood, G.E., and Hickman, C.W. (1991). Research and practice in parent involvement: Implications for teacher education. *Elementary School Journal, 91*(3), 279–288.

Gregory, E., Long, S., and Volk, D., eds. (2004a). *Many Pathways to Literacy: Young Children Learning with Siblings, Grandparents, Peers and Communities.* London, UK: Routledge.

Gregory, E., Long, S., and Volk, D. (2004b). Syncretic literacy studies: Starting points. In E. Gregory, S. Long, and D. Volk, eds., *Many Pathways to Literacy: Young Children Learning with Siblings, Peers, Grandparents, and Communities* (pp. 1–5). London, UK: RoutledgeFalmer.

Guinier, L. (2001). What we must overcome. *The American Prospect*. Retrieved from http://www.law.harvard.edu/faculty/guinier/publications/mass_humanities.pdfr/publications/overcome.pdf

Guinier, L. (2003). Admissions rituals as political acts: Guardians at the gates of our democratic ideals. *Harvard Law Review, 117*(1), 113–224.

Guinier, L. (2004). From racial liberalism to racial literacy: Brown v. Board of Education and the interest-divergence dilemma. *Journal of American History, 91*(1), 92–118.

Guinier, L. (2006). *Voting Rights and Voting Wrongs: An Interview with Lani Guinier.* The Massachusetts Foundation for the Humanities. Retrieved from http://www.law.harvard.edu/faculty/guinier/publications/mass_humanities.pdf

Gutiérrez, K. (2008). Developing a sociocritical literacy in the third space. *Reading Research Quarterly, 43*(2), 148–164.

Gutiérrez, K., and Rogoff, B. (2003). Cultural ways of learning: Individual traits or repertoires of practice. *Educational Researcher, 32*(5), 19–25.

Gutiérrez, K., Baquedano-López, P., and Tejeda, C. (1999). Rethinking diversity: Hybridity and hybrid language practices in the third space. *Mind, Culture, and Activity, 6*(4), 286–303.

Gutiérrez, K., Morales, P., and Martínez, D. (2009). Re-mediating literacy: Culture, difference, and learning for students from nondominant communities. *Review of Research in Education, 33*, 212–245.

Haight, W., and Carter-Black, J. (2004). His eye on the sparrow: Teaching and learning in an African American church. In E. Gregory, S. Long, and D. Volk, eds., *Many pathways to literacy: Young children learning with siblings, grandparents, peers and communities* (pp. 195–207). London, UK: Routledge Falmer.

Halliday, M.A.K. (1973). *Explorations in the Functions of Language.* London, UK: Edward Arnold.

Halliday, M.A.K. (1975). *Learning How to Mean: Explorations in the Development of Language.* London, UK: Edward Arnold.

Halliday, M.A.K. (1978). *Language as Social Semiotic: The Social Interpretation of Language and Meaning.* London, UK: Edward Arnold.

Halliday, M.A.K. (2004). Relevant models of language. In J.J. Webster, *The Language of Early Childhood: M.A.K. Halliday* (pp. 269–280). New York, NY: Continuum.

Halliday, M.A.K. (1980). Three aspects of children's language development: Learning language, learning through language, learning about language. In Y. Goodman, M.M. Haussler, and D.S. Strickland, eds., *Oral and Written Language Development Research: Impact on the Schools* (pp. 7–19). Proceedings from the 1979 and 1980 IMPACT conferences. Urbana, IL: International Reading Association and National Council of Teachers of English.

Harste, J.C., Breau, A., Leland, C., Lewison, M., Ociepka, A., and Vasquez, V. (2000). Supporting critical conversations in classrooms. In K.M. Pierce, ed., *Adventuring with Books*, 12th ed., (pp. 507–554). Urbana, IL: NCTE.

Hart, B., and Risley, T.R. (1995). *Meaningful Differences in the Early Experience of Young American Children.* Baltimore, MD: Paul H. Brookes Publishing Co.

Hart, B., and Risley, T.R. (2003). The early catastrophe: The 30 million word gap by age 3. *American Educator*, 4–9. Retrieved from http://www.aft.org//sites/default/files/periodicals/TheEarlyCatastrophe.pdf

Heath, S.B. (1982). What no bedtime story means: Narrative skills at home and at school. *Language and Society, 11*(2), 49–76.

Heath, S.B. (1983). *Ways with Words: Language, Life, and Work in Communities and Classrooms.* New York, NY: Cambridge University Press.

Heath, S.B. (1990). The children of Trackton's children: Spoken and written language in social change. In J.W. Stigler, R.A. Shweder, and G. Herdt, eds., *Cultural Psychology: Essays on Comparative Human Development* (pp. 496–519). Cambridge, UK: Cambridge University Press.

Heath, S.B. (2012). *Words at Work and Play: Three Decades in Family and Community Life.* New York, NY: Cambridge University Press.

Hensley, M. (2005). Empowering parents of multicultural backgrounds. In N. González, L.C. Moll, and C. Amanti, eds., *Funds of Knowledge: Theorizing Practices in Households, Communities, and Classrooms* (pp. 143–151). Mahwah, NJ: Lawrence Erlbaum Associates.

Hill Collins, P. (2000/2009). *Black Feminist Thought: Knowledge, Consciousness, and the Politics of Empowerment.* New York, NY: Routledge.

Hill, M.L. (2016). *Nobody: Casualties of America's War on the Vulnerable, from Ferguson to Flint and Beyond.* New York, NY: Astria Books.

Hilliard, A.III. (2009). What do we need to know now? In W.Au, ed., *Rethinking Multicultural Education,* (pp. 21–36). Milwaukee, WI: Rethinking Schools Publications.

Hirsch, E.D.Jr. (1987). *Cultural Literacy: What Every American Needs to Know.* New York, NY: Houghton Mifflin Company.

Holdaway, D. (1979). *The Foundation of Literacy.* Portsmouth, NH: Heinemann.

Holland, D., Lachiotte, W., Skinner, D., and Cain, C. (2001/2003). *Identity and Agency in Cultural Worlds.* Cambridge, MA: Harvard University Press.

hooks, b. (1994). *Teaching to Transgress: Education as the Practice of Freedom.* New York, NY: Routledge.

Hull, G. and Rose, M. (1989). Rethinking remediation: Toward a social-cognitive understanding of problematic reading and writing. *Written Communication, 6,* 139–154.

Hull, G.A., and Schultz, K., eds. (2002). *School's Out: Bridging Out-of-School Literacies with Classroom Practice.* New York, NY: Teachers College Press.

Hymes, D. (1972). On communicative competence. In J.B. Pride and J. Holmes, eds., *Sociolinguistics: Selected Readings* (pp. 269–293). Harmondsworth, UK: Penguin.

Hymes, D. (1974). *Foundations in Sociolinguistics: An Ethnographic Approach.* Philadelphia: University of Pennsylvania Press.

Hymes, D. (2004). *"In Vain I Tried to Tell You": Essays in Native American Ethnopoetics.* Lincoln, NE: University of Nebraska Press.

Illinois State Board of Education (2016). *Illinois School Readiness Initiative (revised).* Retrieved from http://www.isbe.net/earlychi/pdf/KIDS-IL-School-Readiness-Initiative.pdf.

Inoue, A.B. (2014). Theorizing failure in US writing assessments. *Research in the Teaching of English, 48*(3), 330–352.

International Reading Association and National Association for the Education of Young Children. (1998). *Learning to Read and Write: Developmentally Appropriate Practices for Young Children.* Newark, DE: International Reading Association.

Irvine, J.J. (1991). *Black Students and School Failure: Policies, Practices, and Prescriptions.* Westport, CT: Greenwood.

Jackson, P.W. (1986). *The Practice of Teaching.* New York, NY: Teachers College Press.

James, A. (2011). Agency. In J. Qvotrtrup, W.A. Corsaro, and, M.S. Honig, eds., *The Palgrave Handbook of Childhood Studies* (pp. 34–35). New York, NY: Palgrave MacMillan.

Janks, H. (2000). Domination, access, diversity and design: A synthesis for critical literacy education. *Educational Review, 52*(2), 175–186.

Jenkins, E. (2015). *A Fine Dessert: Four Centuries, Four Families, One Delicious Treat.* New York, NY: Schwartz & Wade.

Jenkins, H. (1998). Introduction: Childhood innocence and other modern myths. In H. Jenkins, ed., *The Children's Culture Reader* (pp. 1–35). New York, NY: NYU Press.

Jenkins, H. (2007). Going bonkers: Children, play and PeeWee. In *The Wow Climax: Tracing the Emotional Impact of Popular Culture* (pp. 159–184). New York, NY: NYU Press.

Jenkins, H., Purushotma, R., Weigel, M., Clinton, K., and Robinson, A. (2009). *Confronting the Challenges of Participatory Culture: Media Education for the 21st Century*. Cambridge, MA: The MIT Press.

Johnson, A. (1994). *Joshua's Night Whispers*. New York, NY: Scholastic.

Johnson, H.B. (2015). Word play: How "Black English" coarsens culture. *Teachers College Record*. Retrieved from http://www.tcrecord.org/Content.asp?ContentID=18829

King, J.E., and Swartz, E.E. (2014). *The Afrocentric Praxis of Teaching for Freedom: Connecting Culture to Learning*. New York, NY: Routledge.

Kirkland, D. (2008). "The rose that grew from concrete": Postmodern blackness and new English education. *English Journal, 97*(5), 69–75.

Kirkland, D.E., and Jackson, A. (2009). "We real cool": Toward a theory of black masculine literacies. *Reading Research Quarterly, 44*(3), 278–297.

Kliebard, H.M. (1992). Constructing a history of the American curriculum. In P. Jackson, ed., *Handbook of Research on Curriculum* (pp. 157–184). New York, NY: Macmillan Publishing Group.

Kohl, H. (1995). *Should We Burn Babar?: Essays on Children's Literature and the Power of Story*. New York, NY: The New Press.

KQED (n.d.). *Chinatown resource guide*. Retrieved from http://www.pbs.org/kqed/chinatown/resourceguide/story.html

Kress, G. (2003). Perspectives on making meaning: The differential principles and means of adults and children. In N. Hall, J. Larson, and J. Marsh, eds., *Handbook of Early Childhood Literacy* (pp. 154–166). London, UK: SAGE.

Kuby, C., Gutshall-Rucker, T., and Kirchhofer, J. (2015). "Go be a writer": Intra-activity with materials, time, and space in literacy learning. *Journal of Early Childhood Literacy, 15*(3), 394–419.

Kuhl, P. (2010, October). *Patricia Kuhl: The Linguistic Genius of Babies* [Video file]. Retrieved from https://www.ted.com/talks/patricia_kuhl_the_linguistic_genius_of_babies

Kumashiro, K.K. (2012). *Bad Teacher!: How Blaming Teachers Distorts the Bigger Picture*. New York, NY: Teachers College Press.

Kumashiro, K.K., and Meiners, E. (2012). Flip the script. *Bank Street Occasional Paper Series, 27*. Retrieved from https://www.bankstreet.edu/occasional-paper-series/27/part-iii/flip-the-script/

Ladson-Billings, G. (1992). Reading between the lines and beyond the pages: A culturally relevant approach to literacy teaching. *Theory into Practice, 31*(4), 312–320.

Ladson-Billings, G. (1994). *The Dreamkeepers: Successful Teachers of African American Children*. San Francisco, CA: Jossey-Bass.

Ladson-Billings, G. (1995). "But that's just good teaching!" The case for culturally relevant pedagogy. *Theory into Practice, 34*(3), 159–165.

Ladson-Billings, G. (2006). From the achievement gap to the education debt: Understanding achievement in U.S. schools. *Educational Researcher, 35*(7), 3–12.

Ladson-Billings, G. (2011). Boyz to men?: Teaching to restore Black boys' childhood. *Race Ethnicity and Education, 14*(1), 7–15.

Ladson-Billings, G. (2012). *Cultural Competency* [Video file]. Retrieved from https://www.youtube.com/watch?v=XSE8nxxZN5s

Ladson-Billings, G. (2015, April). *Justice... Just, Justice!* [Video file]. Social Justice in Education Award Lecture, American Educational Research Association Annual Meeting, Chicago, IL. Retrieved from http://www.aera.net/EventsMeetings/AnnualMeeting/PreviousAnnualMeetings/2015AnnualMeeting/2015AnnualMeetingWebcasts/SocialJusticeinEducationAward(2015)LectureGloriaJLadson-Billings/tabid/15943/Default.aspx

Ladson-Billings, G., and Brown, K. (2008). Curriculum and cultural diversity. In F.M. Connelly, M.F. He, and J. Phillion, eds., *The SAGE Handbook of Curriculum and Instruction* (pp. 153–175). Thousand Oaks, CA: SAGE Publications.

Ladson-Billings, G., and Tate, W. (1995). Toward a critical race theory of education. *Teachers College Record, 97*(1), 47–68.

Laínez, R. C. (2004). *Waiting for Papá.* Houston, TX: Piñata Books.

Laínez, R. C. (2010). *From North to South.* San Francisco, CA: Children's Book Press.

Larson, J., and Marsh, J. (2005). *Making Literacy Real: Theories and Practices for Learning and Teaching.* Thousand Oaks, CA: SAGE.

Lee, C. D. (1992). Profile of an independent Black institution: African-centered education at work. *Journal of Negro Education, 61,* 160–177.

Lee, J. (2002). Racial and ethnic achievement gap trends: Reversing the progress toward equity? *Educational Researcher, 31*(1), 3–12.

Lesko, N. (2012). *Act Your Age!: A Cultural Construction of Adolescence,* 2nd ed. New York, NY: Routledge.

Lewis, C., Enciso, P. and Moje, E. (2007). *Reframing Sociocultural Research on Literacy: Identity, Agency, and Power.* New York, NY: Routledge.

Lewison, M., Flint, A. S., and Van Sluys, K. (2002). Taking on critical literacy: The journey of newcomers and novices. *Language Arts, 79*(5), 382–392.

Li, G. (2008). *Culturally Contested Literacies: America's "Rainbow Underclass" and Urban Schools.* New York, NY: Routledge.

Licona, A. C., and Chávez, K. R. (2015). Relational literacies and their coalitional possibilities. *Peitho: Journal of the Coalition of Women Scholars in the History of Rhetoric & Composition, 18*(1), 96–107.

Licona, A. C., and Russell, S. T. (2013). Transdisciplinary and community literacies: Shifting discourses and practices through new paradigms of public scholarship and action-oriented research. *Community Literacy Journal, 8*(1), 1–7.

Lindfors, J. (1987). *Children's Language and Learning.* Englewood Cliffs, NJ: Prentice-Hall.

Lindfors, J. (2008). *Children's Language: Connecting Reading, Writing, and Talk.* New York, NY: Teachers College Press.

Long, S., Volk, D., Baines, J., and Tisdale, C. (2013). "We've been doing it your way long enough": Syncretism as a critical process. *Journal of Early Childhood Literacy, 13*(3), 418–439.

Lucas, S. R. (2001). Effectively maintained inequality: Education transitions, track mobility, and social background effects. *American Journal of Sociology, 106*(6), 1642–1690.

Luke, A. (2000). Critical literacy in Australia: A matter of context and standpoint. *Journal of Adolescent and Adult Literacy, 43*(5), 448–461.

Luke, A., and Freebody, L. (1997). Critical literacy and the question of normativity: An introduction. In S. Muspratt, A. Luke, and P. Freebody, eds., *Constructing Critical Literacies: Teaching and Learning Textual Practice* (pp. 1–18). New York, NY: Hampton Press.

Macedo, D. (1994). *Literacies of Power: What Americans Are Not Allowed to Know.* Boulder, CO: Westview Press.

MacGillivray, L., and Curwen, M. S. (2007). Tagging as a social literacy practice. *Journal of Adolescent and Adult Literacy, 50*(5), 354–369. Retrieved from http://graffitistreetart.pbworks.com/f/8sb.pdf

Manyak, P. (2004). Literacy instruction, disciplinary practice, and diverse learners: A case study. *Journal of Early Childhood Literacy, 4*(1), 129–149.

Marsh, J. (Ed.). (2005a). *Popular Culture, New Media and Digital Literacy in Early Childhood.* New York, NY: Routledge.

Marsh, J. (2005b). Ritual, performance, and identity construction. In J. Marsh, ed., *Popular Culture, New Media and Digital Literacy in Early Childhood* (pp. 28–50). New York, NY: Routledge.

Marsh, J. (2010). One-way traffic? Connections between literacy practices at home and in the nursery. *British Educational Research Journal, 29*(3), 369–382.

Marsh, J., and Bishop, J. (2014). *Changing Play: Play, Media and Commercial Culture from the 1950s to the Present Day.* Maidenhead, UK: Open University Press.

Marshall, J. (1989). *The Three Little Pigs.* New York: Puffin Books.

Martin, L.T. (2013). *The spatiality of queer youth activism: Sexuality and the performance of relational literacies through multimodal play* (Doctoral dissertation). The University of Arizona, Tucson. Retrieved from http://hdl.handle.net/10150/293546

Martínez-Roldán, C., and Malavé, G. (2011). Identity construction in the borderlands. In V. Kinloch, ed., *Urban Literacies: Critical Perspectives on Language, Learning, and Community*, (pp. 53–71). New York, NY: Teachers College Press.

Marx, K. (1998). *The German Ideology: Including Theses on Feuerbach and Introduction to the Critique of Political Economy.* New York, NY: Prometheus Books.

Massey, D. (2001). Residential segregation and neighborhood conditions in U.S. metropolitan areas. In N. Smelser, W. Wilson, and F. Mitchell, eds., *America Becoming: Racial Trends and Their Consequences* (Vol. 1, pp. 391–434). Washington, DC: National Academy Press.

Massey, D.S., and Denton, N.A. (1989). Hypersegregation in U.S. metropolitan areas: Black and Hispanic segregation along five dimensions. *Demography, 26*(3), 373–391.

Massey, D., and Denton, N. (1993). *American Apartheid: Segregation and the Making of the Underclass.* Cambridge, MA: Harvard University Press.

Maynard, M. (1994). Methods, practice, and epistemology: The debate about feminism and research. In M. Maynard and J. Purvis, eds., *Researching Women's Lives from a Feminist Perspective* (pp. 10–26). Abingdon, UK/New York, NY: Taylor and Francis.

McCarty, T. (2002). *A Place to Be Navajo: Rough Rock and the Struggle for Self-Determination in Indigenous Schooling.* New York, NY: Routledge.

McKay, T. (2016, March 5). A New York public school is being threatened and harassed over this art project. Retrieved from http://mic.com/articles/137133/a-new-york-public-school-is-being-threatened-and-harassed-over-this-art-project#.GMUIhLWdX

McLaren, P. (1999). A pedagogy of possibility: Reflecting upon Paulo Freire's politics of education. *Educational Researcher, 28*(2), 49–56.

Meier, D. (2004). *The Young Child's Memory for Words: Developing First and Second Language and Literacy.* New York, NY: Teachers College Press.

Merchant, G. (2007). Writing the future in the digital age. *Literacy, 41*(3), 118–128.

Michaels, S. (2013). Déjà vu all over again: What's wrong with Hart and Risley and a "linguistic deficit" framework in early childhood education? *LEARNing Landscapes, 7*(1), 23–41.

Millard, E. (2004). Writing of heroes and villains. In J. Evans, ed., *Literacy Moves on: Using Popular Culture, New Technologies and Critical Literacy in the Primary Classroom* (pp. 121–45). Portsmouth, NH: Heinemann

Miller, P.J., and Goodnow, J.J. (1995). Cultural practices: Toward an integration of culture and development. *New directions for child and adolescent development,* (67), 5–16.

Moje, E.B. (2000). "To be part of the story": The literacy practices of gangsta adolescents. *Teachers College Record, 102*(3), 651–690.

Moll, L.C., Amanti, C., Neff, D., and González, N. (1992). Funds of knowledge for teaching: Using a qualitative approach to connect homes and classrooms. *Theory into Practice, 31*(2), 132–141.

Moll, L.C., and Greenberg, J. (1990). Creating zones of possibilities: Combining social contexts for instruction. In L.C. Moll, ed., *Vygotsky and Education* (pp. 319–348). Cambridge, UK: Cambridge University Press.

Moll, L., and González, N. (1994). Lessons from research with language-minority children. *Journal of Reading Behavior, 26*(4), 439–456.

Monbiot, G. (2016, April). *Neoliberalism—The Ideology at the Root of All Our Problems.* Retrieved from https://www.theguardian.com/books/2016/apr/15/neoliberalism-ideology-problem-george-monbiot

Morales, Y. (2014). *Viva Frida.* New York, NY: Roaring Brook Press.

Morrell, E. (2015). Powerful English at NCTE yesterday, today, and tomorrow: Toward the next movement. *Research in the Teaching of English, 49*(3), 307–327.

Morton, S. (1839). *Crania Americana; or, A Comparative View of the Skulls of Various Aboriginal Nations of North and South America to Which is Prefixed an Essay on the Variety of the Human Species.* Philadelphia, PA: John Pennington.

Munsch, R. (1980). *The Paper Bag Princess.* Toronto, Ontario, Canada: Annick Press.

Muth, J.J. (2002). *The Three Questions.* New York, NY: Scholastic Press.

Myers, C. (2014, March). The apartheid of children's literature. *The New York Times.* Retrieved from https://www.nytimes.com/2014/03/16/opinion/sunday/the-apartheid-of-childrens-literature.html

National Association for the Education of Young Children (NAEYC). (2009). *Where we stand on school readiness.* Retrieved from https://www.naeyc.org/files/naeyc/file/positions/Readiness.pdf

National Council on Teacher Quality (2013). "Teacher prep review: A review of the nation's teacher preparation programs." Retrieved from http://www.nctq.org/dmsView/Teacher_Prep_Review_2013_Report.

National Institute for Literacy (2008). *Developing Early Literacy: Report of the National Early Literacy Panel.* Retrieved from https://lincs.ed.gov/publications/pdf/NELPReport09.pdf

Neuman, S.B., and Celano, D. (2001). Access to print in low-income and middle-income communities: An ecological study of four neighborhoods. *Reading Research Quarterly, 36*(1), 8–26.

Neuman, S., and Celano, D.C. (2012). *Giving Our Children a Fighting Chance: Poverty, Literacy, and the Development of Information Capital.* New York, NY: Teachers College Press.

New London Group. (1996). A pedagogy of multiliteracies: Designing social features. *Harvard Educational Review, 61,* 60–92.

New, R.S., and Mallory, B.L. (1994). Introduction: The ethics of inclusion. In B. Mallory and R. New, eds., *Diversity and Developmentally Appropriate Practices: Challenges for Early Childhood Curriculum* (pp. 1–13). New York, NY: Teachers College Press.

Newman, K., and Wyly, E. (2006). The right to stay put, revisited: Gentrification and resistance to displacement in New York City. *Urban Studies, 43*(1), 23–57.

Nicholls, C. (2005). Death by a thousand cuts: Indigenous language bilingual education programmes in the Northern Territory of Australia, 1972–1998. *The International Journal of Bilingual Education and Bilingualism, 8*(2/3), 160–177.

Nieto, S. (2010). *The Light in Their Eyes: Creating Multicultural Learning Communities,* 10th anniversary ed. New York, NY: Teachers College Press.

Noguera, P.A. (2009). Preparing for the new majority: How schools can respond to immigration and demographic change. In A. Hargreaves and M. Fullan, eds., *Change Wars* (pp. 163–184). Bloomington, IN: Solution Tree Press.

O'Donnell, C. (2008). Defining, conceptualizing, and measuring fidelity of implementation in its relationship to outcomes in K–12 curriculum intervention research. *Review of Educational Research, 78*(1), 33–84.

Olah, L.N. (2000). How language comes to children: From birth to two years by Benedicte de Boysson-Bardies and how children learn the meanings of words by Paul Bloom. *Harvard Educational Review, 70*(4). Retrieved from http://hepg.org/her-home/issues/harvard-educational-review-volume-70-issue-4/herarticle/_134

Orellana, M.F. (2009). *Translating Childhoods: Immigrant Youth, Language, and Culture.* New Brunswick, NJ: Rutgers University Press.

Orellana, M.F. (2016). A different kind of word gap. *Huffington Post.* Retrieved from http://www.huffingtonpost.com/marjorie-faulstich-orellana/a-different-kind-of-word-_b_10030876.html?

Owocki, G., and Goodman, Y.M. (2002). *Kidwatching: Documenting Children's Literacy Development.* Portsmouth, NH: Heinemann.

Oxford Living Dictionaries. (2016). *Translation.* Retrieved from https://en.oxforddictionaries.com/definition/translationhttps://en.oxforddictionaries.com/definition/translation

Pahl, K., and Rowsell, J. (2010). *Artifactual Literacies: Every Object Tells a Story.* New York, NY: Teachers College Press.

Paley, V.G. (1986). On listening to what the children say. *Harvard Educational Review, 56*(2), 122–131.

Paley, V.G. (1987). *Wally's Stories: Conversations in the Kindergarten.* Cambridge, MA: Harvard University Press.

Paley, V.G. (1988). *Bad Guys Don't Have Birthdays: Fantasy Play at Four.* Chicago, IL: The University of Chicago Press.

Paley, V.G. (1990). *The Boy Who Would Be a Helicopter.* Cambridge, MA: Harvard University Press.

Paley, V.G. (1992). *You Can't Say You Can't Play.* Cambridge, MA: Harvard University Press.

Paris, D. (2009). "They're in my culture, they speak the same way": African American language in multiethnic high schools. *Harvard Educational Review, 79*(3), 428–448.

Paris, D. (2012). Culturally sustaining pedagogy: A needed change in stance, terminology, and practice. *Educational Researcher, 41*(3), 93–97.

Pellegrini, A.D. (1989). Elementary school children's rough-and-tumble play. *Early Childhood Research Quarterly, 4*(2), 245–260.

Perry, T., and Delpit, L. (1998). *The Ebonics Debate: Power, Language, and the Education of African-American Children.* Boston, MA: Beacon Press.

Piaget, J., and Inhelder, B. (1969). *The Psychology of the Child.* New York, NY: Basic Books.

Pollock, M. (2008). From shallow to deep: Toward a thorough cultural analysis of school achievement patterns. *Anthropology & Education Quarterly, 39*(4), 369–380.

Powell, T. (2014). My son has been suspended five times. He's 3. *The Washington Post.* Retrieved from https://www.washingtonpost.com/posteverything/wp/2014/07/24/my-son-has-been-suspended-five-times-hes-3/?utm_term=.26a760618c4a

Purcell-Gates, V. (1993). Focus on research: Issues for family literacy research: Voices from the trenches. *Language Arts, 70*(8), 670–677.

Purcell-Gates, V. (1996). Stories, coupons, and the "TV guide:" Relationships between home literacy experiences and emergent literacy knowledge. *Reading Research Quarterly, 31*(4), 406–428.

Purcell-Gates, V., and Dahl, K. (1991). Low-SES children's success and failure at early literacy learning in skills-based classrooms. *Journal of Reading Behavior, 23*(1), 1–34.

Quintero, E. (2013). The "early language gap" is about more than words. *The Washington Post.* Retrieved from https://www.washingtonpost.com/news/answer-sheet/wp/2013/11/01/the-early-language-gap-is-about-more-than-words

Ramsey, P.G. (2015). *Teaching and Learning in a Diverse World: Multicultural Education for Young Children.* New York, NY: Teachers College Press.

Ranker, J. (2007). Designing meaning with multiple media sources: A case study of an eight-year-old student's writing processes. *Research in the Teaching of English, 41*(4), 402–434.

Ray, K.W., and Glover, M. (2008). *Already Ready: Nurturing Writers in Preschool and Kindergarten.* Portsmouth, NH: Heinemann.

Razfar, A. (2005). Language ideologies in practice: Repair and classroom discourse. *Linguistics & Education, 16*(4), 404–424.

Reyes, I., Iddings, A.C., and Feller, N. (2015). Building relationships with diverse students and families: A funds of knowledge perspective. *Journal of Early Childhood Literacy, 16*(1), 8–33.

Rickford, J. (1999). *African American Vernacular English: Features, Evolution, Educational Implications.* Malden, MA: Blackwell Publishers.

Rogers, R. (2002). Between contexts: A critical analysis of family literacy, discursive practices, and literate subjectivities. *Reading Research Quarterly, 37*(3) 248–277.

Rogers, R., and Mosley, M. (2006). Racial literacy in a second-grade classroom: Critical race theory, whiteness studies, and literacy research. *Reading Research Quarterly, 41*(4), 462–495.

Rogoff, B. (2003). *The Cultural Nature of Human Development*. Oxford, UK: Oxford University Press.

Rose, M. (1988). Narrowing the mind and page: Remedial writers and cognitive reductionism. *College Composition and Communication, 39*(3), 267–302.

Rose, M. (1989). *Lives on the Boundary: A Moving Account of the Struggles and Achievements of America's Educationally Underprepared*. New York, NY: Penguin Books.

Rosenthal, A.K., and Lichtenheld, T. (2008). *It's Not Fair!* New York, NY: HarperCollins.

Rymes, B. (2016). *Classroom Discourse Analysis: A Tool for Critical Reflection*. New York, NY: Routledge.

Saegert, S., and Evans, G.W. (2003). Poverty, housing niches, and health in the United States. *Journal of Social Issues, 59*(3), 569–589.

Schiffman, H., and Spooner, B. (2012). Afghan languages in a larger context of Central and South Asia. In H. Shiffman, ed., *Language Policy and Language Conflict in Afghanistan and Its Neighbors: The Changing Politics of language choice* (pp. 1–28). Leigen, the Netherlands: Koninklijke Brill NV.

Scieszka, J. (1989). *The True Story of the 3 Little Pigs*. New York, NY: Viking Kestrel.

Scribner, S., and Cole, M. (1981). Unpackaging literacy. In M.F. Whiteman, ed., *Writing: The Nature, Development, and Teaching of Written Communication* (pp. 71–87). Mahwah, NJ: Lawrence Erlbaum Associates.

Seiter, E. (1995). *Sold Separately: Children and Parents in Consumer Culture*. New Brunswick, NJ: Rutgers University Press.

Shanahan, T. (2015, September). *11 ways parents can help their children read*. Retrieved from http://www.readingrockets.org/blogs/shanahan-literacy/11-ways-parents-can-help-their-children-read

Shapiro, S. (2014). "Words that you said got bigger": English language learners' lived experiences of deficit discourse. *Research in the Teaching of English, 48*(4), 386–406.

Shor, I. (1987). *Freire for The Classroom: A Sourcebook for Liberatory Teaching*. Portsmouth, NH: Boynton/Cook.

Siegel, M. (2006). Rereading the signs: Multimodal transformations in the field of literacy education. *Language Arts, 84*(1), 65–77.

Skinner, B.F. (1957). *Verbal Behavior*. New York, NY: Appleton-Century-Crofts.

Sleeter, C. (2005). *Unstandardizing curriculum: Multicultural Teaching in the Standards-Based Classroom*. New York, NY: Teachers College Press.

Sleeter, C., and Carmona, J.F. (2017). *Unstandardizing Curriculum: Multicultural Standards in The Standards-Based Classroom*, 2nd ed. New York, NY: Teachers College Press.

Smith, C. (2015). *Clint Smith: How to Raise a Black Son in America* [Video file]. Retrieved from https://www.ted.com/talks/clint_smith_how_to_raise_a_black_son_in_america

Smitherman, G. (2006). *Word from The Mother: Language and African Americans*. New York, NY: Routledge.

Snow, C.E., Burns, M.S., and Griffin, P. (1998). *Preventing Reading Difficulties in Young Children*. Washington, DC: National Academy Press.

Souto-Manning, M. (2005, May). *Critical narrative analysis of Brazilian women's schooling discourses: Negotiating agency and identity through participation in culture circles*. Unpublished doctoral dissertation. University of Georgia, Athens.

Souto-Manning, M. (2007). Immigrant families and children (re)develop identities in a new context. *Early Childhood Education Journal, 34*(6), 399–405.

Souto-Manning, M. (2009a). Acting out and talking back: Negotiating discourses in American early educational settings. *Early Child Development and Care, 179*(8), 1083–1094.

Souto-Manning, M. (2009b). Negotiating culturally responsive pedagogy through multicultural children's literature: Towards critical democratic literacy practices in a first grade classroom. *Journal of Early Childhood Literacy, 9*(1), 53–77.

Souto-Manning, M. (2010a). Challenging ethnocentric literacy practices: (Re)Positioning home literacies in a Head Start classroom. *Research in the Teaching of English, 45*(2), 150–178.

Souto-Manning, M. (2010b). *Freire, Teaching, and Learning:Culture Circles across Contexts.* NewYork, NY: Peter Lang.

Souto-Manning, M. (2010c).Teaching English learners: Building on cultural and linguistic strengths. *English Education, 42*(3), 249–263.

Souto-Manning, M. (2013a). Competence as linguistic alignment: Linguistic diversities, affinity groups, and the politics of educational success. *Linguistics and Education, 24*(3), 305–315.

Souto-Manning, M. (2013b). *Multicultural Teaching in the Early Childhood Classroom: Strategies, Tools, and Approaches, Preschool-2nd grade.* Washington, DC: Association for Childhood Education International and NewYork, NY:Teachers College Press.

Souto-Manning, M. (2014). Critical narrative analysis:The interplay of critical discourse and narrative analyses. *International Journal of Qualitative Studies in Education, 27*(2), 159–180.

Souto-Manning, M. (2016). Honoring and building on the rich literacy practices of young bilingual and multilingual learners. *The Reading Teacher, 70*(3), 263–271.

Souto-Manning, M. (2017). Is play a privilege or a right? And what's our responsibility?: On the role of play for equity in early childhood education. *Early Child Development and Care.* DOI: 10.1080/03004430.2016.1266588.

Souto-Manning, M., Lugo Llerena, C., Martell, J., Salas Maguire, A., and Arce-Boardman, A., (2018). *No More Culturally Irrelevant Teaching.* Portsmouth, NH: Heinemann.

Souto-Manning, M., and Martell, J. (2016). *Reading, Writing, and Talk: Inclusive Teaching Strategies for Diverse Learners, K–2.* NewYork, NY: Teachers College Press.

Souto-Manning, M., and Martell, J. (2017). Committing to culturally relevant literacy teaching as an everyday practice: It's critical! *Language Arts, 94*(4), 252–256.

Steptoe, J. (1987). *Mufaro's Beautiful Daughters: An African Tale.* New York, NY: Lothrop, Lee & Shepard Books.

Street, B. (1993). Introduction: The new literacy studies. In B. Street, ed., *Cross-Cultural Approaches to Literacy* (pp. 1–21). Cambridge, UK: Cambridge University Press.

Street, B. (1995). *Social Literacies: Critical Approaches to Literacy Development, Ethnography and Education.* London, UK: Longman.

Street, B. (2003). What's 'new' in new literacy studies? Critical approaches to literacy in theory and practice. *Current Issues in Comparative Education, 5*(2), 77–91.

Strickland, D. (2004).The role of literacy in early childhood education:Working with families as partners in early literacy. *The Reading Teacher, 58*(1), 86–88.

Sutton-Smith, B. (2009). *The Ambiguity of Play.* Cambridge, MA: Harvard University Press.

Swadener, B.B., and Lubeck, S. (1995). *Children and Families "At Promise": Deconstructing the Discourse of Risk.* Albany: State University of New York Press.

Szwed, J.F. (1981).The ethnography of literacy. In M.F.Whiteman, ed., *Writing: The Nature, Development, and Teaching of Written Communication* (pp. 13–23). Mahwah, NJ: Lawrence Erlbaum Associates.

Tafolla, C. (2009). *What Can You Do with a Paleta?/¿Qué puedes hacer con una paleta?* Berkeley, CA:Tricycle Press.

Tafolla, C., and Teneyuca, S. (2008). *That's Not Fair!: Emma Teneyuca's Struggle for Justice/No Es Justo!: La Lucha de Emma Teneyuca por la Justicia.* San Antonio,TX:Wings Press.

Tatum, B.D. (1992). Talking about race, learning about racism: The application of racial identity development theory in the classroom. *Harvard Educational Review, 62*(1),1–24.

Taylor, N. and Vawter, J. (1978). Helping children discover the functions of written language. *Language Arts, 55*(8), 941–945.

Teale, W.H. (1986). Home background and young children's literacy development. In W.H. Teale and E. Sulzby, eds., *Emergent Literacy: Writing and Reading* (pp. 173–206). Norwood, NJ: Ablex.

Tenery, M.F. (2005). La visita. In N. González, L.C. Moll, and C. Amanti, eds., *Funds of Knowledge: Theorizing Practices in Households, Communities, and Classrooms* (pp. 119–130). Mahwah, NJ: Lawrence Erlbaum Associates.

Thiel, J.J. (2015). "Bumblebee's in trouble!" Embodied literacies during imaginative super-hero play. *Language Arts, 93*(1), 38–49.

Thomas, E., and Winger, P. (2010, March 15). The key to saving American education. *Newsweek, 155* (11), front cover.

Tonatiuh, D. (2011). *Diego Rivera: His World and Ours.* New York, NY: Abrams Books for Young Readers.

U.S. Bureau of Labor Statistics. (2014). Labor force characteristics by race and ethnicity, 2013. *BLS Reports, 1050,* 1–59.

U.S. Department of Education Office for Civil Rights. (2014). *Civil rights data collection: Data snapshot (school discipline).* Retrieved from http://ocrdata.ed.gov/Downloads/CRDC-School-Discipline-Snapshot.pdf

UNESCO. (2016). If you don't understand, how can you learn? *Policy Paper 24,* 1–9. Retrieved from bit.ly/MLD2016

United Nations. (1948). *Universal Declaration of Human Rights.* Retrieved from http://www.un.org/en/universal-declaration-human-rights/

Valdés, G. (1996). *Con Respeto: Bridging the Distances between Culturally Diverse Families and Schools.* New York, NY: Teachers College Press.

Valdés, G. (1997). Dual-language immersion programs: A cautionary note concerning the education of language-minority students. *Harvard Educational Review, 67*(3), 391–430.

Vasquez, V. (2001). On our way: Using the everyday to create a critical literacy curriculum. *Primary Voices, 9*(2), 8–13.

Vasquez, V. (2004a). Creating opportunities for critical literacy with young children. In J. Evans, ed., *Literacy Moves on: Using Popular Culture, New Technologies and Critical Literacy in the Primary Classroom* (pp. 78–96). Portsmouth, NH: Heinemann.

Vasquez, V. (2004b). *Negotiating Critical Literacies with Young Children.* Mahwah, NJ: Lawrence Erlbaum Associates.

Vasquez, V. (2014). *Negotiating Critical Literacies with Young Children,* 2nd ed. New York, NY: Routledge.

Vasquez, V.M., and Felderman, C.B. (2012). *Technology and Critical Literacy in Early Childhood.* New York, NY: Routledge.

Vasudevan, L., Schultz, K., and Bateman, J. (2010). Rethinking composing in a digital age: Authoring literate identities through multimodal storytelling. *Written Communication, 21*(4), 442–468.

Vygotsky, L.S. (1978). *Mind in Society: The Development of Higher Psychological Processes.* Cambridge, MA: Harvard University Press.

Watson-Gegeo, K. (1990). The social transfer of cognitive skills in Kwara'ae. *Quarterly Newsletter of the Laboratory of Comparative Human Cognition, 12,* 86–90.

Weatherford, C.B. (2005). *Freedom on the Menu: The Greensboro sit-ins.* New York, NY: Dial Books for Young Readers.

Wells, G. (1986). *The Meaning Makers: Children Learning Language and Using Language to Learn.* Portsmouth, NH: Heinemann.

Wells, G. (2009). *The Meaning Makers: Learning to Talk and Talking to Learn.* Bristol, UK: Multilingual Matters.

Wenger, E. (1998). *Communities of Practice: Learning, Meaning, and Identity*. New York, NY: Cambridge University Press.

Wertsch, J.V. (1998). *Mind as Action*. Oxford, UK: Oxford University Press.

Willis, A. (1995). Reading the world of school literacy: Contextualizing the experience of a young African American male. *Harvard Educational Review, 65*(1), 30–50.

Wilson, T. (2009). *The Princess and the Packet of Frozen Peas*. Gosford, Australia: Scholastic Press.

Winter, J. (2002). *Frida*. New York, NY: Arthur A. Levine Books.

Wohlwend, K. (2007). Playing to read and reading to play: A mediated discourse analysis of early literacy apprenticeship. In D.W. Rowe, R. Jimenez, D. Compton, D. Dickinson, Y. Kim, K. Leander and V. Risko, eds., *57th Yearbook of the National Reading Conference* (pp. 377–393). Oak Creek, WI: National Reading Conference.

Wohlwend, K. (2008). Play as a literacy of possibilities: Expanding meanings in practices, materials, and spaces. *Language Arts, 86*(2), 127–136.

Wohlwend, K. (2009). Damsels in discourse: Girls consuming and producing identity texts through Disney princess play. *Reading Research Quarterly, 44*(1), 57–83.

Wohlwend, K. (2011). *Playing Their Way into Literacies: Reading, Writing, and Belonging in the Early Childhood Classroom*. New York, NY: Teachers College Press.

Wohlwend, K., and Hall, D.T. (2016). Race and rag dolls: Critically engaging the embodiment of diversity in lalaloopsy transmedia. In G. Enriquez, E. Johnson, S. Kontovourki, and C. Mallozzi, eds., *Literacies, Learning, and the Body: Putting Theory and Research into Pedagogical Practice* (pp. 155–169). New York, NY: Routledge.

Wolfram, W. (2004). The grammar of urban African American vernacular English. In B. Kortman and E.W. Schneider, eds., *Handbook of Varieties of English* (vol. 2, pp. 111–132). Berlin, Germany: Mouton de Gruyter.

Wolfram, W., Adger, C.T., and Christian, D. (1999). *Dialects in Schools and Communities*. Mahwah, NJ: Lawrence Erlbaum Associates.

Wood, E. (2013). *Play, Learning and the Early Childhood Curriculum*, 3rd ed. Thousand Oaks, CA: SAGE.

Woodson, J. (2001). *The Other Side*. New York, NY: G.P. Putnam's Sons.

Woodson, J. (2005). *Show Way*. New York, NY: G.P. Putnam's Sons.

Wortham, S. (2004). From good student to outcast: The emergence of a classroom identity. *Ethos, 32*(2), 164–187.

Wyeth, S. D. (1998). *Something Beautiful*. New York, NY: Doubleday Books for Young Readers.

Yelland, N. (Ed.). (2005). *Critical Issues in Early Childhood Education*. Maidenhouse, UK/New York, NY: Open University Press.

Yelland, N., and Kilderry, A. (2005). Against the tide: New ways in early childhood education. In N. Yelland, ed., *Critical Issues in Early Childhood Education* (pp. 1–13). Maidenhouse, UK/New York, NY: Open University Press.

Yelland, N., Lee, L., O'Rourke, M., and Harrison, C. (2008). *Rethinking Learning in Early Childhood Education*. New York, NY: Open University Press.

Yoon, H. (2013). Rewriting the curricular script: Teachers and children translating writing practices in a kindergarten classroom. *Research on the Teaching of English, 48*(2), 148–174.

Yoon, H. (2014). Can I play with you?: The intersection of play and writing in a kindergarten classroom. *Contemporary Issues in Early Childhood, 15*(2), 109–121.

Yoon, H. (2015). Assessing children in kindergarten: The narrowing of language, culture, and identity in the testing era. *Journal of Early Childhood Literacy, 15*(3), 364–393.

Yoon, H. (2016). "Writing" children's literate identities: The meaning of language in multilingual, multicultural contexts. *Multicultural Education Review, 2*, 65–82.

Yoon, H., Llerena, C., and Brooks, E. (2016). The unfolding of Lucas' story in an inclusive classroom: Living, playing, and becoming in the social world of kindergarten. *Bank Street Occasional Papers, 37*, 1–18.

INDEX

Made in United States
North Haven, CT
30 December 2021